A TALE OF
Three Villages

THE ARCHAEOLOGY OF COLONIALISM IN NATIVE NORTH AMERICA

Series Editors
Liam Frink and Aubrey Cannon

Editorial Board
Alice Kehoe
Patricia Rubertone
Stephen Silliman
Katherine Spielmann
Michael Wilcox

A TALE OF
Three Villages

Indigenous-Colonial Interactions in Southwestern Alaska, 1740–1950

Liam Frink

The University of Arizona Press

Tucson

The University of Arizona Press
www.uapress.arizona.edu

We respectfully acknowledge the University of Arizona is on the land and territories of Indigenous peoples. Today, Arizona is home to twenty-two federally recognized tribes, with Tucson being home to the O'odham and the Yaqui. Committed to diversity and inclusion, the University strives to build sustainable relationships with sovereign Native Nations and Indigenous communities through education offerings, partnerships, and community service.

© 2016 The Arizona Board of Regents
All rights reserved. Published 2016

ISBN-13: 978-0-8165-3109-7 (cloth)
ISBN-13: 978-0-8165-5541-3 (paper)
ISBN-13: 978-0-8165-3380-0 (ebook)

Cover designed by Miriam Warren
Cover photo by Liam Frink

Original series design: David Alcorn, Alcorn Publication Design

Publication of this book was made possible in part by funding from the College of Liberal Arts of the University of Nevada, Las Vegas.

Library of Congress Cataloging-in-Publication Data
Frink, Liam, 1962– author.
  A tale of three villages : indigenous-colonial interactions in southwestern Alaska, 1740–1950 / Liam Frink.
    Archaeology of colonialism in native North America.
    Tucson : The University of Arizona Press, 2016. | Series: The archaeology of colonialism in native North America | Includes bibliographical references and index.
  LCCN 2015025703 | ISBN 9780816531097 (cloth : alk. paper)
  LCSH: Yupik Eskimos—Alaska, Southwest—History. | Indians of North America—Cultural assimilation—Alaska, Southwest.
  LCC E99.E7 F735 2016 | DDC 979.004/9714—dc23 LC record available at http://lccn.loc.gov/2015025703

Printed in the United States of America
♾ This paper meets the requirements of ANSI/NISO Z39.48-1992 (Permanence of Paper).

Contents

List of Illustrations	vi
Preface	vii
Acknowledgments	xi
Introduction. Indigenous-Colonial Interactions, Subsistence, and Identity	3
1. Lifeways on the Coastal Alaska Tundra	19
2. Precolonial Warfare and Early Indigenous-Colonial Trade	42
3. Indigenous-Mission Interactions	73
Conclusion	113
Appendix A. Site Comparisons	125
Appendix B. Qavinaq Site	127
Appendix C. Kashunak Site	131
Appendix D. Old Chevak Site	137
Notes	141
References	147
Index	165

Illustrations

Figure 1.	Map of Alaska	6
Figure 2.	Flow diagram of the movement of stone and steel axes among the Yir Yoront	12
Figure 3.	Map of Qavinaq, Kashunak, Old Chevak, and Chevak	13
Figure 4.	Coastal tundra	20
Figure 5.	Salmon drying at fish camp	24
Figure 6.	Houses in Chevak	27
Figure 7.	Butchering seal, Chevak village	36
Figure 8.	Fish smokehouse at summer fish camp	39
Figure 9.	Diagram illustrating the spatial divisions and connections between coastal women and men, and the men's house and family house	50
Figure 10.	Aerial view of Qavinaq village site	52
Figure 11.	Surface and slough bank artifacts from Qavinaq	52
Figure 12.	Qavinaq site map	53
Figure 13.	Remains of the men's house at Qavinaq	54
Figure 14.	Aerial view of Kashunak village mound	62
Figure 15.	Map of Kashunak village site	63
Figure 16.	Eastern side of Kashunak site mound	63
Figure 17.	Kashunak house pit	65
Figure 18.	Father Jules Convert ringing the bell at church complex in Kashunak	66
Figure 19.	Seal-poke pit at Kashunak	67
Figure 20.	Akulurak children and women cutting fish	79
Figure 21.	Drawing by Father Menager of Kashunak village	80
Figure 22.	Kashunak women and men pulling up *The Little Flower* boat with Father Fox	91
Figure 23.	Four of the Little Sisters of the Snow with their subsistence gear	96
Figure 24.	Mission at Old Chevak	102
Figure 25.	Map of Old Chevak	103
Figure 26.	Old Chevak mission building	107

Preface

THIS WORK IS AN EXPLORATION OF LIFE, CONTINUITY, and change among the people on the Yukon-Kuskokwim coast of southwestern Alaska, entwined in the context of issues between and among Alaska natives, colonists, and scientists. My research journey began in 1996, when the Chevak Traditional Council (the primary indigenous governing body of the village) invited the U.S. Fish and Wildlife Service to find an archaeologist interested in conducting research. Thus far there had been limited scholarly research in the area (and it largely remains so), known as a politically challenging region in which to work.

To enjoy long-term research success and secure funding from federal agencies, I worked to foster village collaboration. I had a desire to work with the community and felt an ethical responsibility to be candid about my research objectives. At each stage of the research program, I tried to balance my interests (and requirements for my PhD) with the wishes of the Cup'ik community of Chevak.[1] The acceptance by members of the village of this protocol was double-edged: I was granted access to the archaeological sites but was unable to excavate except to collect very few datable materials.

The three sequentially occupied sites under consideration in this study provide fascinating spatial data that illuminate cultural persistence and change from the late prehistoric through the colonial period. For the native people of Chevak, the old villages manifest their lives before, during, and after incredible and indelible social and economic change. These village sites harbor enduring and powerful memories of youth; of traveling by kayak up a slough; of the first house a young man built for his bride; of Elders' and ancestors' wisdom, trials, and triumphs; of spaces where grandmothers sewed incredible garments with their granddaughters in training; and of places where grandfathers, fathers, and uncles taught boys to be Yup'ik warriors, traders, and hunters. Perhaps more significantly, these places are linked to present heritage and a deep desire and dedication to not relinquish Yup'ikness or Yup'ik land to historical or post-colonial social and economic pressures. The connection to the past is a significant lifeline to the present and future. The boundaries placed on this study reflect a continued local tenacity to incorporate, yet negotiate, the impact of Western goods and ideas—including the imperialism of science.

The limits imposed on this study were made clear at my first meeting with the Elder Council of the Chevak Traditional Council, where I proposed to excavate at the late prehistoric site of Qavinaq. Oral history links this remarkable site to an abandonment episode during a tumultuous time in coastal prehistory, the Bow and Arrow War Days. After enduring an enemy siege and the felling of their warrior leader, the village was abandoned and burned to the ground by the victors. For me, Qavinaq was an incredible opportunity to understand late prehistoric life just prior to indigenous-colonial interactions, but, for Elders, excavation at the old village meant (literally) uncovering buried animosities and potentially rekindling regional violence—a dangerous proposal indeed. As decided by the group of Elders, the tragedies entombed in the murky strata of the tundra should and would remain unexhumed.

Given this cultural context, I developed an alternative research program: a methodology that respectfully, creatively, and meaningfully investigates the spatial and material past within the political realities of the present. Instead of focusing singly on the late prehistoric site, I comparatively examine the sequential occupation of three unoccupied village sites that are all connected to the people of Chevak. The investigation of this sequence of villages has been an opportunity to analyze settlement layout changes over the late prehistoric to indigenous-colonial historic periods. These surficial data are contextualized with ethnohistoric data, local oral histories, and eyewitness accounts from people who lived at two of the villages.

Because of the lack of excavation and artifacts, some readers may be found wanting more evidence to substantiate my interpretations. But given the post-Native American Graves Protection and Repatriation Act realities of twenty-first-century archaeology among indigenous groups as stakeholders of the past, the continued development of innovative methodologies is called for, as is our ability to more creatively situate different kinds of data we can collect (Delle 2007; Oland, Hart, and Frink 2012). It is my hope that if archaeologists and coastal people continue to forge relationships based on mutual respect, trust, and enthusiasm about the past, the possibility of future excavation may yield more fine-grained archaeological data. Nevertheless, even without excavation, I believe this largely ethnohistoric study illuminates issues of the enactment of culture change—what all anthropologists study. In this case, the culture change occurs during the colonial period in coastal southwestern Alaska, but the processes and interactions can be broadly applied to cross-cultural examination of the dynamics of change in any time period (see Dietler 2010).

This study also highlights the incredible potential for indigenous-colonial interaction studies in the Arctic. There remains a real connection among Alaskan native communities and their archaeological villages, and as highlighted in this work, stories and experiences with colonial institutions. There is also a continued intimate association of many people with subsistence and ways of making a living on the land—a crux of this study. Food and the production of foodstuffs is a significant marker of self and identity, and rights and responsibilities throughout a person's life course are firmly entrenched in the relationship with subsistence. A focus on the production and distribution of subsistence foods is critical, as the relationship with self, food, and the land was (and continues to be) a primary locus of the worldwide colonial siege.

Acknowledgments

THIS WORK WOULD NOT HAVE BEEN PRODUCED without an incredible amount of support and encouragement. I owe the deepest debt of gratitude and respect to the Traditional Council Elders and several generous families of Chevak. *Quyana Caqneq*. This project's field research was funded by a National Science Foundation Division of Polar Programs Doctoral Dissertation Improvement Grant (#0094664); many thanks to program director Dr. Anna Kerttula de Echave. In addition, early write-up of this research was supported by a Wenner-Gren Foundation Richard Carley Hunt Fellowship. Support also was provided by the U.S. Fish and Wildlife Service; a heartfelt thank-you goes to Debbie Corbett (who introduced me to the people of Chevak) in the Anchorage office and Mike Rearden in Bethel. Moreover, a significant note of gratitude goes out to the staff of the Bureau of Indian Affairs ANCSA Office in Anchorage, especially Ken Pratt and Matt O'Leary. I also thank David Kingma and staff at the Jesuit Oregon Province Archives, Foley Center Library, Gonzaga University. I also am grateful to the University of Nevada, Las Vegas (UNLV), the College of Liberal Arts (Dean Chris Hudgins in particular), and my department for the sabbatical year to work on this manuscript. I give a special thanks to my mentors Drs. Meg Conkey, Maria Lepowsky, and Doug Price. Thanks also to UNLV PhD students Celeste Giordano for her work on the tables (and all of our extensive conversations about subsistence and identity) and Aaron Woods for creating the illustrations and maps. A heartfelt debt of gratitude to Dr. Allyson Carter, editor-in-chief, University of Arizona Press (UAP), and the outstanding UAP team, and a special debt of gratitude to the anonymous reviewers—your thoughtful comments made this book better, thank you. Finally, this book is dedicated to my parents, Elders Darlene and Joseph Frink. All royalties for this book will be distributed to the Chevak Traditional Council.

A TALE OF
Three Villages

Introduction

INDIGENOUS-COLONIAL INTERACTIONS, SUBSISTENCE, AND IDENTITY

SUMMER DAYS ON THE ALASKAN COASTAL TUNDRA can be peaceful. Stalks of sea-green grass bend gracefully in the gentle breeze, the sky a yawning blue umbrella above the slowly moving yet powerful gray-hued river. Overhead, ducks soar, calling to their mates on the choppy water below. On the grassy bank above a muddy stretch of river, a family relaxes in a warm cozy tent at their summer fish camp, relieved to be away from the pressures of the winter village. Each day, grandfathers, fathers, uncles, sons, and grandsons land their boats along the river's edge, low in the water with fish caught in voluminous nets. The men carry their catch to the shoreline and unload the fish into pits cut into the frozen ground. The fish lay in queue, to be butchered by the women. Back from the shoreline strips of salmon hang over impressive driftwood racks and an Elder woman inspects their progress. The fat red flesh gradually dries in the fresh delta breeze, and nearby, women and girls gut and cut the remaining fish. Boys run about the camp and on the tundra honing their hunting skills, pausing to watch their grandmothers, mothers, aunts, and sisters work. Women sit face-to-face as they deftly slice the plump and oily fish and girls practice their own emerging skills. Before being packed for transport to the village, the curly, desiccated tails of the fish are counted, as women calculate the provisions their family and dogs will need through the long, frigid, dark, yet festive winter months.

For some Yup'ik Eskimo families, this tundra scene happens today much like it has for several thousand years on the riverbanks and adjacent islands of the Yukon Kuskokwim Delta region of southwestern Alaska. Of course, their lives, tools, materials, and social and economic organization today are contextualized by generations of ecological and cultural adaptation—in particular, nearly two hundred years of interaction with market and religious colonialism. Yet, amidst vast change there remains among coastal people an enduring and meaningful connection to the land and subsistence that sustains and defines their bodies and communities. That is what this book is about—it focuses on how foods and identity are intertwined and essential to understanding the trajectory of change, resistance, and persistence during stages of indigenous-colonial interactions. The data collected and interpreted in this study are not your typical archaeology but rather an approach that is taking root in our discipline. Except for the minimalist collection of datable materials, there was no digging—what Matthew Liebmann (2013, 21) refers to as a "noninvasive investigation." The project relies on site spatial and surface-feature comparisons, ethnohistoric and oral historic accounts, my ethnographic observations and experiences, and the very memories of local people. This narrative journey tracks the histories of three villages ancestrally united to the contemporary community of Chevak: Qavinaq, a village just at the precipice of colonial interactions and eventually devastated by warfare; Kashunak, where people lived during the infancy and growth of the commercial market and colonial religion; and Old Chevak, a briefly occupied yet solidifying stepping-stone village occupied just prior to modern Chevak.

The history of these three villages and the people who once lived at them is framed through a current paradigmatic trend in indigenous-colonial scholarship—the connection of local people to their experiences of colonialism. There are three primary themes woven throughout this study that form a theoretical framework to explore the culture history of this group of indigenous people along the southwestern Alaskan coast. First, I investigate how and why indigenous systems prior to the onset of indigenous-colonial interactions set the stage for trajectories of social and economic change; second, I develop how it is imperative to integrate local subsistence food systems and their essential relationship to identity and change; and third, I consider why interactions among native people are as important to analyze as are relations between indigenous people and colonists.

As much as possible, understanding lifeways prior to indigenous-colonial interactions is elemental since prehistory has everything to do with history (Friesen 2012; Mitchell 2012; Scheiber and Mitchell 2009). Undoubtedly, market and religious colonialism kindled transformations among groups in Native North America, but descendant people are no longer presented as helpless pawns but as active participants in historic processes. This revised paradigmatic perspective is not meant to dismiss the very real and destructive symbolic and structural violence of colonial ascendancy (Silliman 2010). Nonetheless, interactions between colonists and indigenous people were enacted on a stage of native cultural expectations and systems. Current colonial scholarship shows that we dare not disarticulate the prehistoric from the historic and that trajectories of transitions rest squarely in indigenous systems prior to contact, such that "present changes are set in the past" (Bayman 2010, 133).

Framing indigenous experience amidst colonial practice as interactive better problematizes the processes and links between the precolonial, early colonial-period, and later colonial-period transitions (Oland, Hart, and Frink 2012). The ways a cultural group responded to colonial events is rooted in the precolonial, a kind of baseline for comparison over time, which provides scholars the opportunity to "measure the rate and magnitude of cultural change" and continuity (Lightfoot, Wake, and Schiff 1991, 7). Therefore, connecting the precolonial indigenous system is paramount to tracing the processes and cumulative outcomes of different stages and types of colonial encounters. By explaining the processes of actions and reactions to colonialism, we are better prepared to inquire about the before-colonial culture and the internal native interactions that set the stage for engagement with colonials. A useful framework for untangling the long-term threads of colonialism and power relationships is to think of indigenous people and colonialists entwined in evolving stages of unfolding and intensifying change in an "emerging colonial arena" (Comaroff 1985, 10). In this light, colonial and indigenous interactions were fraught with varying levels of mitigation, accommodation, resistance, and acceptance—an "entanglement" over time between colonists and locals (Dietler 1998, 298).

Market and religious colonialism was a primer to changed culture played out on a field of indigenous social, economic, and ideological norms and values (Rubertone 2000). The precolonial cultural template helped shape responses and repercussions, especially of early colonialism, when indigenous groups had more space in a relatively more even middle ground of interactions (see Gosden 2004; White 1991). And much of this discourse was configured not only between indigenous and foreigners and their goods but also among native people themselves (see Ehrhardt 2005). It is therefore imperative to integrate material and ideological interactions and changes among native people themselves, and one of the most relevant regions in the world to study these early processes is in Arctic North America.

Indigenous-Colonial Interactions in Southwestern Alaska

A common narrative suggests that not until the mid-twentieth century did coastal Yup'ik Eskimo lives significantly alter because of colonial markets and religious interventions. Customary is an image of fairly isolated people sheltered from the initial maelstrom of Russian government officials, traders, and Orthodox priests; Euro-North American gold seekers; international whalers; and merchants who during the nineteenth century infiltrated much of Arctic North America. For coastal people, their relative sequestration from early colonial impacts delayed major transformations. In the face of indelible cultural revisions to the north, south, and east of them, they remained relatively unspoiled for a late nineteenth-century explorer to discover. Shielded from the stresses of the early market tempest, change came rather in the form of religious colonialism in the early twentieth century, at which time their social and economic lives suddenly transformed.

But, a less "monolithic" viewpoint leads to a more nuanced and realistic narrative of the past and of the scale of historic indigenous-colonial interactions, impacts, and culture change and persistence (Liebmann 2012, 25). Coastal Yup'ik people were in a frontier region relatively buffered by direct interactions with colonists until the early 1900s settlement of Jesuit missionaries. Nonetheless, coastal folks were not without encounters with colonial people, ideologies, and goods that triggered social and economic dialogue

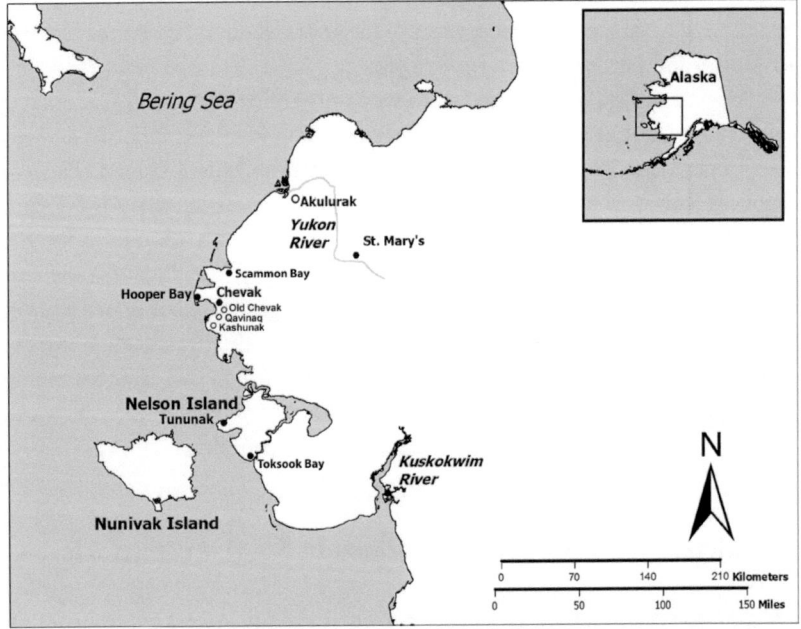

FIGURE 1. Map of Alaska. The Yukon-Kuskokwim Delta is the coastal region between the two rivers.

and change. Their settlement archaeology, native memories and lived experiences, and ethnohistoric documents illuminate an alternative account of a subtle yet enduring and active indigenous interface with colonial commerce that set the stage for their engagement with twentieth-century religious colonialism.

The Arctic North is as yet a relatively underrepresented region of colonial scholarship, but circumpolar north cultural and archaeological research has been at the forefront in the early development of colonial studies.[1] Studies have considered early colonial contexts and mechanisms of cultural change from an increasingly emic perspective. Early on, William Fitzhugh (1985, 5) comments, "Little attention, however, has been given to archaeological studies of early contact from the native point of view." To best approach studies of contact interactions and the directions of transformations, he suggests that we must understand precontact indigenous systems and, in particular, that both colonials and native groups have various intersecting and divergent motivations and agendas.

Subsistence and Identity

The second overarching core theme of this book is that subsistence as it relates to identity (here, gender and age groups) is an essential element of understanding indigenous-colonial interactions and culture process. The colonial project was largely about exploitation and undermining of social and subsistence systems. And it has been through food and identity connected to subsistence foods that Yup'ik people have negotiated among themselves and with colonials.

Subsistence is unequivocally tied to the framing of group and individual identity and in particular gender and age. What a person does and how successfully (or not) he or she does it in large part defines a person's position, rights, and responsibilities through his or her life course. As Eleanor Leacock observes (1986, 114), divisions of labor and production commonly unite subsistence-based communities of "women and men in exchange relations as constituents, each of which is responsible for and controls the conditions of its own production"—elsewhere astutely referred to as "gendered economics" (Eislet and Darling 2012, 424). As individuals and social groups, women and men are interdependent on their mutual social and economic success. This shared dependence tempers but does not negate tensions and negotiations between women and men and their relative access to resources, particularly at points of cultural transformation and stress (Begler 1978, 574).

Gendered and aged divisions of labor and production set up fundamental systems of knowledge, expertise, authority, and access that organize identity groups and unionize them to shelter and improve their interests (Frink 2006). Over time, identity groups can be observed and measured by their relative degree of productive control over subsistence resources. It is crucial to track which collective group(s) control labor and production and the shaping of economic and social relationships. The position of groups can be gauged by at least two factors: (1) the control of resources and/or the means of production, and (2) access to status-building opportunities based on the control and merit of production (see Lepowsky 1993, 32). Productive control includes the direction of processing activities, decisions concerning distribution and manufacture, and overall management of immediate use and surplus. Native North American gendered divisions have been viewed as complementary, each having its own sphere of influence. For instance, among the Plateau Indians, gendered skills were similarly valued, and political voice (stemming from economic production and reproduction) was not limited to men (L. Ackerman 1995). And among some Great Lakes groups, a woman's intimate control over the distribution of meat constituted a large part of her autonomy and authority (Devens 1992).

Though we have become more explicit in our inclusion of gender as a fundamental category of inquiry and native agency (Spielmann et al. 2009; Voss 2008), we still relatively lag on factoring identity and life course in our investigations (but see Kamp 2001; Lawrence and Davies 2010; Park 2005). But age coalitions are one of the most potent elements in modeling dynamics of cultural persistence and revision. Age categories are fundamental boundary markers of privileges and duties among subsistence-based groups. Cross-culturally, Elder men and women are often political, ritual, technological, and economic experts and can gain significant influential ground based on their mastery, knowledge, and junior-senior debt systems wherein young people earn to learn (Cruikshank 1990; Dickerson-Putman and Brown 1994). Elders, especially those who have achieved great expertise, can hold significant political sway (Ellanna and Sherrod 1995). Among subsistence-based groups, there is deep respect and reverence for Elder people, mixed with an important element of trepidation for their power.

In indigenous systems, older people hold much more authority over others—in particular, young people. Traditional age hierarchies keep young people in their place as they acquire access to cultural knowledge, material goods, and marriage partners through homage and debt peonage. Older people are less apt to embrace change if they have subscribed to the traditional system and have reaped the dividends of authority through age. Change, however, can come from those groups, such as women and young people, who have not (yet) benefited from "tradition" and who may rather profit from introduced changes. For instance, Cameron Wesson (2010) shows that during incipient colonial interactions in the southeast United States, native individuals who chose to trade with Europeans effectively undercut the established political economic system.

Indigenous-Indigenous Interactions and Colonialism

The third thematic thread that weaves through this book is that native people negotiated not only with colonials but also among themselves. Native people had already grappled with those who desired to augment their social ranking through monopolization of resources long before Euro-North American colonists arrived. Cameron Wesson (2010, 63) has recently likened native organization to a "moral economy" with a fundamental framework of "self-interested calculation." People do not just endure but also, as Stephen Silliman adds (2004, 3), "work the system to their own benefit"—in particular, through acts of "undermining." In this work this includes colonists actively undercutting native social and economic systems, native peoples undermining colonial tactics, and native communities, families, and individuals jockeying among one another for material and political resources. James Scott (1990, 14–15), too, suggests that the colonial era was rife with internal struggles or "infrapolitics" for the "distribution of power, wealth, and status" among groups. Conflicts stemmed from perceived and real internal advantages or disadvantages and dialogues of negotiating authority. Colonialist-inspired stimulants could exacerbate and enhance already-existing social and economic inequities or could benefit those who had been disadvantaged (Comaroff 1985). Cultural transformation in this context was driven from within as well as from without.

Indigenous-colonial history is at least in part a reconfiguration of opportunity for individual and identity group advancement as two different cultural constructs impacted one another (Frink 2007). Globally, economic and social transformations could be triggered by colonial goods or events, and yet the kinds and directions of change were at times founded in existing group issues sometimes based in systemic inequities (see J. Scott 1990). I do not think, nor do the data support, that colonialism or capitalism converted coastal people to suddenly discover self-interest (contra Sahlins 1985; following Hayden 1995; Maschner 1991); instead, I view complex interactions and contestations as present already and exacerbated by colonial impacts.

Access to resources is a key place to look for internal fissures that colonialism could seep into. A model of inequities persisting within indigenous subsistence-based groups prior to colonial insurgency challenges an idea of locals as sailing through life with divisions of resources that are rarely, if ever, questioned or contested. But, as Elsie Begler (1978, 574) pointed out long ago, an idea of continuous balanced parity among interest factions in subsistence-based communities through time is clearly "political naïvete." In this case study, each stage of indigenous-colonial interaction is focused on how to better elucidate evidence of negotiations among Yup'ik interest groups—and whether their positions, and in particular those based in resource access and control, were hampered or elevated.

The fundamental theoretical framework for this study is a political economy perspective—in particular, contexts and outcomes of access and distribution, of material goods but also of information and ideology. It is also a study to explore how decisions people made were sometimes based on their perceived access (or lack of) to resources. People are able to identify potential change agents, estimate possible economic and social transitions, and make calculated choices in their best interest based on potential economic and social shifts. Indigenous groups and individuals undoubtedly made calculations during the colonial era, with a wide range of responses, including active (violent) or passive resistance (malingering), intensified embracement of the traditional, or adaptation and incorporation of aspects of the new (Ferris 2011; J. Scott 1990; Voss 2000). Any choices in a constrained and transformative context can be rife with peril, as the direction or outcome of a transitory historic period was yet to unfold.

Negotiations and tensions of management over resources were not introduced by colonials but are a fundamental part of human group relations. As coalitions, women and men cooperate but also compete for resources (Devens 1992; Redding-Gubitosa 1992; Ward 2002). The colonial market triggered differential development of roles, responsibilities, and rights for men and women, and "development for one sex may simultaneously lead to underdevelopment for the other" (Bossen 1975, 599; see also Gonzalez 1981, 3). During colonial transition among small-scale groups, the valuation of subsistence resources and relations of production changed significantly. For instance, the decline of women's status (and status-seeking opportunities) is strongly linked to colonial patriarchal market practices, the attendant disintegration of women's subsistence-based productive and distributive control, and the correlative loss of "decision-making power" (Leacock 1978, 247). Women's production, including the control over distribution, is critical to their autonomy and authority and was significantly abridged in the colonial context.

This is powerfully illustrated by the historic Iroquois. Prior to colonial incursion, women held a fair measure of public and private authority based on their jurisdiction over food. But when Iroquois men took up the plow, it was an economic and social boon but a bust for women, who lost a significant measure of their political influence within the transfigured socioeconomic system (Brown 1975).

Women's authority, in cases where it did not deteriorate within the market system parity, largely rested on their continued control of their production and reproduction. For instance, indigenous-colonial sexual unions augmented a trader's access to native economic networks and social alliances and, at the same time, to a strategic union that could amplify a woman's access to goods and opportunities (Fossett 2001; Ray 1975; Sleeper-Smith 2001). Nevertheless, as market systems matured, colonists increasingly circumvented kinship relations, especially those tied to women. As a result, native women's direct involvement could be truncated, and they instead filled auxiliary labor roles and lost a significant measure of direct control over their products (Van Kirk 1980).

The role of women has been little examined in the history of complexity through manipulation of surplus foods, even though, cross-culturally, women store, manage, and transform foodstuffs. When women's roles are factored, it has been in the realm of extracted labor (particularly in polygynous systems) for men's primary activities. But, Michael Dietler (2001) infuses the negotiations and the complexities of women's roles and rewards in past public displays (see also Mills 2007). Critical analyses must bypass the untenable position that inserts women simply as (manipulated) subsidiary support or as (acquiescent) exploited labor to men's public endeavoring. Indigenous women have certainly played both of these parts (and more), but their roles in the dynamics of economic and cultural change are much more realistic, interesting, and complicated. For instance, Judith Habicht-Mauche (2005) explores the common portrait of indigenous North American women as hide-working so-called drudges (first broached by Gifford-Gonzalez 1993), women exploited by southern High Plains men to further their competitive political and economic machinations. But she suggests that we must better understand the path that domestic goods take on the road to becoming commodities in transformed economies. This is critical because women were the producers of these wealth items that became revalued, and their control over distribution was a fundamental building block to their authority and status (see also Hollimon 2005). Therefore, we need to pay attention to the organization of labor and how it may change, potential struggles over the control over resources, and contexts of new exchange opportunities.

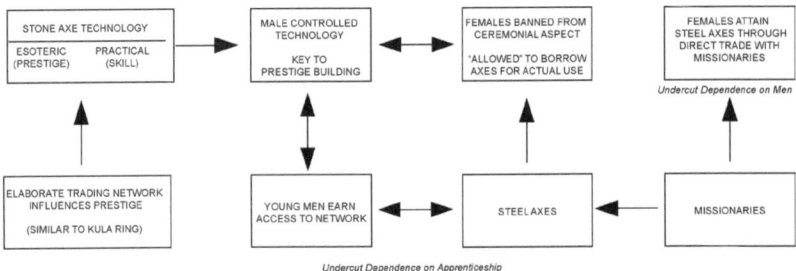

FIGURE 2. Flow diagram of the movement of stone and steel axes among the Yir Yoront. (After Sharp 1952.)

This study also focuses on the political economy of youth in an indigenous-colonial context. Young people are more apt to undermine customary systems of power (see Reedy-Maschner and Maschner 1999); what is tradition but a system of practices, materials, and beliefs that emphasize roles of individuals and groups that set up and maintain forms of social control and authority? Tradition is most closely guarded and reinforced by those who have contributed into the system of authority and especially those who have benefited from that traditional system: older people in a community. They have built their lives on conforming to traditional expectations and have been variably rewarded, but young people are still vying for access to resources and these rewards. Youth were targeted by colonial traders and missionaries, and their (both passive and purposeful) engagement with new technologies, language, and ideologies has significant potential to undermine traditional systems of control.

Both women and young people as allied groups are strongly implicated in indigenous-colonial–era change, not just as the orphaned or helpless but also as actors with power to undermine traditional systems of gender and age discrimination. A classic example of colonialism as a vehicle for internal undermining of a traditional system of material and symbolic status inequity is Lauriston Sharp's (1952) groundbreaking study among the Yir Yoront of Australia.

During the incipient period of colonialism among the Yir Yoront, missionaries rewarded (perceived) compliant interactions with the distribution of steel axes (see figure 2). Women and young men embraced the practical and social tool, but older men eschewed the priests and their offering. Sharp suggests that this was because, as a group, Elder men's arena of prestige building and maintenance was firmly positioned in the ideological and economic control over access and use of the stone adze. In this sense, clinging to tradition meant so much more than fear of cultural loss: it meant saving the Elder men's social, economic, and ritual advantage of access and formal clout over their sons and wives. Colonial missionaries introduced the metal axe, but it was women and young men who ultimately undermined Elder men's position by circumventing their control and effectively renegotiating their social and economic relationships.

So how do we find the subtle yet powerful impact of prehistory on history and negotiations of identity through subsistence both among indigenous and colonials and among indigenous interest groups? This is indeed a tall order, and colonial scholars are now experimenting with different variations of this theme (see Liebmann 2012; C. Lyons and Papadoulas 2002). As my predecessors did, in this book I rally several lines of evidence to weave together a narrative that follows the spatial and architectural structure of the three villages that were occupied from just prior to the beginnings of colonial impacts to 1950. Of particular salience in this work is the importation of the words of Yup'ik people who experienced the indigenous-colonial encounter in their own lifetimes.

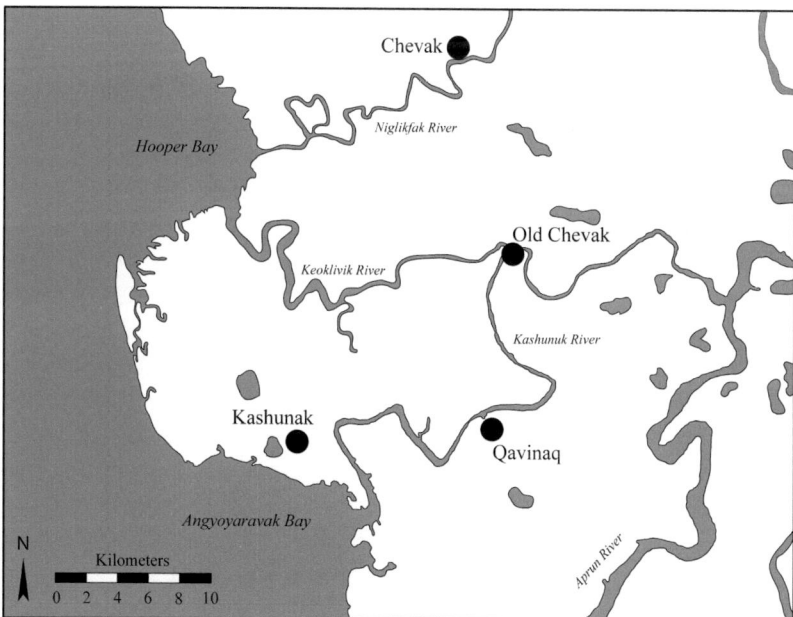

FIGURE 3. Map of Qavinaq, Kashunak, Old Chevak, and Chevak. (To protect the sites, these locations on the map are approximate and show their relation to one another not their precise locations.)

Use of Space and Cultural Change

In this study I compare surface site features among three sites occupied by the people of Chevak and incorporate ethnohistoric, oral historic, and interview data to explore contexts of manifested cultural transitions. Reading cultural negotiations in the past through use of space is a challenging but long-recognized and accepted archaeological practice (Hodder 1982). The built environment is not just structures used by people; it also speaks to observable characterizations of daily life and how relationships may have changed over time. The created environment is commonly identity-group specific, and renovations to structures can have deep cultural implications. Built forms are especially indicative of gender- and age-based interactions and the structural orchestration of social and economic engagement (Blunt and Rose 1994). For instance, in the American Southwest, Patricia Crown and Suzanne Fish (1996) explore the impact of built walls amid the Hohokam Preclassic to Classic transition and suggest that architectural segregation of women would have had repercussions on their networking and status-building activities, especially among older women. The enclosure of houses enacted and reinforced a faint yet compelling structural seclusion, which effectively restricted women's day-to-day direct interactions. As a consequence, women had fewer opportunities to build, display, and reinforce their skills, leadership, and senior standing. The walls figuratively and literally blocked women's prestige- and rapport-building activities among one another and truncated the "distribution of knowledge," an essential element of networking (Crown and Fish 1996, 806).

The examination of the colonially inspired reorganization of space has been a rewarding point of analysis for understanding long-term processes and the "remapping" of people's lived environment (Delle 1998, 3; 2000). Barbara Voss (2000) charts how indigenous lives were structurally redirected and restricted by Spanish missions and how native people differentially responded to colonial encroachment through their contingent choices. Also, use of space can be a medium for negotiating colonial processes—for example, Silliman's (2001a, 194–95) framed "acts of residence" in which indigenous people manipulated space and everyday activities to "stake out a claim" in colonial conditions. These spaces are not necessarily representative of "active revolutionaries out to usurp the powers that oppress them" but are places where folks fashion a place for themselves within a dynamic social, economic, and political context (Silliman 2001a, 195). Religious conversion in highland Peru, according to Steven Wernke (2011; see also 2007; 2013), centered on conscious colonial tactics of reshaping and reordering the built environment—in essence changing the daily rhythms of people's lives to reinforce conformity to a new colonial order. But Wernke shows that at least in the early phases of evangelizing these spaces became indigenous-colonial amalgamations and not simply Spanish structural impositions.

In the following I examine the changed construction, location, and uses of four identity-linked village structures: the men's house, the family house, and associated tunnels and storage facilities. By following the modifications and/or abandonment of these over the sequence of site occupations, we can surmise elements of cultural persistence and change, interactions among interest groups and with colonists, and potential long-term implications of the revisions of these structural forms. The four features highlight the external and internal strains among people for access and control of resources amid the increasingly modified economic and social landscape of commercial and religious colonialism.

Introduction of the Three Sites

To weave together this narrative of change over time, I draw from several lines of evidence to bring meaning to the site surface patterns and the comparison of features. I incorporate ethnohistoric evidence, including secondary and primary interviews with Alaskan native people, many of whom have lived at two of the villages. The deeply enduring connection of indigenous people and their ancestors' village sites is common in the Alaskan Arctic (Griffin 1996; Oswalt 1952; Oswalt and VanStone 1967). Chevak villagers trace their lineage to Qavinaq, an ancestral village lived in just prior to the emergence of the indigenous-colonial experience; Kashunak, a village that spans both the precolonial and historical; and Old Chevak, where people lived prior to their move to contemporary Chevak (see appendix A; figure 3).

The now unoccupied village of Qavinaq was occupied just prior to colonial settlement into Alaska (circa 1740 to prior to 1833). The village is on a raised terrace located on a narrow slough that flows from the Kashunak River. Because of tides, seasonal flooding, and ice scouring, the eastern edge of the site is eroding; nevertheless, much of the site remains intact. The site features are on two distinct sectors of raised ground. On these mounds are classic house pit features and two larger pit structures identified by local people as men's houses and aboveground interments on the adjacent crowberry tundra. Data from oral histories, surface and midden artifacts, site layout, and radiocarbon dates show that this winter village site is typical of precontact coastal culture. Among people in the region Qavinaq is best known as a site that was destroyed by warriors from the north and a place that represents late precolonial life at the precipice of cultural change.

As the story is told, after the infamously disastrous battle at Qavinaq, the survivors relocated to Kashunak (also known locally as Nunaraluq), never to return to their homes. On the Kashunak River, one can see the grand mound of Kashunak village from quite a distance. An ever-narrowing slough snakes along the tundra and eventually ends, and a foot trail through the marshy grasses marks the remainder of the journey to the village. Kashunak (circa AD 1640 to AD 1950) has archaeological, oral historic, and eyewitness evidence of prehistoric, protohistoric, and colonial occupation. People lived at Kashunak when traders, and following them the Jesuit missionaries, entered the region in the later 1800s and early 1900s. Its complex architectural conglomeration shows evidence of typical Yup'ik buildings as well as revised colonial-era additions. The Chevak connection to Kashunak was quite viable since at the time of my study some Elders were born or lived at Kashunak.

In 1947, the people of Kashunak left their village mound and brought their belongings upriver to Old Chevak, conveniently located at the confluence of the Keoklivik and Kashunak Rivers. This area had long been used for fishing and hunting, and it was the location of an early colonial commercial store. There are some pit house features at Old Chevak, but most others are hybrid-style house features that were shallowly dug or even set upon stilts, similar to today's manner of construction. A Jesuit chapel still stands at the site, as do some remnants of the colonial store. Unlike its predecessors, Old Chevak looks little like a typical prehistoric or early historic coastal village, and it is a place where local people knew life had irrefutably and irrevocably changed. Shortly after establishment of the village, Old Chevak was vacated in 1950, and the entire group moved to the present village of Chevak.

The Data

Matthew Liebmann (2012, 21) writes that non-excavation-focused archaeological practice may lead us to "learn more by digging less." In this study, I explore how and why four surface features—the men's house, family house, and associated tunnels and storage facilities—change among these three villages (see appendix A). The surface survey data collected for this study have proved particularly appropriate for Arctic archaeologists, as aboriginal architecture and features are commonly visible (Darwent, Darwent, et al. 2007; Darwent, Mason, et al. 2013; Dawson 2001; Schaaf 1995). Staying within the strictures of community wishes (i.e., no invasive testing or excavation except minimally for dating), I define the surface settlement characteristics at each site. All three sites were mapped by a U.S. Bureau of Indian Affairs (BIA) crew in the 1980s, and I re-measured and re-mapped them, using meter tape and a compass. None of the sites had previously been carbon dated, and in line with permissions from the village Traditional Council, the very few datable samples I collected are from eroded areas at each site (the Old Chevak sample is most likely near but off-site).

Complementing the site surface data, I integrate ethnohistoric information, including several kinds of archival records of the Jesuit Catholics, the first missionaries in the area. I studied these sources at the Jesuit Oregon Province Archives (JOPA) in Special Collections, Foley Center Library, Gonzaga University, Spokane, Washington. I incorporate notarial records from the Jesuits' daily logs at the Kashunak and Old Chevak missions. The notations (in English) are interesting vignettes of some occurrences at the missions with aspects of the priests' observations of village life and Yup'ik interactions with the Catholic Church. I also integrate official and unofficial correspondences, in particular among the village mission priests and their superiors at Akulurak and St. Mary's main missions. In addition (beginning in the early 1930s with Father John P. Fox), I draw information from black-and-white photographs as well as a published memoir by Father Frances Menager (1962), the first priest to establish the mission in Kashunak.

These data are a significant literary and visual record of life at Kashunak and Old Chevak. Study of the colonial period in the Americas has relied on ethnohistorical documents, critical evidence to understanding colonial perspectives and practices. Nevertheless, as Michael Dietler cautions (2010, 20), the slanted perspective of these kinds of documents can lead to a biased "tyranny of the text." Part of the challenge is that when colonials did record and comment on local activities it is commonly "exotic" behavior that is noted, not the mundane activities that make the material past we later observe (see Liebmann and Murphy 2011, 4). But the mission logs provide a relatively more fine-grained view of everyday life at the villages.

Over the past several decades, archaeologists have continued to develop theoretical frameworks and methodological best practices to examine and give expression to a broad spectrum of native lives prior to and during the colonial era (N. Lyons 2013; Mitchell and Scheiber 2010; Panich and Schneider 2014; Silliman 2004). An additional data set this study incorporates is indigenous perspectives on and experience with colonialism, drawing from two kinds of native data: oral traditions (generationally passed histories) and oral histories (accounts of one's own lifetime; see Vansina 1985). Undoubtedly, these data are influenced by the issues of memory and the politics of culture and change. But these kinds of data are a valuable "insider's view on the past" and can "hint" at the perceptions of indigenous people and their interactions with and interpretations of colonials and their practices (Lightfoot 2005, 16–17).

There are two sets of oral evidence that I integrate into this study. First, I draw from archived oral interview data from the Alaska Native Claims Settlement Act (ANCSA) 14(h)(1).[2] During the late 1970s and 1980s, there were hundreds of interviews conducted with Elders in Alaska by teams of men and women from the U.S. Bureau of Indian Affairs, U.S. Bureau of Land Management, and U.S. National Park Service Cooperative Park Studies Unit (CPSU) (see Norris and Saleeby 2009). In many cases the Elders did not speak English in the interviews; therefore, the interviewers worked with local interpreters. The focus of the interviews was generally on the use of landscape (and land claims), but there are other topics covered as well. The documents I use were first recorded on cassette tape during the interviews (these interviews were in people's homes and also in the field); they then were often translated by local interpreters from the cassette tapes and typed to produce hard copies.[3] For this study, I focus on interviews with Elders from the "Triangle Area" (Funk 2010) of Chevak, Hooper Bay, and Scammon Bay. Though there are limitations to these data, they are a treasure trove of oral historic accounts of the Bow and Arrow War Days and eyewitness perspectives of land use and subsistence, and intersections with indigenous-colonial interactions and outcomes.

Second, I incorporate my own interviews and participant observation studies with Yup'ik women and men. Most of my interview data derive from my discussions with Yup'ik women, a relative rarity of perspective in academic scholarship.[4] These folks were appropriate to interview for this project since most had lived at both Kashunak and Old Chevak villages. Of course, eyewitness accounts have issues of memory distortion and bias; nevertheless, the complementary ethnographic data set in this study is a valuable and rare contribution to better explore and situate the complexities of the colonial period from an indigenous point of view.

I

Lifeways on the Coastal Alaskan Tundra

AT HEART, THIS BOOK EXPLORES THE LIVES of people in coastal southwestern Alaska just prior and during the early stages of the indigenous-colonial period. Of utmost importance for the reader to understand is the fundamental role that food has in this local history. Subsistence is one of the more critical lynchpins of the indigenous-colonial experience and one that is not oft incorporated fully into our narratives of the past. This chapter explores the environmental context of life on the tundra and specifically focuses on subsistence as not just what people harvest, process, and eat, use, or wear but also fundamentally who people are through their life courses. The substrate of entwining subsistence and identity is critical since much of indigenous-colonial interactions and change are centered on food.

The delta is a coastal maritime environment bounded by the Yukon River in the north and the Kuskokwim River in the south. From above, the tundra is a majestic and intricate tapestry of moving and standing waterways, continually carving and reshaping the landscape. Storms, tidal flow, and scouring spring ice continually alter the topography of the tundra. Over three-quarters of the massive alluvial fan is composed of wetlands with rivers, sloughs, ponds, and marshy areas.

The winters are long, dark, and cold, and summer days are generally cool, wet, and windy. The climate is regulated by the Bering Sea, and mean monthly temperatures range from 10°C to −14°C, with an average precipitation of 43 cm, with 27 cm of rain and 160 cm of snowfall (Jorgenson and Ely 2001, 125). For part of the year, flowers, sedges, lichens, mosses, grasses, and other hardy, low-lying plants create a seemingly endless carpet of spongy, lush, and colorful tundra. Below the thin ground surface is a discontinuous layer of permafrost. Alder and willows grow patchily farther upland along tributaries. Elevation is everything on the tundra, with the slightest rise from a wet marsh ceding to relatively drier crowberry tundra. There are

FIGURE 4. The coastal tundra, July 2001. (Photo by author.)

limited areas of higher ground suitable for habitation, and prehistoric settlements can be found among the remains of old alluvial deposits.

People have lived along the Yukon-Kuskokwim coast for several thousand years. The first culture group to settle here was the Norton tradition, thought to have entered from north Alaska (Giddings 1964; Larsen and Rainey 1948). This culture group occupied the coastlines of western Alaska and the Canadian border to the Alaska Peninsula from around 2,400 years ago to AD 1000. On the Yukon-Kuskokwim coast the earliest Norton sites have been identified on Nunivak and Nelson Islands (Nowak 1982; Okada et al. 1982). Don Dumond (2000, 5) refers to these groups as "river fishing folk," and they also subsisted on caribou and sea mammals. They built semisubterranean driftwood-framed sod houses, included men's houses in their larger villages, and used well-made ceramic pots (Dumond 2000, 2011; Lutz 1972). People expanded up into the interior river systems possibly 2,000 to 1,500 years ago. Based on his work at the Manokinak site, Robert Shaw (1983, 1998) suggests that upriver migration may have been a response to population pressures and higher investment in fish harvests.

The site of Manokinak shows a fairly uneventful and rapid transition (around AD 1000) from Norton to a community of people archaeologists refer to as Thule. Prehistoric Thule are generally accepted as ancestral to contemporary Arctic Eskimo communities across northern North America (Dumond

2011), but this direct line of descent is more difficult to understand in the eastern Arctic (Helgason et al. 2006). Maybe several hundred years later than Alaskan Thule, these people colonized occupied lands of the Canadian Arctic and Greenland (Friesen and Arnold 2008).

Thule people along the Alaskan coast lived much like their Norton predecessors. They harvested sea mammals, fished along the coastline and the rivers, and hunted caribou (Dumond 2011). They likely used skin tents in the summer and built driftwood-framed and sod-covered homes to stay warm and dry during the long winter months. These homes often had deep cold-trap tunnel entrances, perfectly adapted to the sometimes-bitter wind and cold. Families tended to live in large winter villages and dispersed for seasonal harvesting camps on the tundra (Okada et al. 1982). Their technology was much like that of historic Alaskans; people used ground slate for their knives and fished and hunted sea mammals using skin kayaks on the open water and along the shore ice. The Thule people thrived along the coast for hundreds of years—but their lives were soon to irreversibly change.

Early Indigenous-Colonial Encounters

Beginning in 1741, Russian entrepreneurs rushed to the "Great Land," targeting the Aleutian archipelago for fur seals and sea otters and trading to elites in northern China in return for tea (Crowell 1997). The Russian-American Company (RAC) was established in 1799 as an administrative and mercantile body. After over-hunting the Aleutians, the RAC turned its extractive attentions north. Beaver, fox, sable, martin, ermine, and river otter pelts were in high demand on the European, southwest Asian, and Chinese markets. The RAC built trade locations as early as 1818 along the Nushagak River and fortified their posts, as some indigenous people on both continents resisted Russian settlement and the usurping of their trade networks (Pierce 1988).

Official colonial markets across the Bering Strait were inaugurated with the establishment of the St. Michael and Kolmakov Redoubt on the Kuskokwim River in 1833 and, several years later, the Russian Mission along the shores of the lower Yukon River (Ray 1975). However, similar to the commerce activities in other regions of North America (i.e., Ehrhardt 2005), foreign goods moved amid native people well before Russian émigrés settled. The Bering Strait was an intercontinental route for travel and trade between the east and west, as well as inland and coastal groups. Inland Athabaskan furs, coastal Eskimo sea mammal oil and skins, walrus tusks, and frozen and dried fish were traded for Chuckchi reindeer hides from the Siberian coast for

European and Russian tobacco, iron, glass beads, knives, copper, and cloth (Black 1984; Michael 1967).

The coastal delta was edged by these trade posts to the south and north, but the Russians did not officially occupy the study area. During the 1840s, the RAC established smaller trade outposts, or *"odinochkas,"* which were maintained by Russian men, and even smaller posts stationed with native managers, trading partners of the RAC employees. These native managers, or *"zakazchick,"* controlled the flow of goods to and from the RAC to locals in their trade districts (Black 1984). But the RAC sought to bypass these local traders and worked to persuade villagers to trade directly with Russians at the forts (Michael 1967). Both men and women would travel great distances to the Russian posts to trade, including one indigenous woman who, with "infants at the breast," alone hauled a sled of caribou meat to Nulato (Michael 1967, 155).

Russians also traveled to villages in an attempt to circumvent local traders. They were particularly interested in securing dried fish—the essential fuel for people and dogs and one that women fully managed. For example, Zagoskin commented that women could negotiate "very cleverly" for their fish (Michael 1967, 130, 133, 135, 145, 197). The RAC was determined to monopolize trade of furs since the informal native market was economically formidable (Michael 1967). For instance, in one year (1842–1843) at the post of Nulato, the Russians moved 3,125 beaver pelts but estimated that indigenous entrepreneurs traded at least 5,500 (Gibson 1988, 379).

The breadth of imports into Alaska increased throughout the 1800s to include alcohol (forbidden for trade with indigenous people by the RAC), Russian tobacco, molasses, rice bread, and "Indian sugar," a blend of half sugar and half bran (Gibson 1988, 388). The trade in luxury items increased with blue glass beads, buttons, and "China cash" (holed coins). These were traded for fish, wildfowl, berries, greens, and fresh water, along with sea mammal oil, used as an essential condiment and for ships' lamps (Gibson 1988). Trade for women's foodstuffs and their labor was substantial because the RAC had difficulties provisioning their Alaskan employees. Native entrepreneurs included women such as Kuropatka, who traveled with Zagoskin and did "all kinds of women's work," including stringing glass beads used for trade and hunting partridge to feed the Russian and native crew (Michael 1967, 185). Russian men were encouraged to marry indigenous women, and their descendants were critical to the RAC's success, birthing an essential creole class (Crowell 1997).

The pace and kinds of indigenous-colonial interactions changed after 1867, when Russia sold Alaska to the United States. The RAC withdrew, and the American Commercial Company (ACC) and numerous independent venture capitalists poured into Alaska. Russians had restricted trade in firearms and alcohol, but by the 1850s, American whalers distributed various hardware, alcohol, and firearms for walrus ivory (VanStone 1972, 90). Along with increasingly diverse networks of exchange and a growth of available goods in the latter part of the nineteenth century came an influx of development and exploration in Alaska, including the Western Union Telegraph Expedition based in St. Michael. By the end of the 1800s, St. Michael also became the staging area for gold prospectors who traveled to the Klondike, Nome, and Kotzebue Sound. At the peak of the boom in gold, St. Michael's population ballooned to twenty thousand people. Native people were actively engaged in these new commercial opportunities. The U.S. Navy hired Alaskan men as interpreters, and wives, along with their children, would accompany their husbands and produce food and "assist in various ways" (Ray 1966, 19). These women were not paid but rather were "fed and occasionally given small presents" for their work (Ray 1966, 19).

Partner to this rapid demographic expansion were outbreaks and the spread of epidemic and chronic diseases such as tuberculosis (Fortuine 1992). There were waves of lethal plagues of smallpox (1837–1839) and influenza (1852–1853, 1900). The "Great Sickness" eruption of measles in 1861 and the pandemic outbreak of Spanish influenza in 1918–1919 were cataclysmic to native villages, and the number of casualties could be staggering (Wolfe 1982). The timing and impact of epidemics along the delta coast is sketchily reported, but, undoubtedly, villages were struck with major losses of life by the early twentieth century (Griffin 2004).

Coastal delta villages were fairly shielded from direct interactions until the latter 1800s when Euro-Americans began to arrive. The first documented Euro-American to travel along the delta coastline was Edward W. Nelson. As a member of the U.S. Army Signal Corps, he collected over ten thousand ethnographic specimens for the Smithsonian Institution (Nelson [1889] 1983). With an indigenous guide and American trader, he ventured 1,200 miles into "little known country" along the coast, from the mouth of the Yukon River to the Kuskokwim River, during the winter of 1878–1879 (Nelson 1877; 1882, 660). On this arduous journey, Nelson visited the village of Askinuk (modern-day Hooper Bay) and stayed four days in Kashunak, where he witnessed the Bladder Feast, a principal celebration among the Yupiit (Lantis 1946). Each December villages hosted this large affair that honored the seals caught that year (the seal's soul rests in the bladder). Upon arrival in each village Nelson offered dried fish, tobacco, ammunition, glass beads, brass, jewelry, metal needles, cotton thread, iron knives, cloth, buttons, and metal axe

Figure 5. Salmon drying at fish camp, July 2001. (Photo by author.)

blades to use as barter for stone knives, wooden masks, and dolls. He later regaled his trading prowess; nevertheless, locals crowned him the "man who buys good-for-nothing things" (Nelson [1889] 1983, 373).

His collections and commentary challenge the paradigm that people along the coast were largely sheltered from colonial influences. For example, coastal folks possessed foreign goods when Nelson arrived, and Yup'ik men apparently accumulated more than did the women. For example, steel traps and guns were used primarily by coastal men, even though "ancient devices are still sometimes used" (Nelson [1889] 1983, 121–22). In addition, iron and steel were noteworthy in the villages he visited, and metals had "superseded to a great extent the more primitive implements" of ground slate, ivory, and bone (Nelson [1889] 1983, 80). However, whereas men's stone tools were "almost entirely displaced," metal was only "gradually displacing the old stone and slate implements" of the women (Nelson [1889] 1983, 109). For example, women were still using primarily the ground slate ulu knife, or *kegginnalek* (Frink 2002; Frink, Hoffman, and Shaw 2003).[1]

This gendered differential dispersal and access to metals was also observed by H. M. W. Edmonds to the north in 1898. He notes that except for metal cooking pots, native women "constantly" used stone, bone, and ivory tools while men using metal "saws, axes, planes, augers, and knives are seen everywhere" (Ray 1966, 53–54). Metal tools were so abundant at this time that men routinely sold stone tools to Euro-North American buyers, and they often had "three, or even more guns" (Ray 1966, 62–63).

Contemporary Village Life

To better contextualize and map indigenous-colonial experiences and outcomes, we must as fully as possible understand not only regional history but also subsistence systems and linkages to identity. Getting and producing food and goods is not only a way of life but also the framework for one's life and relationships in subsistence-based systems—and a crucial context in which to understand indigenous-colonial interactions over time. To varying degrees, coastal people continue to move to seasonal harvest areas,[2] but their relocations are far curtailed compared to their prehistoric and early historic mobility. In the past at the larger aggregate winter villages like Qavinaq or Kashunak, families relocated to coastal, early-spring seal camps, where men hunted seal on the ice floes and all eagerly awaited the fresh eggs of migratory birds. After the spring ice breakup and the increasingly longer days of warming sun, families moved to fish camps located along the extensive river systems. Men would catch herring, the first fish to arrive along the coastline, and then, soon after, salmon and other species (see figure 5). As the late summer tundra colors turned a subtle autumn brown, women gathered tundra berries, and families would camp and collect together at the height of the season. Soon after berry picking, people returned to the villages, and men would travel inland to fall hunting and trapping camps. The cycle would begin anew with a move to winter camps where men would opportunistically hunt and all would fish through the ice either with traps or jig fishing.

Much of this rhythm of harvesting foods across the landscape is practiced even today. But a significant change is that the people of Chevak and other coastal communities are permanently settled. Some families still move out to summer fish camp, and some will still travel to berry camp. However, where previously a family would have all moved out to seal camp in the spring, now it is the men who foray out for hunting expeditions and return on their snowmobiles (locally known as snowmachines). Villages are now occupied year-round by all. Smaller villages like Tununak on Nelson Island have some three hundred residents, while larger villages like Chevak have around one thousand. Most of the people one meets in a village (except for some in the Elder and younger generations) are bilingual (English and a dialect of Central Yup'ik, or Cup'ik in Chevak), and in the home people tend to speak Yup'ik.

Chevak is typical of other contemporary villages. The only way in or out of the community is by plane, snowmobile, or boat. If the weather is amenable, both people and goods travel in and out on several daily flights from the main inland hub of Bethel. The streets of Chevak are unpaved and in the summers can be quite dusty; when it rains, they are thick with the dark and sticky tundra mud. When the streets are wet, it is best to rely on the substantial planked boardwalks that connect many of the village homes. Instead of the semisubterranean sod houses that were used into the early/midcentury, people today live in aboveground houses. Older homes are noted by their smaller size and materials (such as tin roof sheeting) and by the fact that they are on the ground. Newer homes are built on substantial wooden stilts to alleviate the danger of spring flooding. However, because of the permafrost, the stilts must be readjusted with blocks. The metal-grated staircases to house entrances can be quite sheer due to the height to which some have been raised. All Yup'ik homes that I have had the pleasure to visit or stay in have all the appointments of a standard Western home, including satellite-fed flat-screen televisions, computers, and the ever-present (and continuously on) marine radio. The houses generally have some sort of plumbing and some have running water.[3]

LIFEWAYS ON THE COASTAL ALASKAN TUNDRA

FIGURE 6. Houses in Chevak, July 2001. The two-story building at the center back is the Catholic church. It is centrally located in a relatively high location. (Photo by author.)

The village of Chevak is located along the banks of the Ninglikfak River. In the summer, aluminum boats with powerful outboard engines line the water's edge and men wait for the tide to rise in order to go fishing and hunting. Down along the broad, flat shoreline plain are old-style wood-plank storage sheds on stilts. Men use them to store fishing and other harvesting gear. On a ridge above the river is the old Sheppard Company trade store building, moved from the site of Old Chevak, and farther toward the river is the Wayne Hill Company store. During the summer, barges moor in front of the store and men unload goods and fuel. All of the villages have stores ranging from more extensively provisioned businesses, such as Wayne Hill, to smaller stores in homes. Goods (food and hardware) are expensive (generally three times that in the lower 48) and limited in choice and freshness (especially fruits and vegetables). Residents buy equipment (e.g., plastic buckets, rain gear, boat parts) and supplement this with online ordering (especially from stores in Bethel and Anchorage) of goods and foods, which are flown in.

Depending on the village, people use store-bought foods to stretch a meal but still rely on subsistence or traditional so-called country foods (Usher 1976). For example, a common strategy for many women is to prepare a one-pot meal. On a gas stove (or out at fish camp on a propane stove or wood fire), in a large metal pot, women will combine broth, meat (seal, bird, caribou, or purchased frozen meat), and frozen vegetables with a carbohydrate filler like ramen noodles, pasta, or rice. The percentage of subsistence foods in a person's diet varies with each family, the particular village, and age of the consumer. At a meal I partook of in Toksook Bay, a village on Nelson Island, the adults ate Canada goose while the teenagers and young children dined upon Hot Pockets®.

There are several institutional mainstays in each Alaskan native village. Along with at least one store, villages have a state-funded school (K–12), at least one church, and a Traditional Council (TC) building. The churches tend to be Catholic, although there are other sects increasingly moving into the villages. Inside the church is often a syncretic mix of symbolism. For instance, hung behind the altar in the Chevak church is an impressive bearded sealskin stretched out on the wall. Village schools are fairly well appointed, with computers, big kitchens, and other basic school equipment. People often meet for events in school gymnasiums, especially during the winter months. In particular they play basketball, an extremely competitive and celebrated sport. The gym is also used for community events such as dances. Year-round, the stores are favored places for hanging out, and village business is conducted in each village's TC building, as are community events such as dances and, especially for the women, the ever-popular evening bingo games.

For all of the modernity in the villages, there are persistently strong and valued connections to the past, particularly through the acquisition, processing, distribution, and consumption of subsistence foods. For the contemporary residents of the coastal villages, harvested food continues to be a fundamental, practical, and ideological benchmark of Yup'ik livelihood and individual, group, and community identity. Today, the last vestiges of familial seasonal relocation are summer fish camp and berry camp, where families spend a week or so gathering berries in the late summer and early fall. Children eagerly await the freedoms of the tundra, and adults anticipate getting away from the closeness of village life for a while. Each June, many Chevak extended families load up their boats with supplies and head out to their fish camps. Some stay for weeks, some for only days at a time, and still others tack back and forth each day. However, I have been told by Chevakers that the amount of time spent out at fish camp is generally decreasing, and families are tending to set their camps closer to the village.

Several factors have influenced seasonal mobility trends. Waged labor in the villages is a significant agent of change, with two major (but limited) opportunities for paid work: construction and education. Construction jobs are few and seasonal, and men generally fill these positions. In the school system women tend to be clerks and teachers' aides and men are the coveted year-round janitorial custodians. The school calendar has differentially tethered women and children to the village; for example, no longer do entire families move to the coast for spring seal camp—it is men that travel to the harvest. Technology has also played an important part in the changes in mobility patterns, as has the rising cost of fuel. Today, powerboats and snowmobiles allow hunters and fishers to procure food at distances without moving the entire family; however, the cost of fuel is very high in the villages.

Subsistence, Life Course, and Group Identity

Subsistence as a complex ecological and social system must be incorporated and contextualized in any exploration of native people and colonial interactions and change. Spend some time in a coastal community and it becomes exceedingly apparent how fundamental subsistence is to people even today. In many ways Yup'ik people define themselves by their relationships with one another via subsistence. Because subsistence is a primary marker of self and group identity and negotiations, any change in a subsistence system has repercussions for relationships of authority, power, and decision-making. At a base level, colonial commerce affected subsistence systems by revaluing some subsistence as commodities or by replacing others with technological or material imports.

We can better understand, track, and model culture change by fleshing out the social relationships among people and food. Interaction with the subsistence ecology is fundamental not only to an individual's life but also to his or her life course. It can be reasonably argued that, in the Arctic, subsistence defines a person and his/her relationships with others. A Yup'ik Eskimo person's sense of self was (and to a large degree continues to be) enmeshed with his/her relationships with subsistence. A man's influence in a village, his position in the men's house, and his attainment and maintenance of a marriage were all largely built on his subsistence activities and contributions. Essentially, he was what he caught. Even today, a coastal boy is not considered a social man and, in the recent past, marriageable, until he kills a bearded seal.[4]

The Yup'ik maintained and negotiated gendered and age relations principally through their subsistence systems. A woman's sphere of economic and social activity was complementary to that of a related man, but it was autonomous and an avenue for her own status-building. Women were (and generally continue to be) the primary producers and managers of all subsistence harvests, including seal, waterfowl, and fish. A man brings his catch to a grandmother, mother, wife, or sister, and she assumes productive oversight and distributive control. In the words of an Elder Chevak woman, after men caught the fish, women were "in charge" of the harvest. During seasonally intensive harvesting periods, women had to efficiently process a large amount of fish for winter human and dog consumption, as well as for ceremonial distribution.[5] Alaskan Eskimo women presided over the household economy and internal labor, and Elder women could achieve substantial authority through their management and distribution of foods. Linda Ellanna and George Sherrod (1995, 33) observe that effective northwestern Inupiaq seniors could become "big women." An Elder Yup'ik woman can build a reputation (with attendant authority) for industriousness, expertise, and generosity, and she is revered as *pinituq* (Frink 2010). Of course, many gender relations and achievements are founded in mutually satisfactory cooperation, accommodation, and interdependence. However, the cultural meaning and value of divisions of production are not timeless or without conflict, and among Eskimo people there are indications of stress between gendered groups. For instance, a Russian observed that Eskimo women sang songs of discontent and that "they already knew that their husbands were lazy, that they first steam themselves and smoke pipes" (Michael 1967, 120), hinting at internal jockeying for resources. This "hidden transcript" (J. Scott 1990) gives voice to tensions between women and men and potential cleavages not only between indigenous people and colonialists but also (perhaps even more significantly) between native women and men as groups.

Yup'ik women and men are clearly interdependently linked through the subsistence system. However, it is critical to uncouple the particular points along the continuum of handling and managing foods to fully appreciate the social and economic implications of what people do and what it means. Important in this system also is to explicate the full spectrum of gendered and aged skills, technologies, and distribution of resources (see Brightman 1993; Spector 1993). Those who have studied subsistence-based groups have tended to explore the procurement system (hunting = men) to the relative neglect of the production (processing = women) side of subsistence systems. Scholars can tend to go through a laundry list of subsistence foods that indigenous people harvested, with little recognition of what is done with the foods once they are secured (see, for instance, Bruce Smith 2011). But understanding a subsistence procurement and processing system as a continuum or package of behavior is essential to understanding aspects of both harvest decision-making and a wider comprehension of what subsistence means, economically and socially—and how it is an integral element in all indigenous-colonial interactions.

Indigenous women are most often the processors of subsistence harvests. However, they are not ancillary labor but rather critical to decision-making and distribution, and men's harvesting decisions can be influenced by Elder women. For example, during the early runs of herring in Tununak on Nelson Island, men ready to harvest the fish are in constant discourse with women (especially Elder women), who actively gauge the oil content of herring in each of the several seasonal runs. This example highlights two parts of harvest decision-making: women's essential expertise about the food to be procured and the fact that women can only properly process so much. Women's calculation of what can be done in the most efficient manner is critical to the success of the procurement and processing system. For instance, with herring, if the fish brought in are too oily, they take longer to dry and are a riskier investment. Connecting field decision-making to input by women who are intimate experts on the catch has significant implications for our models of indigenous use of the landscape. This case highlights not only the interdependence of women and men in the subsistence harvest and processing system but also the fact that women and their expertise are intimately conjoined in decision-making procedures, even if not always physically present in the field. One of the primary places that women exert incredible influence is over stored foods—one of the most important aspects of Arctic adaptation.

Storage in the Arctic

In the extreme Arctic environment, being able to find and harvest your foods is crucial. But just as important is the attendant processing of the harvested animals. Without the proper processing of foods, the harvest would be meaningless. Women have perfected the art of processing foods for appropriate consumption and storage in the Arctic climate for thousands of years. The following section will briefly discuss some parameters of storage and then focus on seal and fish harvests and their requirements for storage. Seal and fish are critical harvests to understand since they are subsistence resources heavily affected by indigenous-colonial interactions.

Margaret Lantis (1946, 245) neither minces words nor undersells a subsistence reality when she states, "Storage and preparation of all food was [women's] most essential contribution to the economy, and seasonally a big task." Even though descendent people continue to use a range of traditional approaches, there has been relatively less focus on storage and women's activities than we would expect (but see Binford 1980; Friesen and Stewart 2013; Frink 2007; Jarvenpa and Brumbach 2006; Stopp 2002). This relative oversight may be connected to a general scientific malaise concerning taken-for-granted technologies typically connected to women and the perceived value of the domestic sphere (Frink 2009a, 2009b; Frink and Harry 2008; Skibo and Schiffer 1995).

The implications of gender-demarcated subsistence storage are heightened in environments of extreme abundance and scarcity, such as the Arctic. Here, effective systems of processing and management of storage were essential for successful adaptation to a variety of ecologies. The kinds of storage techniques used in the Arctic varied with the kinds of resources in a specific area (see Darwent and Bjorneboe Johansen 2010; Stopp 2002). For example, Arctic people have deployed both underground and aboveground storage to stock foods for daily consumption, feasting, and regional trading. Ingenious ice cellars are used in the northwest and stone-lined caches in the east, and the stilted cache is ubiquitous (Dall 1870; Geist and Rainey 1936; Lee and Reinhardt 2003; Spencer 1959). Successful storage often depended on the right kind of processing of a meat or plant. Commonly, subsistence resources were either air dried, smoked, salted, frozen, boiled, or fermented, or some combination of these. And women have developed and used an exceedingly clever array of containers for processing and storing foods such as the bladders and stomachs of sea mammals and caribou (Eidlitz 1969).

Storage and the management and distribution of subsistence foods in Arctic communities had an undeniable impact on social status for both women and men. The direct connection for men was their provisioning of families and community. For women, it was their expertise in handling and distributing the subsistence resources (whether for the table, a feast, or garments) that brought them significant renown. Middle-aged and older people I have talked with remarked how, unlike the present day, their mothers and grandmothers had complete control over the stores and what their families ate. Even today, women primarily remain in control of the distribution of subsistence foods, although access to cash and market foods has significantly undermined their overall management of foodstuffs.

On the delta coast, pit storage is common, but we as yet know little of the range of storage facilities represented in the archaeological record. The identification of subfloor pits can be problematic, as we have had few studies of the site morphology of storage and uses over time (Jarvenpa and Brumbach 2006). We do know that women used a variety of storage techniques to keep a broad array of foods edible. Today, women use electric freezers but also keep foods cold in their house porches or storage sheds. In the past, women used pits to store grass baskets full of berries; deep, dry storage pits to keep the hard-to-dry late-season fish; and small round pits to ferment "stinky heads," the heads and other parts of fish.

The examination of the steps involved in the preparation and storage of subsistence foods is essential (Ingold 1983; Testart 1982). The complexity and variability of women's storage-processing activities have been understudied relative to other aspects of subsistence (but see Binford 1980; Steward [1938] 2002), but recently there has been a renewed focus (Friesen and Stewart 2013; Kuijt 2009; Kuijt and Finlayson 2009; Morgan 2012; Tushingham and Bettinger 2013; Whelan et al. 2013). The ability to keep foods edible is an incredibly time-consuming and expert-level undertaking, and understanding the processing methods along with the consequences of improper processing is critical. For example, for many years, I thought that simply placing fish in a permafrost-lined pit would be sufficient to keep them edible, but I was wrong. A U.S. Fish & Wildlife crew I had contact with in the field had tried to use pits to store their foods but found that they spoiled or were ruined by freezer burn. To mitigate spoilage, Lantis (1946) reports that Nunivak Island women carefully packed their fish in layers of grass and wood, ostensibly to retain some airflow.

Harvesting of a resource was but the earliest stage in a series of steps to preserve and transform subsistence foods. When a coastal man handed his catch to a woman, it became her responsibility to handle it properly and to make a series of decisions concerning that resource. Foods had to last through a long winter of feeding an extended family and the working dogs and supplying provisions for communal winter feasting. Expert management could confer great esteem upon a woman, and mismanagement could prove disastrous (see Shnirelman 1994). Therefore, storage represents women's undeniable roles in subsistence, and women's aspirations were intimately connected to their processing, management, and distribution of harvested resources.

Seal Harvesting

One of the most important resources that North American Arctic men capture and women manage is seal. Along the Yukon-Kuskokwim coast, food is at its low point in the very early spring (in the past famine could strike), and there is excitement in the air. People know that soon, along with bird eggs and eventually fish, fresh seal meat and blubber will be available. In the early spring, seal hunting is a delicate balance between the movement of the sea ice and the particular proclivities of each sea mammal species that are known to the expert Yup'ik hunters.

Into the mid-1900s, men still used single-holed sealskin kayaks to hunt on the open waters of the Bering Sea, in the bays, and up the mouths of the rivers. Light, maneuverable skin kayaks that required an astonishing range of skills (see Walls 2012) gave way to durable but heavy wood-plank and plywood boats. Today, men hunt and fish from aluminum and fiberglass boats with outboard or inboard motors. In the early spring, men are busy servicing their boats, engines, and other equipment (see Lantis 1946, 193). Into the mid-1900s families would move to spring seal-hunting camp; today, the boats are pulled by snowmobile to the edge of the shorefast ice. The hunters expertly gauge the constant movement of the ice, steering themselves through the open water. Seal hunting was and continues to be a cooperative venture, with social frameworks of hunting partners and scripted meat distribution; however, it is also highly competitive. For instance, each Nunivak Island man knew the number of others' seals, "and everyone was rated thereon" (Lantis 1946, 173).

The earliest seal to arrive (end of April/early May) via northerly migration is the bearded seal. As the largest seal, an adult can range from 7 to 8 feet long and 575 to 800 pounds (males weigh slightly more than females). Two-year-old juveniles (each weighing approximately 200 pounds) arrive after the adults and are also hunted. Adults tend to respite and birth their pups on ice floes, giving an advantage to hunters, who today shoot them with rifles but not long ago used harpoons. One of the (many) challenging aspects of seal hunting, particularly if the seal is shot in the water, is that it may quickly sink if dead or swim for escape if wounded. Therefore, after shooting the seal, the hunter must quickly get near enough to harpoon it with a detachable point (even today made of ivory) and line attachment. In the past this line attached to the seal was buoyed by a sealskin float.

There are two primary seal that Yup'ik men target for harvest: the spotted and the ringed seal. The spotted seals are open-water seals and migrate in the winter, but the ringed seals tend to stay along the shorefast ice and are available through the fall and winter. The adults of each of these species weigh around 100 pounds. In the fall, Yup'ik men also set nets in open waters and at river mouths to snare the seal (Fienup-Riordan 1983, 125). In the open waters of the bay or the rivers, they surround the animals, shoot them with .22-gauge rifles, and then get close enough to secure them with the harpoon. (A Yup'ik man I worked with in Alakanuk village to the north of Chevak still uses his throwing board to jettison his harpoon.)

After spring break-up in May, when the rivers and the Bering are clear of ice, the area is a cacophony of subsistence harvesting, including the capture of birds and their eggs. Before the rifle, blunt-headed arrows and bird spears were used by men and boys to hunt emperor and Canadian geese (Nelson [1889] 1983). On the tundra, ptarmigan (a year-round resident) and the Arctic hare are sought, and women and girls harvest the previous year's berries that were not picked. Both men and women are aware of any bird eggs that may be available, a delicacy that people absolutely savor. However, this early-spring complex coupling of subsistence activities will be curtailed once seals start to be harvested in earnest. For instance, in Toksook Bay (on Nelson Island to the south of Tununak), "the hunt was on, and for the next four weeks everything else was suspended" (Fienup-Riordan 1983, 72). Other sea mammals, such as the sea lion or walrus, may be caught, but these are not primary targets of the hunters—they are a supplementary or coincident harvest. The larger sea mammals, such as the bearded seal, are deftly field butchered by men on-site, which allows for easier transport and, later, for full processing by the women in the village (see Barker 1993).

Seal Processing

As fundamental as the harvest is the processing of the catch, for without proper preparation, the seal would spoil and be worthless beyond immediate consumption. While men multitask as they harvest several species simultaneously and in queue, women juggle the demands of processing different kinds of foods concurrently in different seasonal clines. Each subsistence resource has species- and seasonal-specific demands of handling, butchering, and preserving.

Generally, there are two ways that Yup'ik women butcher seal, which depend on the species as well as the intended uses of the animal. (This decision-making regarding the use of the product is critical for how a woman will process subsistence foods.) A smaller seal will be cut in the house, or outside if the weather permits. One method of butchering is for the woman to use a sharpened ulu to slit the seal open from throat to anus. The blubber is then cut from the skin (a very delicate process) and placed in plastic buckets to render into oil. The seal meat is cut into strips and hung to dry on racks; when dry it is jet black. Women would have thousands of pounds of seal meat to dry; Fienup-Riordan (1983, 83–84) estimates that one hundred pounds of meat and oil were processed in Toksook Bay per day. People enjoy this meat for months, especially dipped in seal oil made from the blubber.

Another kind of seal-butchering technique was more time-consuming for women (see Eidlitz 1969; Frink and Giordano 2015). Much of descendent

FIGURE 7. Butchering seal, Chevak village, June 2004. (Photo by author.)

women's work was dedicated to making containers for "wet preservation" (d'Anglure 1984, 491). For instance, foods were dried and then stored in animal stomachs (such as reindeer, seal, and beluga) that had been processed and dried. The seal-poke system was an innovative and multifaceted wet-storage technology—whole sealskins wherein seal blubber was rendered to oil and other meats and plants were stored, marinated, and preserved for winter consumption. It was apparently the only means people had to render and store quantities of oil. Sea mammal oil was (and continues to be) arguably the most important element in northern cuisine and diet and was well-known as an "essential condiment" (Lantis 1984b, 176; Starks 2007). Margaret Lantis (1984b, 175) comments that "without seal oil, no matter how many fresh or dried fish they had, they thought they might starve or become ill." Seal oil maintains its prominence as an essential accompaniment to dried foods, among other uses, but it is no longer necessary as fuel for lamps. The sealpoke storage system demanded an impressive set of knowledge and skills. The proper making, filling, and maintenance of these bags was "based on the experience of generations," and the "preparation of a blubber bag of this kind was, in reality, a great art with which only the old people were completely familiar" (Høygaard 1941, 21; in Eidlitz 1969, 114).

As Lantis (1984b, 214) recounts, "An effort was made to store large quantities of dried or frozen seal meat and oil, the oil in 'pokes' made of whole sealskins, as well as fish for winter consumption." The seals that were used as seal pokes are opened at the throat, and the insides of the seal are cut from the skin. Once the seal body is free from the skin, it is literally turned inside out. Any tears or holes (bullet or harpoon) in the skin are sewn tight, and the skin is inflated and hung to dry. The ingenious pokes were used for preserving, marinating, storing, transporting, and rendering the fat. The key to the success of the poke was to keep the contents (which could include herring fish, greens, and other foods) cool in the summer in streams or in submerged pits to reduce spoilage. There are very few women who continue to make these pokes since now women render their seal blubber in five-gallon plastic buckets.

Given their primacy across the Arctic North, we know too little about the origins or technology of the seal-poke storage system; based on J. Louis Giddings's (1967) work, Zona Starks (2007, 43) suggest they may have been made and used for some four thousand years. The bags were ideal containers for oil but were eventually supplanted by wooden containers and, eventually, five-gallon plastic buckets. The implications of this technology are significant; I have been told independently by several Elders that the contents of the seal bags could be edible for up to five years. The system was an ingenious invention and had multiple functions. The rendered train oil was essential not only for consumption but also for heat and light in the ubiquitous oil lamps.

Up until the early 1900s, sea mammal oil was vital for lamp fuel and as a fundamental trade item of coastal and non-coastal groups (Hughes 1984; Spencer 1984). Bags of oil were traded into the interior and to colonists. The pokes were perfect vessel containers for long-distance trade. For instance, Nunivak men "took pokes of oil and seal skins . . . up the Kuskokwim River" and received "squirrel, wolverine, and other furs from the interior regions" (Lantis 1984b, 215). Significant trade of oil continued into the colonial era where as early as 1891 on Nunivak Island (to the east of Nelson Island) pokes of oil were a leading trade good for such items as leaf tobacco, flour, matches, and metal needles (Lantis 1984b, 215). The coveted oil continued to be traded into the 1950s, and Nunivak men "sold the much-desired oil for a high price in cash" (Lantis 1984b, 215).

Fisheries

Equally important to the subsistence economy was the harvesting, processing, and storage of an array of fish. Amazingly, given the magnitude of the significance of fish along the Arctic and North American coast, scholars are just beginning to intensively investigate the complexities and impactful subtleties of a variety of subsistence fisheries (Frink and Knudson 2010; Moss and Cannon 2011). Like seal, some species can be harvested all year long. For instance, a fisher will jig through the ice with a barbless hook for a day and bring up fifty to one hundred pounds of tomcod or set wire mesh or wooden traps under the ice for the ubiquitous blackfish. The blackfish are known as an "insurance" fish because they are able to survive in the underwater traps for weeks, giving the fishers flexibility in their coordination of disparate and distant harvesting activities (Barker 1993, 27, 38, 116).

The most intensive and productive subsistence season for fisheries is during the summer months. Just after ice breakup in late May or early June, the salmon begin their spawning run up the rivers. There is much activity along the shoreline in Chevak, with men readying their nets and boat engines, and families eagerly anticipating their time at fish camp. Though people today tend to camp closer to Chevak and for briefer periods, the family I stayed with spends considerable time during the summer at their fish camp along the Kashunak River. These summer camps are an opportunity for families to be on their own, away from the bustle and dust of the village, and to harvest the bulk of their winter food.

The primary fish species caught during the summer months is salmon (although in some areas such as Tununak the primary species and first to run is herring). The first and largest (30-plus pounds) salmon to run up the rivers is the king, which last into early July. The chum or dog salmon follow and have both a summer and fall run. They are smaller and weigh in at around 6 pounds. Smaller yet, at 4.5 pounds, are the pink or humpies, which run mid-summer and are a preferred fish for their relative ease of drying. The final run of salmon is the coho, or silver, salmon, which run in August and September and weigh in at around 10 pounds. Along with salmon, harvests will include other fish, such as whitefish and flounder.

Men, women, old people, and young people all catch fish. Traditionally, fish could be caught with a fish spear (see Nelson [1889] 1983), but set nets are the preferred means of catching salmon and other fish, although drift nets are used as well. Dip nets are still used to dunk for smelt in the summer and for needlefish in the winter months under the ice. Salmon nets are typically set along the shorelines of the rivers and at the mouths of smaller sloughs and set to take advantage of the direction of the tidal flow.

Of course, all of the harvested fish must be properly processed. Fish processing is not a simple task; it requires incredible expertise and knowledge of the ecology of the fish and the seasonal conditions. This is important, for

FIGURE 8. Fish smokehouse at summer fish camp, July 2001. (Photo by author.)

it is not only the butchering of the fish that must be done but also, just as importantly, the storage preparation—the smoking and drying. If these are not done correctly, the fish can rot, and until not that long ago, this could leave a family exposed to the dangers of spring hunger, for, in the later spring, the ice is too far for hunters to get to seal, too dangerous to be on for fishing, and the birds have not yet arrived for their northerly migration (see Fienup-Riordan 1986).

Fish camps, like villages, have some standard features that have likely persisted for generations (Frink 2002). Depending on the number of people in the extended family, there are one or two canvas tents. A rectangular pit is located near the river shoreline, where men deposit the fish to be put into the cutting queue. Often, related women sit face to face and butcher the fish on pieces of plywood. The fish is cut to optimize drying and hung on fish racks to hang in the wind. Today, bright-blue tarps are hung over the driftwood and rack complexes, but in the past, women used grass mats to protect the fish from rain and blowflies and their maggots, which can infest and ruin fish. Salmon are commonly cut with their tails still in place and hung; however, herring are commonly strung with their heads intact on braided lengths of grass. After the fish are dried, some are smoked in plywood sheds enclosed by plastic tarps (see figure 8). Before these structures were used, women would smoke the fish with willow wood (still used as fuel) in small, sod-covered pits. After the fish are properly prepared, they are stored in five-gallon plastic buckets, which have largely replaced the use of woven grass bags.

Chapter Summary

This chapter outlines the fundamental role of subsistence as not just food but also a fundamental aspect of individual and group identity. For Yup'ik people, the harvesting and production of food, and especially of sea mammals and fish, is so much more than what food people eat. The subsistence procurement and processing system is a foundational framework upon which to understand the past and how and why culture changed during the early colonial-indigenous era. Subsistence as identity helps us understand the initial inroads of market colonialism, in particular how the Russians traded with both women and men and how supplies of fish and sea mammal oil—women's products—were critical for the Russian colonial project. But, the mid-century shift to American control of commerce ushered in increasing differential development—for instance, when Nelson traveled along the coast, men, not women, were privy to foreign goods.

The following chapter extends this initial analysis and explores the connections between the sequentially occupied villages of Qavinaq and Kashunak. Qavinaq is in many ways a quintessential coastal winter village, with two big men's houses and family houses linked by tunnels. Tragically, it was a village mired in the endemic warfare of its day, where the harvest could be curtailed by threat of a tundra ambush and whereby the clever maintenance of food stores within the homes was an essential feature of winter life. However, the structures at Kashunak, where the survivors of a tragic battle at Qavinaq fled to, reflect a vastly different story. It is a conglomeration of the prehistoric with that of the historical interactions with colonial markets and then religion. It is at Kashunak that Nelson first wrote about the people of the coast, and though in popular tropes thought to be tundra isolates, the people of Kashunak were clearly already linked with the emerging colonial arena.

2

Precolonial Warfare and Early Indigenous-Colonial Trade

GENERALLY, IT HAS BEEN THOUGHT that people's lives on the coast were largely unchanged until Jesuit missionaries arrived in the early 1900s. But when we integrate the sites and add several lines of evidence, a different story unfolds, one that indelibly indicates coastal people's interactions with colonial markets before the churchmen arrived. Of specific interest is the dramatic transition from prehistoric indigenous warfare to early historic competitive commercial trade. These changes are essential to parse and integrate since they impact interactions among Yup'ik people and mission men when the Jesuits settled on the coast at the turn of the century.

There are two critical early periods during this transitory phase on the coast. The first is the Late Prehistoric Period (1740–1833), which encompasses life on the tundra prior to any colonial enmeshment and ends at the point at which the Russians begin their trading in the regions to the north and east of the delta coast. At this time, the ancestors of modern Chevak lived in the village of Qavinaq during a tumultuous time of endemic regional warfare. The second, the Early Trade Period (1833–1927), represents life at the village of Kashunak, a prehistoric and historic village where the survivors from the Qavinaq massacre fled, warfare was no longer practiced, and early commercial opportunities were available prior to the settlement by the Catholic Church.

To best understand the economic and social transitions represented at the sites, I track the changes at each based on four significant features: the men's house, the family house, site tunnels, and storage facilities. In the next section, I briefly describe and contextualize these archaeological features and how they are different at each site. The architectural and feature modifications between the sites are then contextualized with oral historic, archival, and eyewitness information and framed within the Late Prehistoric Period and the Early Trade Period.

Specifics of Four Village Features: The Men's House

One of the grandest elements of coastal villages was the men's house (kashim), or *qaygiq*. It was a complex structural and ideological construct found among both Yup'ik and Inupiaq groups and used into the early to mid-1900s (Lantis 1946; Larson 1995). It was the place where men of a village large enough to support it slept, socialized, relaxed, and worked, clearly an institution of "gender-based politics" (see Mason 2012, 77). An early account of the men's house comes to us from Nelson, who stayed in one during his trek across the coastal tundra (Nelson [1889] 1983, 249–50):

> At this place there are two kashims, the smaller one being about 30 by 30 feet on the floor and 20 feet high at the smoke hole. The walls are of split logs placed vertically, with their plane faces inward and resting at their upper ends against the logs, which form the framework of the roof; the floor is of heavy hewed planks. Extending around the room on the floor, and about 3½ feet from the walls, are small logs, serving to mark off the sleeping places of the men and at the same time as head rests, the sleepers lying with their heads toward the middle of the room. Three feet above and 6 inches nearer the walls other logs extend around the room, with planks between them and the sides, affording a broad sleeping bench, supported in the middle by upright posts and at each end inserted in the wall of the structure. The roof is made by the usual arrangement of logs forming a rectangular pyramid with a flat top, in the middle of which is the smoke hole. The entrance passage is unusually high and roomy, opening directly into the kashim above ground by means of a round hole in the front of the wall.

Variability in the sizes of the buildings may be due both to the availability of driftwood (Nelson [1889] 1983, 251) and to membership. They were not only significantly larger than family houses but also architecturally more elaborate. The roofs were rectangular and pyramid-like and "unusually high and roomy" (Nelson [1889] 1983, 250, figure 78). The building was framed with whole and hewed driftwood logs, and these were covered with sod blocks. Depending on the number of men who lived within, there could be more than one row of hewed driftwood logs set against the walls that were used for sleeping and eating. In addition, a piece of wood covered a hole in the floor of the men's house that led to a long, deep tunnel. At one of the men's houses at Kashunak, the subterranean winter tunnel sported two impressive walrus tusks used to hoist oneself from the chamber to the main floor.

Larger villages could have allied yet competitive lineages, each with its own men's house association. For instance, at the village of Kashunak, the two men's houses were "side by side" on the village mound, and "half of the village belonged to each" (Nelson [1889] 1983, 321). The space was the village men's ritual and practicum center (to instruct younger men and boys) and the venue for public ceremonial events and exchange. For instance, when Nelson arrived at Kashunak village, he was immediately ushered inside and received gifts, and he likewise distributed tobacco to the men inside.

The men's house was central to a man's sense of self and negotiation of his identity through his life course. Nelson noted that "there is scarcely an occurrence of note in the life of an Eskimo man which he cannot connect with rites in which the kashim plays an important part" ([1889] 1983, 245–46). It was "essentially the house of the men," and when in the village, a man was "nearly always" in the qaygiq: he was working, visiting, sleeping, or enjoying a daily firebath (Nelson [1889] 1983, 245–46). But men's inclusion into the activities of the family house was limited by custom. "All lie down to sleep at sunset, the adult males in the kazhim [men's house], the women, children, old men, the sick and the shaman in their huts" (Pierce 1984, 65).

There was no institutionalized leadership in the men's house or village such as a chief, but clearly accomplished men were respected above the others. These men demonstrated "superior shrewdness, wisdom, age, wealth, or shamanism" and exhibited prosperity and generosity (Nelson [1889] 1983, 304–5). The men's house was internally arranged based on status and age, and a man could track his social and economic progress and prospects based on his position within (Lantis 1946). Less successful men and orphaned boys sat near the entrance on the floor, where it was colder and draftier. Closer to the light and heat emitting from the seal oil lamps in the rear of the building were the older men: the prominent warriors, hunters, and shamans (Nelson [1889] 1983, 304).

Today, Yup'ik men mourn the loss of their largely exclusive space and consider the disbanding of the men's house as a significant negative change agent in traditional village life. In particular, Elder men regret the inability to collectively instruct young men of the village on matters of hunting and other subsistence teachings and appropriate rituals. Women tend to sympathize with their men's sense of loss of the men's house, but I have been told women, too, appreciate having men in the house, particularly for easier access to their labor.

The limitations to women's access to the space and men were ritually and spatially reinforced. While affiliated kinsmen had access to the men's house, women's pursuits within were highly prescribed, and if decorum were breached, they could be subject to harassment (Fienup-Riordan 1988; Lantis

1946). In general, women entered for three secular and sacred purposes: to serve food to men, as integral participants in ceremonies, and as temporary work groups to adroitly attach sealskins to the men's wooden kayak frames (Lantis 1946). Yup'ik women generally entered the men's house to feed their kinsmen. Nelson ([1889] 1983, 286, 289) observed that "each woman places a quantity in one or more wooden dishes, takes it to the kashim, and sets it beside her husband, father, or whoever she has provided for." Women could sit on the floor until the men finished their food or would leave and return to retrieve the dish. One Chevak Elder I spoke with recalled, "There were no girls at the qaygiq, it was all men, and their teaching was done by the men." Decades before her, a woman Elder (Aloralrea 1981) reminisced that, other than feasting, "the only time they [women] would ever go into the *kasigig* was when they would bring food to their husbands. They'd be always there. The men, the men, the men sleep in *kasigi* and the women bring them their food." Another Chevak Elder woman said that men "used to stay in the qaygiq all the time, the women used to cook at their house and the men are at the qaygiq; they cook and they bring them food over there—the men sitting there." And an Elder man recalled that women would "bring them food, like you go to the barn to feed horses" (Nanok 1981).

A very important element of women's inclusion in the men's house was during the annual ceremonial cycle during the winter months. For example, each village would invite people from other villages to ceremonies such as the Messenger Feast and the Bladder Feast (Koranda 1968; Morrow 1995). Ceremonial activities centered on reverently recognizing animals, storytelling and competing through dancing and games, and distribution of special foods and goods. Extended families would try to outdo one another, displaying their industriousness and capacity for generosity and what they caught and processed during the previous season. Fish and seal products were a substantial element of feasting and gifting activities (Burch 1985; Ray 1966). At the Feast of the Dead ceremony near St. Michael, Edmonds saw gifts of fish "in rolls, in baskets, and strung on sticks" and remarked that "great numbers of frozen fish are eaten, bundle after bundle being brought out" (Ray 1966, 101–2).

Women were integral to many of the parts of ceremonies as practical and symbolic participants in the feasts. For instance, a wife carried the seal bladders (which she would have dried and cared for) into the men's house, their essences later to be released beneath the river ice. During the ceremony, women compensated for a household's low number of bladders (a signal of relative poverty) by hanging grass mats. In addition, the women controlled the distribution of the prodigious amounts of special foods they had prepared. One Elder woman (George 1981) recounted the centrality of women during the Bladder Feast:

One of the women will enter wearing a sealskin raincoat, bringing in with her a bunch of bladders wrapped in woven grass. She will first push a bowl full of food and seal oil in front of her in the entrance. When she emerges, she gets up and goes to her husband and hands him the bladders wrapped in woven grass. The man takes those and places them in front of himself. Then the women enter the *qaygiq*, two and sometimes three at a time, doing the same thing as the first woman. They would exit and others would come in and do the same thing.

Upon Nelson's December arrival at Kashunak, the Bladder Feast was in session. This ceremony was primarily a tribute to seal "shades" (their essences) that had generously offered themselves to each Eskimo hunter (Nelson 1882, 666; [1889] 1983, 380–83). Successful hunting was, of course, based on the skills of a man, but the renewed cooperation of seal was essential. The hope was that, if treated well (by the wife of the hunter as well), the seal would be pleased and once again return to the hunter (Bodenhorn 1990). If a man had not observed the appropriate rituals and/or his grandmother or wife had not treated the seal well, subsequent hunting could be in jeopardy.

Women were essential characters in the community drama of ceremonies like the Bladder Feast; nevertheless, there were times when they were unyieldingly denied access to the men's house and the men therein. As young girls, several of the middle-aged women I spoke with were acutely aware of the unspoken but fully recognized gendered limits to the men's house. For instance, Nelson ([1889] 1983, 393) observed that men slept within the walled-off space "rigidly apart from the women," and if this proscription were broken, the hunters could lose their future subsistence yield (Nelson [1889] 1983, 393). During the sequestered periods, men would avoid all contact with women, except to be fed. For instance, while the bladders hung in the men's house, the hunters were instructed to "avoid all intercourse with women, saying that if they fail in this respect the shades will be offended," thus jeopardizing hunting for all (Nelson [1889] 1983, 440).

Family House

Another architectural aspect that is important in this study is house features. The women's space in a winter village was the family house, or *ena*. Early in my career, I referred to these archaeological house features as "women's houses" but was summarily corrected by women in Chevak, who consider them family houses. Men's access to the family house was less restricted than that of women to the men's house; this is a familiar scripted fluidity common cross-culturally where men and women are separated by space (Herdt 1994). Yet, these were strongly matrifocal households, such that "a man always was something of an outsider in the house where his wife lived" (Oswalt 1990, 21).

The classic house structure is typically rectangular in shape and set approximately 50 cm or more into the permafrost. Different materials would be used given the environment (such as whale or walrus bone in the northwest or driftwood on the delta) (Lee and Reinhardt 2003). An underground tunnel led into the low-ceilinged main chamber. Roofs were held aloft with wooden corner posts, and near the center of the floor was the hearth. Houses were generally framed with driftwood covered with sod blocks and insulated with packed snow. Raised wooden platforms were set in the sides, and up to three or four related family groups could live in one house. Each woman had a stone oil lamp, wooden cooking utensils, and bentwood dishes, with stocks of oil and food in storage. The matrilocal extended family's authority rested with the eldest woman of each social unit in the house; even in a composite grouping, the eldest woman in the house had considerable decision-making influence based on her age, prosperity, and expertise (Lantis 1946).

Since the later 1800s, houses in general have become more shallowly dug until they were finally set on the ground with sod covering the foundation for increased insulation (see Oswalt and VanStone [1967] for an early discussion of historic house architectural transitions). In addition, over time, the entrance/exit tunnels were truncated and eventually transformed into a porch structure in the historic period. People remember living in the sod houses, as they were used into the early 1960s, albeit in hybrid form (Knudson and Frink 2010). Similar to the buildings' structural transformations, the social structure has profoundly changed to nucleated/extended households with women and men living together. In an ANCSA interview, an Elder woman remembered, "The whole family would be in one house. The grandma would be there, if her husband was still alive he'd be there, the daughter with her husband would be there. Her son would be there with his wife." But in her childhood home it was women. She had her grandmother, mother, and two aunts, plus their children in the same household: "It was the noisiest house she'd ever been in" (Aloralrea 1981).

Village Tunnels

The third feature I focus on in this study is the village tunnels, of which there are several different kinds. What is known for the region from archaeological survey, ethnohistoric, and ANCSA data is that village buildings could be connected through a series of tunnels (for critical survey data and discussion of these tunnels, see Pratt 1995). The village tunnel system consisted of at least three types: (1) entrance/exit passages to quarters, (2) tunnels that linked village buildings, and (3) escape tunnels. The oldest and best-known form of underground passageway is the dwelling tunnel, found in many regions of the circumpolar north. The other two features, linking tunnels and escape tunnels, are noteworthy to the region and largely associated with the late prehistoric Bow and Arrow War Days. The constant threat and acts of internecine violence had substantial impact on both site location and organization, and the connecting and escape-tunnel features may have been, according to Caroline Funk (2010, 548–49), "invented during the war," as "being ready to escape or hide from attack was a constant requirement."

Entrance/Exit Tunnels

The most ancient of tunnels, found across the Arctic, are building entrance and exit tunnels, an archetypal northern structure that is thousands of years old (Dumond 2011). Tunnels were commonly dug into the permafrost and shored with horizontal logs or hewed planks on the sidewalls of the chambers, and short vertical retainer logs braced the sides. People had to crouch-walk under the low roofs, which were constructed of short split logs and covered with sod blocks (Oswalt and VanStone 1967). Some buildings would have a warm-weather entrance and, below this, a cold-weather entrance that was dug deeper than the house floor to create a cold trap. The length of the tunnels could vary regionally, and according to Nelson ([1889] 1983, 248), those on the coast had "extraordinarily long entrance passages." Margaret Lantis (1946, 157) notes that, on Nunivak Island, "one entered a house or kazigi [men's house] through a long underground passage, coming up through the floor at the front of the structure."

The entrance/exit passages had several purposes. The low cold-weather tunnel was a cleverly engineered means to minimize loss of heat by creating a cold trap. The warm-weather passage allowed for some cross-ventilation into the building and reduced the entrance of suffocating swarms of mosquitoes and other bugs. And tunnels could be used as places to cook and for storage (Nelson [1889] 1983, 253). Tunnel entrance/exits could also confuse a visitor. Nelson noted that, at Askinuk (today Hooper Bay), "houses are clustered together in the most irregular manner, and the entrances to the passageways leading to the interiors open out in the most unexpected places.

Sometimes one of these passages opens on the top of another house built lower down on the side of the mound, or it may be between two houses, or almost against the side of an adjoining one" (Nelson [1889] 1983, 249). Similar to a fence, the tunnels would have hindered the entrance of unwanted visitors. This may be why the entrance/exit tunnels, unlike the secret crawlways and interlinking tunnels (see below), were built well into the historic period. For instance, colonists, such as the first priest at Kashunak, were keenly aware of the protective low growls of the dogs that lined house tunnel entrances (Menager 1962). This gatekeeping purpose would no doubt have mitigated unanticipated, undetected, or unwelcome access to the house (as do dogs stationed outside homes today).

Warfare Tunnels

A less common style of tunnel construction was the clandestine tunnel. Given the secretive nature of these escape warrens, we can imagine that they may have had other surreptitious economic and/or social purposes, such as expediting a secret liaison or undetected storage. However, as discussed in oral histories, these tunnels were used for two purposes in the study area: to escape or to avoid smoke and fire during an attack (Frink 2006; Funk 2010). These tunnels could be so cleverly built that they could even be hidden from house residents. There is an instructive tale of a wife who spent a summer covertly building a tunnel extension from her house. Her husband wondered what she was spending her time on and even chastised her for not working more diligently during the fish-harvest and -processing season. Nonetheless, her efforts soon were rewarded when marauding raiders surrounded their house; the woman told her husband to flee through the passage, which he did successfully (Buster Smith 1984).

Another kind of sub-floor passageway connected village buildings. Nelson was told of "underground passageways leading from the kashim to adjacent houses" ([1889] 1983, 250–51). There could be extensive underground tunnels throughout a community, such as the village Lantis (1946) was told of, where people could traverse from house to house without surfacing (see also Pratt 1995). A primary purpose of the tunnels was to be able to move about during an enemy siege (Nelson [1889] 1983, 327). One of the main tactics of a raid was to surprise and surround a village men's house. But tunnels would have expedited the unobserved movement of trapped men from the men's house to other buildings. We can imagine the defensive power of the villages' planning strategy. If the tunnels were deeply built, they likely

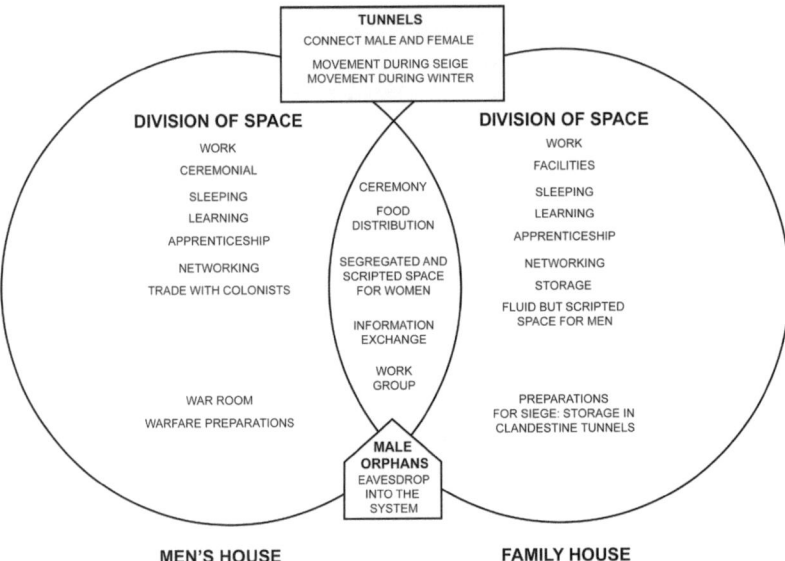

FIGURE 9. Diagram illustrating the spatial divisions and connections between coastal women and men, and the men's house and family house.

could not have been detected, even in warmer months, and during the winter, under the cover of snow, the layout of the village would have been nearly impossible for an outsider to discern. For example, Nunivak Island men used their tunnels to "pop up" and shoot the enemy (Griffin 2004, 73). The village tunnel system with entrances and exits, interconnecting passages, and escape crawlways was a highly effective structural design for evasive and defensive movements and offensive tactics during a battle siege.

Certainly the development of the village tunnel system was likely prompted at least in part by the endemic threat of warfare on the coast. Nonetheless, the tunnel complexes would have served other, more everyday purposes for the village residents. On a pragmatic level, these tunnels would have been a welcome respite from the bitter cold and wind of an Arctic winter, which can stubbornly sequester people in their homes even today. The tunnels enabled people and goods to move no matter what the external circumstances (warfare or weather). This purpose would have been a significant element of use and may have been particularly appreciated by women since they were expected to leave their homes to feed their male relatives. Additionally, the tunnels would have expedited communication among the households as well as in the men's house (see figure 9).

Storage Features

The final archaeological elements under consideration are storage features. As previously discussed, storage of foods is prevalent across the Arctic, with a diversity of applications with common themes (see Jarvenpa and Brumbach 2006). There are two customary storage applications along the coast and under consideration in this work—underground and aboveground storage facilities. Foods were often stored underground in pits in baskets, or another tactic was to stack the foods, such as fish, with layers of grass. As well, people used wet pits to store their seal pokes in cool water. Across the Arctic and in the study area, people also did (and continue to) use aboveground storage caches. These caches were typically made with driftwood logs with sod roofs and were like little houses placed on stilts.

These four features and their purposes are critical to contextualize how people lived at the prehistoric village of Qavinaq and, as covered in this chapter, to compare them with the historic village of Kashunak (and later with Old Chevak). In the following section I will more fully describe life at the village of Qavinaq, focusing, in particular, on aspects that inform how early commerce was experienced on the coast.

Late Prehistoric Period (1740–1833)

Qavinaq is a late prehistoric[1] coastal winter village site (see figure 10; appendix B) which is well-known in the region, partially because of its connection to the Bow and Arrow War Days. Today, Chevak people generally don't travel much to the old village, except some families who gather fall berries on the surrounding crowberry tundra. The ancient village is located approximately five miles downriver from Chevak on a relatively wide slough that flows from the Kashunak River. I clearly recall the first time I was taken by boat to the village. I was filled with anticipation as we glided upon the high tide in the slough, eventually seeing the rise of the grassy village mounds. At low tide, the erosion of the site along the slough bank is stunning. Artifacts protrude from the shoreline strata, and on the slick slough floor are well-preserved pieces of wood, various tools, and clumps of animal hair and bones (see figure 11).

Tall grasses on the site announce human occupation. The village is parsed into two primary sections and edged on the south by a rise of crowberry tundra and over one hundred small old burial mounds (see figure 12). There are three fairly indistinct features to the east of Area A, and a group of pits to the

FIGURE 10. Aerial view of Qavinaq village site, July 2001. (Photo taken for author by BIA pilot.)

FIGURE 11. Surface and slough bank artifacts from Qavinaq. From left to right: bone whitefish sinker, antler point, wooden figurine, pottery piece, ground-slate point (partial), and ground-slate ulu knife. (All of these items remained with the Chevak Traditional Council.) (Photo by author.)

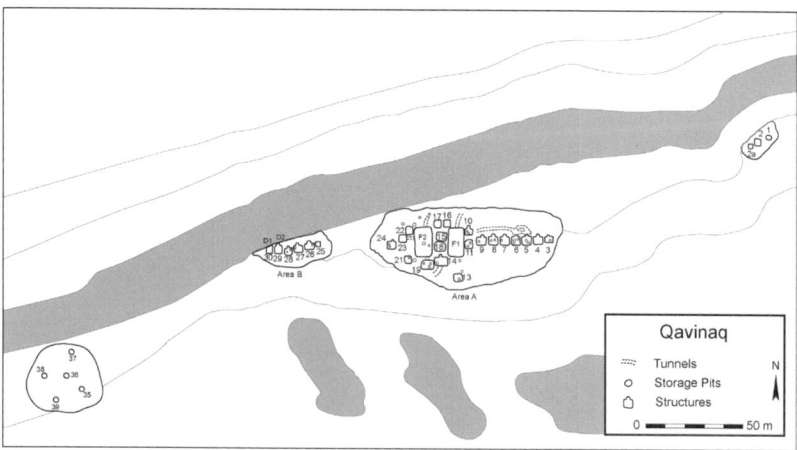

FIGURE 12. Qavinaq site map.

west that are likely modern and possibly wet storage pits for seal pokes (Ziff, Pratt, and Drozda 1982). In total, at the site there are twenty-eight house pit features (average size 28 m²) and two large men's houses (F1 and F2, appendix B; average size 177 m²).

Area B is the tract nearest the tidal slough and under continuous erosion from relentless tidal flow and spring thaw ice scouring. Likely the site was even larger than it is today. When I surveyed the site, there were five intact house pits in Area B and one being eroded, but there are no cultural features across the opposite slough side. Elder consultants remarked that at least "two or more" house features were absent when Robert Ackerman (1972, 9) surveyed the site, and four houses have disappeared since his work. The four undisturbed and intact house pits in Area B have tunnels that extend toward the water's edge and are dug into a rise of land (48 m x 20 m) approximately 2 m above the marshy tundra. A wooden corner post on the floor of house 29 (figure 12) is a typical structural feature of prehistoric Yup'ik houses. In addition, there are subsurface storage pit depressions on three of the house floors.

Approximately 40 m to the east of Area B is Area A. It is an appreciably larger (90 m x 50 m) mound that rises 2.5 to 3 m above the surrounding tundra. There are twenty-seven house pits and two men's house features. Several houses edge the men's houses (two of which may be attached by tunnels), and seven others cascade in a linear suburban row. Of the twenty house-pit depressions in Area A, eleven have subfloor depressions, some quite deep. Six of these houses have two pits, and two of the houses have three pits on the floors.

FIGURE 13. Remains of the men's house (F2, figure 12) at Qavinaq, July 2001. (Photo by author.)

Of the total of twenty-nine intact house features, nearly half (48 percent) have subfloor storage pits.[2]

The side-by-side men's house buildings have attached tunnel entrance/exit depressions that extend beyond the mound (see figure 12). These structures were likely even more profound, as it is typical for surrounding berms of sod to collapse in on features, making them appear smaller than when in use. A distinct tunnel depression of 8.5 m extends almost the entire length of the row of houses, and a tunnel depression extends out from house 14. The Elder man whom I interviewed at the site suggested these tunnels were constructed to manage and mitigate a violent siege, as previously discussed, a standard raiding tactic during the Bow and Arrow War Days.

There are two late prehistoric and early historic changes that are critical to chronicle in coastal Yup'ik culture history prior to permanent colonial settlement and that are etched in the physical layouts of the villages of Qavinaq and Kashunak. These are (1) the architecture of regional warfare and (2) identifiers of colonial market intensification. The effects of warfare and the nascent beginnings of market trade can be better understood by comparing organizational changes between the two villages. Here I will contextualize the site of Qavinaq by exploring how the site structure reflects late prehistoric life under siege and why this matters when we compare it to how people lived at Kashunak.

The Bow and Arrow War Days

Northern scholars are increasingly evaluating the chronology, extent, and impacts of native Arctic violent conflict (Mason 2012). Like other regions of the world, Arctic groups were saddled with a colonial label as peaceable people. Archaeological, bioarchaeological, and oral historic evidence confirms significant interregional conflict in northern North America prior to Russian pacification (Maschner and Mason 2013; Melbye and Fairgrieve 1994; Nelson [1889] 1983, pl. XCII; and see Burch 1985, 1988). Wars were waged among coastal villages south of the Yukon River mouth and groups that lived upriver closer to St. Michael. The "Triangle" region included the antecedent villages to modern Chevak, Hooper Bay, and Scammon Bay (Funk 2010, 526–27). These villages allied for raids against enemies to the north. To date, our understanding of the Bow and Arrow War Days on the delta comes primarily from accounts recorded by Nelson ([1889] 1983), the Russian lieutenant Lavrentiy Zagoskin (translated and recounted in Michael 1967), and oral histories (Fienup-Riordan 1994; Funk 2010).

The intertribal conflicts may have begun during the seventeenth century (Griffin 2004) and could be as old as Thule settlement of the region, circa AD 1000 (Funk 2010). Raiding activities ceased probably by the 1830s, coincident with Russian occupation. Oral histories recount endemic fighting along the Yukon-Kuskokwim coast; there are two oft-told indigenous stories linked to the inauguration of the time of violence (Funk 2010, 538–41). One is the story of a murdering son-in-law, who had a penchant for stealing other men's seals; the other is a story of an eye-poking affair between two boys. Although the elements of the historic account remain consistent, the villages these incidents took place in vary according to the region in which the story is shared. The following is the version told to Nelson ([1889] 1983, 328):

> The old man said that the main war between these people started in a great village located near Ikogmiut. Two boys were playing with a bone-tip dart, and one of them accidentally pierced his companion's eye; this so enraged the father of the injured boy that he caught the other and destroyed both his eyes. The fathers of the two boys then fought, one armed with a beaver-tooth knife and the other with a bone bodkin, the fight resulting in the death of both men. The quarrel was taken up by relatives and friends on both sides, the village became divided, and the weaker party was forced to leave the Yukon and go southward, where they settled. From that time continual warfare was carried on between them.

The Russians did not witness indigenous warfare. However, both Zagoskin (Michael 1967) and Nelson ([1889] 1983) were told of brutal battles among coastal, interior, and Siberian groups. Nelson's description of the fighting corresponds with many elements Elders shared with BIA crews (ANCSA interviews) nearly one hundred years later:

> A favored tactical mode of ancient warfare was to lie in ambush near a village until night and then to creep up and close the passageway to the kashim, thus confining the men within, and afterward shooting them with arrows through the smoke hole in the roof. Sometimes the women were put to death, at other times they were taken home by the victors; but the men and the boys were always killed. . . . The defeated party was always pursued and, if possible exterminated. (Nelson [1889] 1983, 327, 329)

There are two oral accounts of the cessation of warring, but according to Funk (2010), these, in fact, may be the ends of different periods of warring: one prior to the entrance of the Russians and the other associated with Russian efforts at quashing regional unrest. The more ancient story of resolution involves hunger and two hunters who come together in peace based on sharing seal and dried fish; the other account is linked to the Qavinaq village massacre (Funk 2010, 556):

> Two boys escaped the carnage at Qavinaq; nonetheless, some Yukon warriors tracked them to a close by village. The younger brother witnessed the raiders stretch his brothers' limbs at the wrists and ankles until he died. The surviving brother was taken north as a captive son to a warrior responsible for taking him. However, as he grew older, Panik (the captive son's name) killed the young, potentially good warriors in the northern village. He was eventually told to return to his original home and while journeying downriver the Russians arrived.

The cessation of warfare was due to multiple contextual factors. The Russian control of an arms race and their reluctance to sell them to indigenous men was a significant element of pacification. Native Elder Wassilie Evan (1984) suggested that "people quit the wars because of contact with the white men. The weapons that the white men used were no match for the bows and arrows the natives used. The natives were scared of guns." Elder Joe Friday (1984d) added that the Russians threatened the Yukoners, stating that they would "side" with the villagers that stopped raiding and be "against" those that continued to wage violent forays on their neighbors.

Clearly villagers prepared in several ways for warfare. Considerable effort was devoted to the training of warriors. Boys were educated from a young age to be "agile, swift, and strong," and they would demonstrate their progress and prowess during competitive displays at public feasts (Fienup-Riordan 1994, 328). Agility and speed were used to dodge arrows, and young warriors would run and bait the opposing team to exhaust their arrows. Dodging also was a last-chance strategy if a warrior was surrounded by the enemy:

> When one of the warriors had shot away all his arrows and chanced to be surrounded by the enemy, he could sometimes escape death for a long time by dodging and leaping from side to side, but finally would be killed by some of them striking him upon the head with a warclub having a sharp spur of bone or ivory on one side. (Nelson [1889] 1983, 329)

The ability to wage a successful raid or counter a siege was closely linked to positions of leadership. According to an ANCSA Elder, some men were "reputed to be so powerful that arrows could not hit them, and they often were in at least nominal charge of the warriors of a village" (Funk 2010, 542). Soldiers were known to tattoo small marks on their faces to denote a kill, and "great warriors" could have them across their foreheads (Fienup-Riordan 1994, 332). For the Yukoners, select consumption of a slain enemy was a rite of passage for a young warrior: "When young men fought in their first battle, each was given to drink some of the blood and made to eat a small piece of the heart of the first enemy killed by them, in order to render them brave" (Nelson [1889] 1983, 328).

Warfare and hunting demanded very similar skill sets and technology, such that "the tools of the hunt were the tools of war" (Fienup-Riordan 1994, 329). Men styled a special thin, triangular-shaped ground-stone point, which was designed to shatter in the body of the opponent (see figure 11). Wooden clubs used by fisherman to stun fish could bludgeon a foe. Warriors learned to wield spears and knives and were protected by bentwood headgear and shields made of bearded sealskin (Fienup-Riordan 1994, 329; Nelson [1889] 1983, 328–30). Northwest Alaskan Inupiaq men wore walrus ivory-plated chest armor (Nelson [1889] 1983, 330), but coastal men wore shell armor under their seal-gut parkas or light rabbit-skin garments (Funk 2010).

The men's house was the village command center and the focal target of the enemy. The goal of a raiding party was to outnumber an enemy; consequently, men were recruited from allied villages to join a raid. Nelson was told when the warriors of one village wished to make up a party to attack an enemy, a song of invitation was made, and a messenger sent to sing it in the allied villages' kashims. Meanwhile, the men of the village originating the plot set to work and made supplies of new bows and arrows and prepared other weapons (Nelson [1889] 1983, 327). Much energy was devoted to preventing and planning raids, and men could become quite prominent based on their organizational and motivational skills (Nelson [1889] 1983). The people of Qavinaq village relied on two renowned warriors named Qillerkavialuk and Kinguk who "would advise the warriors when they were going to fight" (Funk 2010, 555). Prominent leaders had to vie for followers because they did not always agree on strategy (Funk 2010).

Generally, a raiding party would sneak up on a village and surround the men's house. Raiders used "brutal, annihilation-oriented raiding techniques" (Funk 2010, 544; see also Melbye and Fairgrieve 1994). Nelson ([1889] 1983, 328) recounts:

> When possible, night raids were made by the villagers on both sides, and the people were usually clubbed or speared to death. The conquered village was always pillaged, and if a warrior saw any personal ornament on a slain enemy which pleased him, he seized it and wore it himself, even placing in his lips the labrets [lip plugs] taken from the face of a dead foe. If one of the conquerors chanced to see a woman wearing handsome beads or other ornaments, he would brain her and strip them off.

There were several defensive strategies used during a raid, including avoidance, concealment, and flight (Funk 2010). ANCSA interviews suggest that these stratagems were particularly pertinent for women, as they would hide their husbands and sons during an attack. Women could be quite clever, including one who helped her husband elude capture by dressing him as a woman and then helping him escape. She was left alone, and when the raiding men began to "make passes at her" (i.e., possibly threatening rape), she alluded to her menstruation. She cunningly cut herself with grass and revealed the blood between her legs, at which time the warriors left her alone (Napoleon 1984). Women, too, would hide their sons and husbands inside storage spaces in the house, such as the woman who "made a hole somewhere in the house to duck under," and this "little cave" was used to hide her husband when the Yukoners attacked (Aloralrea 1981).

Women also calmed men, helped them during a battle, and could plan strategy. Because men were ambushed and trapped in the men's house, they did not always know the best way to confront an enemy that lay in wait. In an ANCSA account, an Elder woman instructs the warriors to emerge from the men's house with the sun at their backs, effectively blinding the enemy.

The next day, when the sun began to rise, the Elder woman returned and announced to the men that they should "go out and give themselves to be killed." Before they embarked on their quest, she soothed their battle anxieties by applying seal oil to their lips. The first two warriors to emerge from the men's house were slain by a rain of enemy arrows, but when "all of the warriors had gotten in front of the rising sun, they started fighting back. The Yukon warriors were dazzled by the sun and they were killed off quickly" (Bunyan 1984). During the ensuing battle, this Elder woman let out a "wailing cry" that caused the Yukon raiders to run away. And as they fled the field of battle, the Askinuk and Qavinaq warriors dispatched them.

But even though Qavinaq was an oft-victorious village, stories tell of a tragic battle that ultimately led to survivors relocating to the neighboring village of Kashunak. It is a familiar historical event in the region and recounted in ANCSA interviews (see especially Funk 2010, 554–56). This rendition is a combination of ANCSA accounts, other published versions (Funk 2010), and what I was told by an Elder Chevak man while at the site of Qavinaq.

One delta evening, a group of raiding Yukon warriors slipped their kayaks up the smooth dark waters. Stealthily, they paddled their boats up a little inlet that cut parallel to the village but just far enough out of the line of sight. They lay in wait near the small tributary named Itqarissiq west of the village. The Qavinaq community had settled in for the evening—men would have been enjoying the pleasures of firebathing, and, in the small warm houses, grandmothers would have been telling stories to children settling in for the night. Little did they know that many of their lives would be lost once the sun rose above their beloved tundra.

As they crept forward toward Qavinaq, the attacking Yukoners were emboldened by earlier events and the foretelling of the fall of the distinguished village. Qillerkavialuk, a powerful Qavinaq warrior, had received a messenger from the north. This Yukoner was *ilaliyaq*, "the one making allies" (Fienup-Riordan 1994, 329), and the Qavinaq warriors could not harm him or raid the northern villages while the enemy was a guest of the village. This regional practice of hosting an enemy warrior may have been a strategy to allow for safe hunting (Fienup-Riordan 1994) and surplusing of foods (which could be severely affected by threat of raids). However, the Yukoner took Qillerkavialuk's woven grass boot liners (*aliqsaqs*) and wore them in his men's house when he returned north to his people. The enemies of Qavinaq hung the great warrior's grass liners in their men's house. They had ceremonies and used the village shaman's bows and arrows to pierce the grass liners. With each strike, the people witnessed a drop of blood emerge from the liners. This, they knew, presaged victory for their raiding party.

As the Yukoners crept forward to position themselves for the stealth attack (a favored strategy), they moved past the deftly built defensive barricade of tightly woven grass and wood made by Qavinaq women and set around the perimeter of the village. Eventually the raiders were detected, and so the enemies lined up across one another for battle. As was standard, the warriors conducted "ritualized taunting" of the enemy (Fienup-Riordan 1994, 331; Funk 2010). One of the goals of this culturally specific taunting was to entice the enemy to waste their arrows. As Nelson recounts: "When any of the men exhausted their supply of arrows, they would stand in front of their comrades and break those of the enemy with their spear shafts by striking them as they flew past. No shields were used. They said that if an arrow was coming straight at a man he could not see it, so it was very hard to avoid being hit, but that a man could readily see one flying toward another" (Nelson [1889] 1983, 328).

On this day, the Yukoners called out the warrior Qillerkavialuk. Though several Qavinaq men bravely volunteered as the leader, the Yukoners saw past this ruse because they knew what Qillerkavialuk wore in battle: a seal-gut raincoat, considered far superior to the Yukoners' fish-skin garments, with his face smeared with black embers (Friday 1984e).[3] Qillerkavialuk stepped forward, believing that his gear would make him immune to arrows, for in the past they would hit his coat but were unable to penetrate. However, on this fateful day, the Yukoners let loose a torrent of arrows into the air directed at the leader. (Nelson [(1889) 1983, 329] was told that "at times, volleys of arrows were fired in order to render it more difficult for the enemy to escape being hit.") His body took so many arrows to the front and back that Qillerkavialuk did not touch the ground when he succumbed and fell. With their powerful leader lost, the Qavinaq men were overwhelmed and fled; however, the raiders pursued them across the river and killed them, many while still in the river. Others escaped, but the raiders chased them to a nearby village. This is where they found two boys, one of whom was killed and the other taken as an adopted captive (in another story this boy eventually slays his captors).

After slaughtering the warriors, the Yukon raiders set out to burn Qavinaq down. Amidst the violent melee a brave woman arose from the tunnel of her sod house and yelled at the warriors, trying to stop them from burning the houses, saying, "Don't do what you're doing so excessively" (Friday 1984d). This same woman told them to "quit tormenting your sister's children," leading people to believe she was a relative-captive in Qavinaq.[4] The Yukon raiders ignored any pleas for mercy and placed wood at the entrances of the houses and set them ablaze; displacement and annihilation of the village were the goals of a successful raid (see Burch 2005; Mason 2012). The survivors left the devastation of their village and relocated to Kashunak—the once-vibrant village of Qavinaq never to be occupied again.

Early Trade Period (1833–1927)

The site of Kashunak encapsulates coastal Yup'ik life prior to and during the early stages of market and religious colonialism on the delta. Several generations of Kashunak residents experienced the Bow and Arrow War Days and imports of foreign goods and materials and hosted the first Jesuit missionaries. Kashunak has an incredible and complex tale to tell—a story told by oral histories, eyewitness accounts, and a settlement and subsistence system bookended by that which came before (Qavinaq) and after (Old Chevak). Chevak people are connected to the site of Qavinaq through stories of their ancestral homestead, but even more palpable is their allegiance to the site of Kashunak, where some of today's Elders were born and lived their early years. Kashunak village embodies the old ways and gives clues to some of the complex processes of indigenous-colonial interactions and transitions. In this section, I explore the settlement and subsistence systems of Kashunak and contextualize them within the historic framework of the Early Trade Period that began before missionary settlement.

Tracking and modeling life and change at the site of Kashunak is substantially more complicated than at either Qavinaq or Old Chevak. Qavinaq and Old Chevak are far edges on a continuum of historic process—the first just prior to change and the latter when considerable cultural revisions are distinct. Indeed, social and economic changes in the region occur in concert with religious-colonial interactions, but subtle yet significant transformations were happening before the missionaries settled in the area. The occupying Jesuits did not step onto a naïve or virgin landscape at Kashunak, a tabula rasa for their moral, social, and economic manipulation. Rather, they walked on indigenous ground that was already fertile with contestation and change due to the end of warring and new goods coming into the native marketplace.

In this section, I explore how indigenous internal interactions previous to missionary settlement influenced the historic trajectory of twentieth-century processes. Though the Bow and Arrow War Days were past, the community of Kashunak was still under siege, internally and externally, from social changes stimulated by ripple effects of Russian regional pacification, imports of foreign technology and materials, and eventually the Catholic Church.

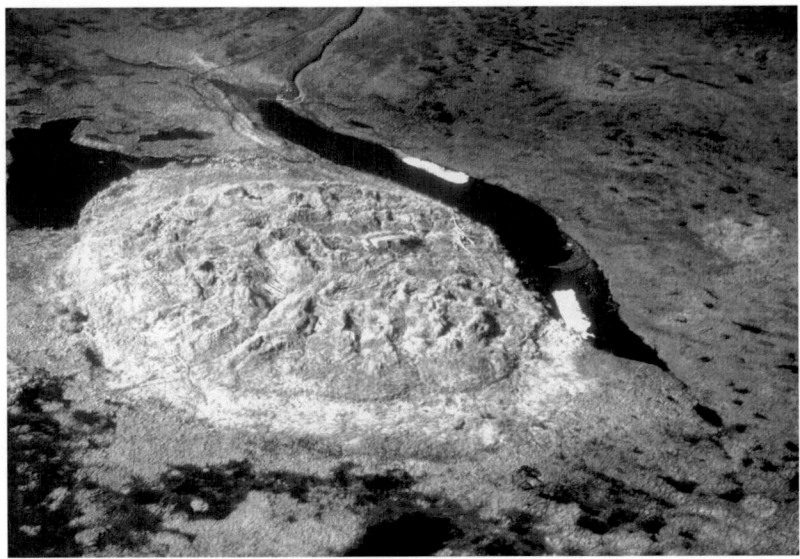

FIGURE 14. Aerial view of Kashunak village mound, July 2001. (Photo taken for author by BIA pilot.)

Entangled contexts that must be included are increased commercial trade, differential access to resources, and redefined relationships to subsistence. Some of the changes the community experienced prior to the arrival of the missionaries were a benefit to some members but a conduit for the undermining of the position of others.

The village of Kashunak is a boat ride southwest from Qavinaq along the Kashunak River (see figure 14). Like a telle on a desert floor, the village mound rises amid wet and marshy tundra plain. Unlike Qavinaq, which is hidden from view and far from the main river, the majesty of Kashunak can be seen from quite a distance. Once turned into the slough, the boat travels a half a mile or so through ever-narrowing tidal sloughs to the mounded village site. Passage must be correctly timed for high tide, for if not, the crew is stuck for hours waiting for the tidal waters to release the boat from the relentless grip of the mud on the slough floor.

Approximately one hundred yards from the site, the waterway becomes impassable, necessitating foot travel on a narrow, well-worn path through wetland to the site. The village is more impressive with each step. Today, the mound is approximately 12 m high, with a base of 63 m x 54 m (see figure 15). According to Elders, it was even higher in the recent past but has since

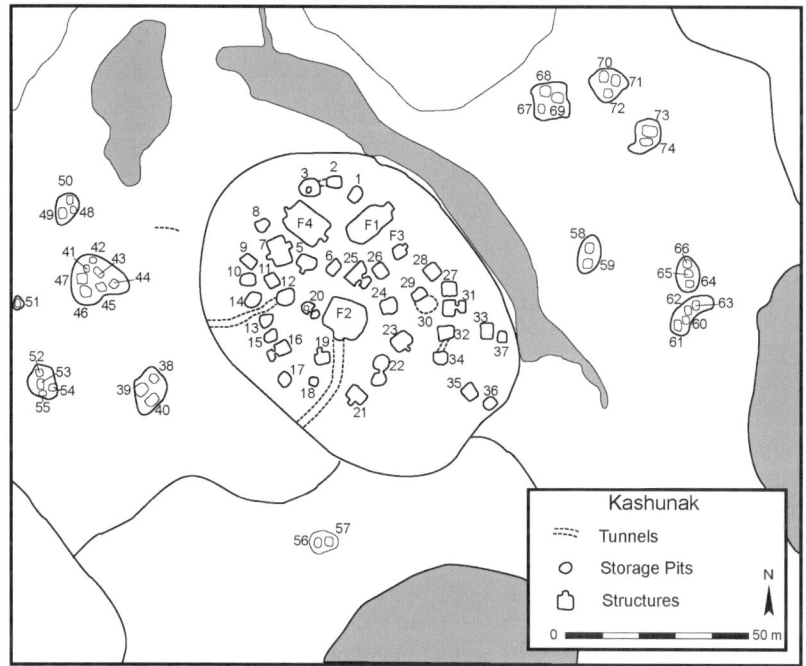

Figure 15. Map of Kashunak village site.

Figure 16. Eastern side of Kashunak site mound, 2002. (Photo by author.)

melted deeper into the tundra. The Bow and Arrow War Days spring to mind as the eastern face of the mound comes into view (see figure 16). It is 37 m long, with a graduated peak of 6 m high, and it is a slippery and difficult ascent. The defensive wall of mud and dirt is reminiscent of what Funk (2010) suggests as conventional for delta conflict-site architecture. Directly below the steeply inclined earthen wall is a shallow, mucky, moat-like pond, perhaps the result of the excavation of soil to build up the village mound out of the swampy surrounding landscape (Nanok 1981).

Unlike the prehistoric village of Qavinaq, Chevak people visit Kashunak regularly. In particular, hunters use a pit house as a base of operations (figure 15, structure F3; figure 16) for spring and fall seal hunting, fox trapping expeditions, and whitefish ice fishing. Instead of a sod roof, tin sheeting covers the house, but the sides are still mounded earth, and inside, vertically placed driftwood logs form the walls. The old village is also frequented by USFWS crews who monitor birds' nests on and around the village. As at Qavinaq, there is scattered corner disturbance in a few of the houses from fox digging.

Unlike in Qavinaq, some people collect cultural memorabilia from Kashunak. While in Chevak homes, I was shown items gathered from the exposed eastern wall. The Elder whom I accompanied to Kashunak (who was born there) remembered well that during his youth he would find pieces of old ground-slate tools and Russian trade beads. A Jesuit (Convert 1979, 13) found that "whenever you dug in to build new houses you found lots of artifacts, spear heads and wood dishes, flint and bone." Crews from the two archaeological surveys identified a range of prehistoric and historic materials eroding from the side of the site. These included parts of a kerosene lamp, Russian glass trade beads, enamel pot pieces, and prehistoric ceramics (R. Ackerman 1982; Ziff, Pratt, and Drozda 1982); these and two radiocarbon dates from the site (see appendix C) corroborate several hundred years of occupation at Kashunak village.

Kashunak village, unlike the more linear design of Qavinaq, is a tangle of features. When Nelson visited, he noted that it was built in a "straggling manner" with about 25 houses and approximately 125 people (see figure 17; appendix C). On average, the house features tend to be smaller than their Qavinaq counterparts (see appendix A for comparison). There are a total of 73 pit features; of these, 38 are off the main mound on 13 small raised mounds built up from the swampy land that surrounds the village.[5] Scattered on the main mound are 35 pit features; 2 of these (figure 15, structures F1 and F2) are reported as men's houses. Farther from the village (similar to Qavinaq) are small raised crowberry and sedge tundra areas, with over 100

FIGURE 17. Kashunak house pit (feature 21 on figure 15), July 2001. Note that the driftwood plank framing is still intact. (Photo by author.)

internments that dot the landscape (Pratt 1981; Ziff, Pratt, and Drozda 1982).

Unlike at Qavinaq, there is evidence of colonist settlement at Kashunak. There are no signs of the first mission building that was erected in 1927,[6] but there are remains of the Jesuit pit compound (with a chapel, shed, and small house) built in 1944 (figure 15, structure F4) (see figure 18).

The site also has distinctly dissimilar patterns of storage from Qavinaq. This is indicated by the overall absence of pit features on the house floors. Of the thirty-six house features on the main mound, only two have shallow pits on the house floors; these actually may be hearth depressions, as they are nothing like the deep pits present at Qavinaq (see appendix A for comparison). Instead, there are two other kinds of storage features that were used at Kashunak. One form of storage is the series of squarish pits found on the thirteen mounds that surround the village (see figure 19). The pits, many of which are partially submerged, were most likely used as seal-poke storage units. According to Chevak Elder Ulric Nayamin (1983), people "used to make pits on fairly good mounds and fill those pits with water. Then they would store their seal poke and oil to keep them fresh." I've been told the breadth of the pits corresponds with the number of seal pokes it could hold. Typically, the caches were lined with driftwood logs and then, when filled,

FIGURE 18. Father Jules Convert ringing the bell at the top of the church complex in Kashunak, 1946. (Courtesy of Jesuit Oregon Province Archives, Special Collections, Foley Center Library, Gonzaga University.)

were covered with logs and dirt (Friday 1984a; Nayamin 1983). The pits were generally dug in swampy areas; the water kept the contents cool (oil spoils quickly if in the direct sun or too warm) and pests and animals out, and assisted in the rendering process. During the warmer months, the "pokes of blubber were placed in a spring if possible and left for several weeks, the blubber being broken down into oil by the constant gentle movement of the pokes in the running water. This apparently was the only method for rendering fat" (Lantis 1946, 179). The poke could remain in the pit through the winter, but most bags were removed prior to freeze-up.

Another method of storage not found at Qavinaq is the aboveground storage facilities that were used at Kashunak. There are no identifiable surface remains of these at Kashunak, but they are noted in historic photographs, Nelson's account, and memories of people who lived there. (These storage facilities may have also been at Qavinaq but no remains have been identified.) These "elevated storehouses" were wood-framed, sod-covered storage houses, raised on four driftwood pilings (Nelson [1889] 1983, 250). This style of raised cache is common in many areas of the Arctic and may have

FIGURE 19. Seal-poke pit at Kashunak (figure 15, structure 73), July 2001. (Photo by author.)

been a colonial introduction into the subsistence regime among Alaskan natives (Fair 1997).

Along with different kinds and locations of storage between Qavinaq and Kashunak, the use of tunnels significantly changes. There are surface depressions that may be remains of tunnels at Kashunak; one of the house features has a long, trailing feature that may indicate a long tunnel (figure 15, structure 12). And the men's house has a long tunnel-like feature that leads from it down to the base of the village mound (which could be an entrance/exit tunnel or an escape tunnel).[7] For instance, Russian traders "who visited this district say that the people in these large villages [like Kashunak] had underground passageways leading from the kashim to the adjacent houses, for use in case of a sudden attack by an enemy." But Nelson ([1889] 1983, 250) did not record the use of interconnecting tunnels at Kashunak. There is a slight indication of tunnels between several of the house features. I was told by a middle-aged Chevak man (who accompanied me to the site) that, when he was young, he fell into one of the ancient and dilapidating underground burrows, but that he had not used them.

Quite distinct at Kashunak, compared to Qavinaq, is the scarcity of house exit/entrance tunnels. Of the few houses that have some remnant of tunnels, these are abbreviated and shallow compared to the house tunnels found at Qavinaq. Instead, there is a new architectural form that appears: the front porch. Four of the house features have extended rooms (F16, F22, F25, F31), which are standard in historic and contemporary household construction. Essentially, over the historic period the tunnel entrance transformed into this attached veranda space (see Oswalt and VanStone 1967). The porches are used today for storing a variety of gear and food since they stay cool in the summer and cold in the winter. In addition, the porch guarantees that an individual must enter the portico space before she or he enters the house through another door—an entrance buffer somewhat akin to a tunnel.

The sites of Qavinaq and Kashunak are different—with different kinds of storage, use of tunnels, and house architecture. To better understand the linking of these shifts in regard to colonialism, I parse out the history of Kashunak into three phases to try and map connections of indigenous-colonial interactions and change (see, e.g., Liebmann 2012). In the remainder of this chapter, I focus on the Early Trade Period, when foreign traders and goods were available to coastal people prior to religious settlement at Kashunak. In particular, I explore the possible associations between the finality of active warfare at Qavinaq and the subsequent intensification of commercial trade opportunities. Certainly the cessation of the resource allocations for the preparation and practice of warfare would have been welcomed, but it also would have cut off an important avenue for status pursuits. Nevertheless, the market boom stimulated by the flourishing colonial trade would have been a viable outlet for strivers. But this would have had repercussions for the traditional control of older men over younger men as well as truncating women's absolute control over their subsistence products.

To contextualize the archaeological changes between the two sites, I draw from two additional kinds of evidence: the first will be Nelson's field notes[8] concerning material objects he collected from the area in the late 1880s. The metals and other objects he amassed and his comments demonstrate that coastal Yup'ik people had a pipeline to foreign goods prior to the in-migration of missionaries. The second line of evidence is the ANCSA oral histories of Alaskan Native people's own accounts of Euro-American, creole, and indigenous traders and their activities in the region's early market commerce.

Early Indigenous-Colonial Market Interactions

With a native guide and a Euro-American trader, Nelson (1877; 1882, 660; [1889] 1983) traveled 1,200 miles through the Yukon-Kuskokwim delta, then a "little known country" to colonists. During his winter journey, he recorded lifeways and collected a variety of objects from coastal villages, including at Askinuk (modern-day Hooper Bay) and Kashunak. He reflected that, amid this "barren waste," the people were "among the most primitive people found in Alaska, and retain their ancient customs, and their character is but slightly modified by contact with whites" (Nelson 1882, 670). Notwithstanding this element of perceived isolation, there is evidence from Nelson's collections and observations that colonial technologies and materials were essential to coastal lives prior to his arrival.

And what is apparent is that foreign goods were accessible (or accepted by) men and women at a differential pace. As discussed previously, Nelson notes that men's traditional subsistence tool kits were largely replaced with foreign technologies. The men Nelson met at Kashunak and elsewhere hunted with steel traps and guns (Nelson [1889] 1983, 80, 121–22). Men used metal knives instead of the "crooked knife" for woodworking, and "the stone knives [for hunting and skinning], formerly in universal use among the Eskimo, have been almost entirely displaced by the ordinary butcher knives sold by the traders" (Nelson [1889] 1983, 85–91, 171). But this supplementation of traditional materials for metal or contemporary tools took place at a dissimilar gendered pace.[9] Nelson noted coastal women were still using the ground-slate *kegginnalek*, or ulu, for skinning and cutting up fish and game, and these "women's knives" were made of a "broad piece of slate, roughly concentric in shape, with the curved side ground to a thin edge" (Nelson [1889] 1983, 108).

Alongside Nelson's information there is also evidence from native oral histories (ANCSA records) that indicate indigenous people were engaged directly with market commerce before missionaries arrived. Kashunak and other delta coastal villages were peripheral to the Russian trade posts, and yet, oral history points to inclusion within these trade networks, not seclusion. For instance, there are memories of men who traveled north to St. Michael for trade opportunities (Friday 1984c). An Elder (Evan 1984) recounted stories of how remarkable the colonial steamboats in the north were, and when the gold prospector boats used all of the available wood, they "took the fish caches along the river to use for fuel." As a young man, Joe Friday worked for the ACC trade store in Kashunak and would travel north to St. Michael and Unalakleet to trade. During this period, workers were paid in wages rather than what occurred earlier when Russians bartered. At St. Michael, native men were paid fifty cents an hour to unload merchandise from the boats. Local traders were hired for their work; for example, Friday was paid one hundred dollars for a summer's work and, with his earnings, was able to purchase a rifle for twelve dollars. There is also mention of Euro–North Americans "looking for money from the ground" (possibly gold?) on Nelson Island (Friday 1984c; see also Tunutmoak 1984).

According to ANCSA Elder accounts, before the missionaries arrived, coastal folks also had access to tobacco, tea, and even firearms (Nayamin 1981a). As Nelson, too, noted, Russian muzzle-loaded rifles were used "before the qasaqs came" (Henry 1984). When the first one was bought, "many people gathered to see how the gun worked," and the shot was so big that "people saw the bullet as it traveled in the air and as it hit the target it fell on the ground and started rolling" (Henry 1984). Other items that entered Yup'ik material culture have been less discussed but were no doubt influential to the workings of the subsistence system—for instance, canvas. Women began to sew summer tents of canvas instead of hides when it became available from a Tununak trader in the late 1800s (Friday 1984c, 1984d).

Apparently, coastal people both traveled to trade posts and were visited by Russian, Euro-North American, and creole traders prior to the missionary arrival. A well-known creole trader was Aluska (Aluskaq), who, among a cadre of traders, exchanged "supplies in their sleds" (Bell 1984). Additionally, Nelson ([1889] 1983, 250) writes of his discussions with "early Russian traders" about underground village tunnel systems. According to oral sources, a Russian entrepreneur named Natriuluk, who worked for Billy (Nagteqaq), set up shop in Kashunak village. Natriuluk, a "white man" (he had a native wife), sailed to the village and is said to have built the first aboveground framed house, which he traded out of (Friday 1984c). Elder Joseph Friday (1984c) was born circa 1895 and remembered traders "since he became aware." He first encountered Natriuluk after he returned to the village from egg hunting. He said that Natriuluk had several companions and had covered all of his lumber and supplies. Friday did not know how long he operated his store, but the Jesuits who arrived in 1929 do not mention him or a trade store at Kashunak.

After leaving Kashunak, Natriuluk was replaced by Tuntuvak, also Russian. He was a "kass'aq but fluent in Yup'ik" and would "fight people all the time" (Friday 1984c). His strong temper was unnerving because "people were supposed to be quiet" (Friday 1984c). The Kashunak men did not tolerate his bad behavior and expressed their displeasure toward his comportment while they communed in the men's house—a conversation which he overheard and frightened him into fleeing the village. The white trader, Frank Willie, replaced Tuntuvak with a young American named Patrick. But Patrick failed to return from one of his many trips to the north, even though he was a "young man with good dogs" (Friday 1984b). Apparently, the store was not manned after Patrick left, and everything was cleared out by a Tununak trader in 1930 after the Jesuits had arrived in 1929.

Chapter Summary

There are similarities and significant organizational differences between the village sites of Qavinaq and Kashunak. Qavinaq is a site built for warfare, with two large men's houses, utilitarian and strategic tunnels, and storage that denotes a group poised for the need to draw upon siege surplus. Warfare conferred special privileges on men, who planned and engaged in battle, and on women, who provided protection and provisions, while the village was under siege.

After the burning of Qavinaq and survivor relocation to Kashunak, coastal people experienced two historic cultural transformations before religious-based colonial engagement: the end of endemic warfare and the start of interactions with the capitalist market. By the time Russians entered the Alaskan north, warfare had ceased and native traders were well-versed in asserting themselves into foreign commerce. When Nelson traveled along the delta coast in the late 1880s, there were no signs of warfare, and men had been able to get foreign goods and find work in areas to the north. And it is evident from the ANCSA data that there were traders (among them native, mixed, and non-native men) who actively engaged in commerce in the region before the missionaries' arrival. Quite remarkable at this time was the differential access men had to foreign goods (especially metals) compared to women.

There are several key shifts in the four archaeological features at the sites. Kashunak has two men's houses, yet they are smaller and less defined than Qavinaq's men's houses (see appendix B). This shift is coincident with the decline of the primacy of the men's house, which may begin in the early period when senior-junior hierarchies began to be undermined by new technologies (such as firearms that would have altered subsistence practices and traditional knowledge expertise) and commercial opportunities for young men (Frink 2009b). Senior men's authority probably was impacted also by the end of the Bow and Arrow War Days and the shift to market competition. In addition, connection between the family houses and the men's houses is vastly different since there are no surface indications of connecting tunnels. The end of tunnel building probably was precipitated by the end of warring. However, it would have had important repercussions during this transitory period. For instance, women would not have been as privy to commerce or political negotiations taking place in the men's house. This would have proven a subtle yet substantial change, especially during the rise of market commerce in the region and the apparent differential development between women and men in the early American commercial system.

Finally, the storage features at Kashunak are very different than those at prehistoric Qavinaq. At least within the memories of Elders (early 1900s), women were no longer storing foods in pits on their house floors. Instead, aboveground caches were used, and these may be tied to the increase in the privatization of fur commerce by men and the intensification of frozen fish for trade. Also, unlike at Qavinaq, there are many seal-poke storage pits on mounds adjacent to the village. This possible change in storage practices is likely related to the end of warfare (women did not need to save and hide foods or their menfolk), and the seal-poke pits may indicate increased demand for oil for food and fuel. The externalization of women's direct control over their stores (and commercialized fox pelts) is coincident with their relative disengagement from commercial opportunities and the increased emphasis on men in the colonial market. In the next chapter I explore how these transformations set the stage for the settlement of missionaries along the coast.

3

Indigenous-Mission Interactions

WHEN THE FIRST JESUIT PRIESTS TREKKED to the coast in the late 1800s, Yup'ik lives were already in flux—not in some mythical precolonial stasis. They had been adjusting to the end of warfare and the rise of commercial trade. In this light, interactions among the Jesuits and the people of Kashunak were predicated on a dynamic cultural landscape. Instead of lumping this time into one period of history, I discuss three phases of indigenous-mission interactions: the Advent Phase, the Retrenchment Phase, and the Transfiguration Phase. In the earliest Advent Phase of mission settlement at the site of Kashunak, the priests were not in a strong position. This is especially shown by the general rebuff from men and the building of the church in the swampy marsh off of the village mound. The exasperated Catholic Church eventually abandoned its Kashunak mission and thrived in the neighboring village of Hooper Bay. Upon their return to Kashunak during the Retrenchment Phase, the priests were in a much better position to negotiate with village men. The Transfiguration Phase encompasses the very brief resettlement of the Kashunak villagers to Old Chevak. It was at Old Chevak that people knew that a return to the old ways of life was no longer a viable option.

In the exploration of this early to mid-twentieth-century period, we expand the available data and I integrate firsthand indigenous accounts and colonial records. The colonial Church perspective is represented in mission logs, published memoirs, correspondence between priests, and drawings and photographs curated at the Jesuit Oregon Province Archives (JOPA) in Special Collections, Foley Center Library, Gonzaga University, Spokane, Washington. These data are of course biased and extremely partial, but the writings of the priests bestow hints of tactics, frustrations and attitudes, and interactions in the community, and early photographs show village structures. The colonial record is balanced with data from ANCSA recordings and with my primary interviews with people who lived at Kashunak and Old Chevak—indeed a rare and valuable inside perspective. Prior to discussing these sites, in this next section I outline the overall scheme of Jesuit missionary practice, critical to contextualize interactions on the coast.

Colonial Mission Standard Operating Procedure

The Jesuits' plan to convert their Alaskan native flock mirrored their Christian brethren's tactics employed throughout the world. A most significant element of a colonial religious undertaking was to convince and coerce indigenous people to settle near church stations (E. Scott 1991). This was often accomplished by interlocking (spatially and conceptually) three primary systems together, what I term the triad of colonial siege: the trade post, the religious mission, and colonial education. The colonial triad is a strategic wedge that effectively disrupted, delayed, or redirected many indigenous practices. When combining forces, the powerful centripetal influences drew people into centralized and more settled populations—often resulting in limited access (spatially or because of time constraints) to subsistence foods and a curtailment of seasonal relocation (particularly for family units) (see Murphy and Murphy 1985).

Indigenous mobility was also infringed upon by commercial subsistence demands. Though at times enslaved and coerced, indigenous people were not just victims to colonial insinuation; they also, for their own benefit, sought opportunities of engagement with the colonial triad and enhanced access to resources (material, social, and ritual). For instance, Athapaskan communities routinely asked the American Fur Company to bring missionaries to their posts (Devens 1992). Though missionaries could be at odds with traders, priests were often points of access to foreign goods, labor opportunities, and bilingual training. Access to foreign goods was a strategic hook, such that the Jesuits in the Great Lakes were "much freer with material aid to those who expressed an interest in conversion," and converts enjoyed special privileges at local trade posts (Gonzalez 1981, 15). It was often younger people that first populated colonial settlements (Devens 1992). While the missionaries rewarded special access to converts who performed measures of seeming acquiescence, they also introduced aspects of structural violence and publically and privately could dispense threats and abuse (Lutkehaus 1999, 223). Resolute in their goals, missionaries could be unflinchingly aggressive "spiritual police" (Gutierrez 1991, 80). Displays of zealous emotion and direct intervention could be quite unsettling for indigenous North Americans (Lutkehaus 1999).

At mission schools, boys were trained in wage-earning skills, and girls were instructed in domestic (non-wage) service. The Catholic Church dissuaded women from seeking paid employment. For example, Tsmishian women were discouraged from working in the canneries but instead were kept on as "servants" within the missions "under the guise of training for future life" of obedience as wives (Bowie 1993, 13). Of significant emphasis was a reinforcement of the ancillary contribution of women to the work of men. These roles were modeled by priests and sisters, who replicated the "subordinate role of women within the hierarchy of the Catholic Church" (Lutkehaus 1999, 212). Though women could gain relatively more access to religious teaching through the colonial Church, they were also the backbone of free labor for the Church (Gutierrez 1991, 78).

Another subterfuge of the churchmen was to undermine customary kinship systems. For instance, even though it was traditional to give children an indigenous name, it was a common practice for missionaries to claim naming rights to a newborn through baptism. Churchmen also interrupted age grades of authority and access both to goods and ritual knowledge. For instance, among the Pueblo of the American Southwest, young men would apprentice with older men to gain experience and skills required for initiation into the kiva. However, priests undercut this gatekeeping system of indigenous authority by offering young men fast-track access to esoteric knowledge, thereby becoming beholden instead to the priests (Gutierrez 1991). Priests also emphasized the sanctity and permanence of nuclear units, to the detriment of indigenous matrifocality and polygynous and arranged marriages. Particularly among matricentric indigenous communities, older women could command significant economic and political sway, especially having to do with marriage. According to the coastal women I have spoken with, the second marriage was not necessarily arranged, which the women liked. The priests at Kashunak were also troubled by the apparent ease with which a person could initiate a divorce. A Yup'ik woman signaled her desire to leave a marriage by not feeding her husband in the men's house, and a man withdrew from a union by leaving the village for a period of time and withdrawing subsistence production (Fox 1939, July 1929–May 1952). The Jesuit extreme emphasis on nuclear family units undercut women's authority in marriage negotiations. As a comparative case, older Montagnais Innu women of northern Quebec resisted mission efforts to eradicate polygyny, but young women commonly sought "sanctuary" from arranged and polygynous unions (Leacock 1980; Lutkehaus 1999, 228).

Women's sexual activity and sexuality was a thorny issue for missionaries since it could be an accepted native instrument of negotiation and economic capital. For instance, Pueblo women used sex as a gift of "cooling," with an expectation of a reciprocal gift (Gutierrez 1991, 51). However, in Native

North America, priests were "systematic and unrelenting" in their degradation of women's sexual economic parlay as "sinful, shameful, and depraved" (Fiske 1991, 524; see also Voss 2005). In their diatribes, men of the cloth insisted upon marital fidelity and, especially, the "elimination of the right to divorce," which they saw as too autonomously chosen by indigenous women (Leacock 1980, 27–28). Emphasis was instead placed on women's obligation for obedience to the colonial Church and men.

Colonial Religion on the Coast

Religious colonialism on the delta coast arrived relatively late compared to other areas of Alaska, but their imperialist tactics were similar to those around the globe. The first religious sect to occupy Alaska was the Russian Orthodox Church, which in 1794 settled Kodiak Island. Coupled with indigenous-colonial commerce, the Church was part of a significant period of change in southeastern Alaska (Veltre and McCartney 2002). However, like the Russian occupation overall, the Church made few tangible inroads into southwestern Alaska, even though Russian priests had briefly visited parts of the coast in the mid-1800s (Fienup-Riordan 1983, 9). Not until the late 1880s did Jesuit Catholic priests begin to travel and eventually settle in several coastal Yup'ik villages. The following section outlines some of the challenges the priests encountered during their early years of deployment into coastal territory. These included the extremely demanding travel logistics on the tundra, provisioning predicaments at outlier mission stations, and difficulty in convincing Yup'ik people to curtail their seasonal relocation patterns. The priests were also met with "indifference, if not outright hostility," from some residents (Fienup-Riordan 1983, 16). However, on closer examination, not everyone was completely unreceptive to the priests. Quite to the contrary, women were relatively open to engagement with the Church.

As Eleanor Leacock (1980) points out, one of the most critical systemic associations for missionaries was the coupling of churches with colonial education. In 1884, the U.S. Congress passed the First Organic Act for Alaskan education, which provided funding for churches to establish schools in Alaska (Flanders 1984). The Jesuits first infiltrated Alaska in 1887 and, unlike their Russian Orthodox predecessors, were very concerned with spiritual conversion and efforts to change indigenous cultural practices. Like missionaries around the world, the Jesuits viewed their prospective spiritual converts as child-like innocents, yet dissolute and in need of saving in both the esoteric and practical worlds (Fienup-Riordan 1983, 12).

Initially, there were very few Jesuits on the coast: itinerate travelers who stayed but briefly in a village. However, by the early part of the twentieth century, the Catholic Jesuits, along with several other Christian sects, had settled in coastal villages, a profound shift in native negotiation of ever-encroaching colonialism. Wendell Oswalt (1990, 93) suggests that Yup'ik people tolerated these new settlers because they "applied their customary pattern of accommodation to the new development without realizing the subtle shifts in goals taking place," but when missionaries (and traders) permanently occupied villages, the "dominance of western culture had begun." But the so-called dominance was not as straightforward, as there were complex responses to the priests. The early indigenous-mission period is the story of the complicated interactions of the people of Kashunak, among both themselves and the emissaries of the Church.

Jesuit Settlements and the Mission Boarding School

The first Jesuits to arrive on the coast went to the village of Tununak on the northern shores of Nelson Island. In their initial attempt to settle, Father Pasquale Tosi (in 1888) and Father Joseph Treca (in 1889) established the third Alaskan mission (the Holy Cross and Nulato missions were established in 1888) in Tununak. However, in 1892, a mere four years after it was established, the primary administrative mission was moved north to Kanelik and then a year later to Akulurak. One of the most difficult issues for the early mission system on the coast was logistics—the challenges of travel and having enough food. The delta is a difficult landscape to safely traverse and successfully live on without a lifetime of training.

As in other indigenous regions, the Jesuits created a system of missions, including primary centers and smaller, village-based, satellite missions to help them deal with logistical challenges. Very early, they established boarding schools at Akulurak and Holy Cross to help them settle the region. The Akulurak mission operated in the study area from 1890 until 1951, when it was moved to a location on the Andreafsky River and renamed St. Mary's Mission (where many middle-aged people I consulted with were schooled as youths). In 1888, the Jesuits opened the larger Holy Cross boarding school, the "mother of the Jesuit missions in interior Alaska," along the Yukon River (Llorente 1988, 26).

The Church applied the stratagem of education, and some indigenous children were removed from their villages and relocated to the mission school. They were exposed to rigid schedules, disavowment of their language, and adherence to colonial gender roles. There was an amalgamation of coastal and upriver/inland children who lived at Akulurak. Some children were recruited by priests, and others were orphans, a large available population during the early twentieth-century waves of epidemics and chronic illness (Fiske 1991). According to Elder Dick Bunyan (1984), the priests would recruit from the surrounding villages, and the "young people that went away to Akulurak and Holy Cross to go to school would seem to learn and know more than the students that went to school in Hooper Bay." Some would be "away for a long time," and some remained at the mission. Two Elder men whom I met in Chevak were the first children from Kashunak to be taken to the boarding school at Akulurak.[1]

The mission schools also functioned as labor camps and feeder systems to the smaller missions. Because the delta was a major logistical challenge to the early Church, these primary hubs provided supplies to the scattering of priests out on the tundra. For much of the early twentieth century, boarding schools such as Akulurak supplied food, fuel, and supplies for the outlying village-based missions, distributing freight coal, tea, tobacco, and foodstuffs such as canned goods, rice, flour, and sugar to the priests.

The Church relied heavily on unpaid child labor to make the system work. Along with cooking, laundry, farming, and fuel and water collection at the mission, the children would harvest and process many salmon and other fish each summer workday. The boys would work the wooden fish wheel, and girls stood for untold hours at raised wooden platforms butchering thousands of fish to be hung to dry in enormous covered structures. A JOPA photograph shows girls and young women with the caption, "busy cutting fish for drying, about 18,000 hung up already" (Fox n.d.-d; see figure 20). The children salted and packed dried fish in wooden barrels. These provisions were essential for winter use by the main and satellite missions and some were canned for sale.

While some of their children were being reeducated and their labor exploited, the Church tried in vain to curb seasonal movements of relatives living on the tundra. During the late 1800s and early 1900s, chapels were built in several villages, but people largely retained their seasonal subsistence rota. "Actually, we did build some chapels in some strategic places," remarks Father Llorente (1988, 108) on early efforts to settle the Alaskan natives, "but they [satellite chapels] became useless in a short time, since those people were quite nomadic." Each spring the priests were left alone in the village while kin groups traveled to the coast for spring sealing and summer fishing. As Elder Ulric Nayamin (1981c) recalled, even though his family was "established at Kashunak, we were always migrating out to other

FIGURE 20. Akulurak children and women cutting fish. Note the drying fish in the background. (Courtesy of Jesuit Oregon Province Archives, Special Collections, Foley Center Library, Gonzaga University.)

areas." The inability to get folks to settle frustrated the first priests at Kashunak. Father Fox lamented that the move to spring seal camp "brings with it the break-up of the missionaries' spiritual activity if he has no boat," and salmon camps were perceived as places of "moral danger" (Fox n.d.-f). The resistance by people to settle down in the village was the primary Jesuit explanation of the withdrawal from Kashunak village. Nonetheless, the reasons are far more complex, and they illuminate both local resistance and entanglement with the Jesuits, especially in the context of competitive economics.

The large district from the south of the Black River to the Kuskokwim River was referred to by the Jesuits as the Kashunak District, and Kashunak village had one of the more important early satellite missions. The Jesuits initially chose the village as their outlier base of operations in lieu of the neighboring village of Hooper Bay, in which a U.S. government school had been founded in 1913. The construction of the Mission of the Sacred Heart at Kashunak was at least in part motivated by competition from a Swedish Lutheran missionary who had been working as a government teacher (Flanders 1984; Fox 1939). However, the Protestants relinquished Kashunak and invested their energies in neighboring Hooper Bay. But soon after their settlement the Jesuits, too, relocated to Hooper Bay—their initial mission a

FIGURE 21. Drawing by Father Menager of Kashunak village with the mission to the right off of the main mound. The larger sod building at the apex of the mound village is the men's house. (Courtesy of Jesuit Oregon Province Archives, Special Collections, Foley Center Library, Gonzaga University.)

failure. The most salient challenge to the mission occupation was the placement of the church complex. It was built not at the center of the village (where it was raised in the following Retrenchment Phase), or even in a marginal area on the village mound, but rather out on the unoccupied marshy fringe. This location of the first mission and the reticence of Kashunak men to embrace the Church would contribute to the eventual withdrawal of the Church.

The Advent Phase at Kashunak (1927–1932)

In September 1927, Brother Hess, along with Father Delon and "some of our big [native] boys" from Holy Cross, traveled three hundred river miles south to construct a chapel at Kashunak.[2] The group traveled in a wood-planked boat pushed by a small gasoline engine (commonly referred to as a *tuk tuk* due to its sound). With them they brought three hundred logs and other building materials, and upon arrival, there was "no room left for a mission without much crowding, and having the mission surrounded by noisy dogs and children on every side" (Fox 1939). Therefore, the mission building was set approximately three hundred yards east of the main mound (Menager 1962; see figure 21). Hess confessed that the "low tundra made construction exceedingly difficult" (Fox 1939, n.d.-c). The Jesuit brother and his crew raised the foundation of the wood-framed chapel building 1.2 m high by "placing heavy logs down on the soggy, mossy tundra" (Fox 1939, n.d.-a). The logs settled, and a pool of water subsequently formed under the building. The men filled the walls with moss and a layer of paper for insulation. The colonial compound occupied about 11 x 14 m in area and included a chapel, classroom, recreation/waiting room, priest quarters, and a second-story kitchen. But it was not long until Father Francis Menager (the first Kashunak priest) realized the mission building was "poorly located" (Fox n.d.-c). On the village mound, people could stay relatively dry, but the mission's location on the floodplain proved to be a consistent irritant to the priests.

Logistics, too, proved very difficult, and supplying the Kashunak mission was a challenging and expensive proposition for the Church. Not only was Kashunak in a remote location, but the narrow tidal slough also flowed only partially to the mound. The slim slough was fine for the skilled kayakers and their boats with little draft, but the Jesuits' overburdened wooden boats commonly bogged down in the muddy bottom of low tide. During the early years, the priests had limited options for transportation, for both supplies and tundra proselytizing. Menager, who unlike his successor Father John Fox failed to master the dog team and did not have a boat, was essentially landlocked for the seven months he served at the Kashunak mission (September 1927 to March 1928). But Fox (at Kashunak from 1928 to 1932) was well-known for his tundra skills. To get his supplies and mail, he rented native dog teams for a ten-day winter trek north to Holy Cross. Fox had a wooden-hulled boat, *The Little Flower*, and each summer hired men to accompany him for his northerly supply run. Boating took more time and was quite expensive, requiring up to 580 gallons of fuel (Fox n.d.-f).

Also vexing the Kashunak priests was the fact that the Sheppard trade store was upriver at Old Chevak, hindering their access to provisions for themselves and their soul bartering. Area traders and the missionaries were often linked in their colonizing efforts through trade goods. Traders monopolized access to provisions in a relationship of dependency and exploitation. The Jesuits used their access to the traders as leverage for local loyalty and conversion. However, this was frustrated during the early phase of occupation at Kashunak, as the trade store was located at Old Chevak.

The store was supposed to be located at Kashunak, but apparently the store owner realized the difficulties of operating out of Kashunak before the

Church did. George Sheppard was a creole who was fluent in Yup'ik and operated several trade stores in the north. As the story is often told, Sheppard had planned to set up a store at Kashunak but, because of a storm, decided to stay where he stopped, at the site of Old Chevak, a local seasonal hunting and fishing encampment based at the confluence of two major riverways. Sheppard had accompanied Menager on his initial voyage to Kashunak, but instead of remaining there, he built his store at Old Chevak (Fox July 1929– May 1952). For his assistance to Menager, the crew dropped three or four logs to be used as the foundation of his store. Though the official story is that he chose the site out of storm-induced desperation, the location of Old Chevak was superior to the logistically daunting location of Kashunak, although without an ancient village mound much more prone to flooding.

The Sheppard trade store sold rifles and other equipment and Western foods for local furs and fish. The store also controlled the mail, a powerful position of access. The ability for the priests to get food and supplies from Sheppard's store was critical for their own provisions and for bartering with locals. This was particularly important during the early spring, when families usually had limited stores and fresh harvests were at a bare minimum. Dick Bunyan (1984) recalled that his family "always worried about getting fish and food" during this period. In March 1929, Fox returned from Sheppard's store with eight bundles of fish (five hundred pounds), and "lots of natives come immediately at Father's return to trade curios for flour and fish" (Convert n.d.).

Like Sheppard, Fox was regularly involved in swapping with folks at Kashunak. He explained that when people "wanted to buy something, they had their skins, they'd bring their furs to the trader, and in return for their fur they got tea, shot, primers, powder, flour sugar, shells and whatever they needed. So I had to do the same thing, I bought what I needed from the natives in barter" (Fox n.d.-a). An important distinction is that Fox, unlike Sheppard and other traders (see VanStone 1982), traded with women for their products. During his early years at Kashunak, he needed dried fish (for himself and his dog team) and firewood. He bought dried fish, wood, and seal pokes filled with oil and fish, with "things from my own provisions for the winter," like tobacco, tea, yards of cloth, flour, sugar, cornmeal, and oatmeal. He also traded with tea and cloth for "curios," such as women's fish-skin bags, boots, bird-skin parkas, gut-skin raincoats, and skin boats and ritual masks from men.

In addition to being engaged in economic exchange for indigenous foods and goods, the priests were conspicuous, competitive consumers. Fox, in particular, was known for having the latest technology such as the kerosene lamp (which eventually replaced the oil lamp), the shortwave radio, plank wooden boats with gasoline engines, and even a gas-powered moped (Convert n.d.). Gasoline engines were highly sought after because "when they didn't have outboard motors, it took a long time to get from place to place" (Friday 1984c). The materials for the plank- and sheet-wood boats and the gasoline engines were not widely available until later, during the Transfiguration Phase, when folks settled at Old Chevak. Fox observed that coastal people traveled primarily in "large skin boats or by kayaks during the summer, and by dogs during the winter. A few outboard motors are beginning to be used. But so far they are still a negligible quantity" (Fox n.d.-f).

During the nascent period of religious incursion in the area, villager labor was crucial to the provisioning and functioning of Jesuit satellite missions like Kashunak. As discussed previously, colonials were more likely to pay native men for their work. Unlike Sheppard, who was reluctant to pay cash,[3] priests paid Kashunak men for their work (Convert n.d.; Fox n.d.-a, July 1929–May 1952). Sometimes they were paid in barter, like altar wine, but generally they were paid with currency. Men were hired as guides, to move goods to and from Holy Cross mission, and (bypassing Sheppard) to retrieve mail. Fox would pay sixteen dollars to rent a dog team for his long winter trip to Akulurak or Holy Cross. Men's labor was especially important for unloading the priests' freight at Kashunak. For example, when Fox arrived in 1928 at the village, he paid fifty cents per hour to unload his boat (Convert n.d.). Nonetheless, the men did not always acquiesce to the priests' requests for help, even if they were promised a wage. For example, Menager was unsuccessful at hiring anyone to haul bags of coal that had been dropped off on a distant shoreline. Some men started to move the coal but soon quit, deciding that the labor was not worth the pay. To Father Menager's palpable alarm, the large pile of his fuel coal remained marooned (Fox 1939).

The priests also had a difficult time persuading men to donate their labor to the Church. Fox lamented that it was "hopeless" in the early days at Kashunak to find boys willing to volunteer their labor toward the operation of the mission, as this work was "not for money but for the love of God" (Fox n.d.-c). In addition, men were more reticent with the priests, and much of this was mitigated through the men's house. Though changes were afoot, the men's house as an institution had flourished during the earlier period and had continued to have a strong influence over economic, social, and ritual aspects of people's lives. When the missionaries settled, the men's house institution was still a dominant influence in the community—but, without doubt, an institution under revision.[4] The men's house was the center for public ceremony and display and trade with outsiders. The patriarchal colonial market, including differential-gendered access to wages and the Yup'ik discretionary system of economics (see also Hensel 1996), had created an environment that rewarded men. However, late nineteenth- and early twentieth-century commerce also would have undermined the authority of the men's house, particularly among young men who could bypass some of the authority and expertise of older men through trade and new technologies.

Early on the missionaries strove to destabilize the solidarity of the men's house system by emphasizing the need for nuclear households (Oswalt 1990). However, even before their efforts, the number of men who exclusively stayed in the men's house was already waning at Kashunak. Like one Elder woman I spoke with, others, too, reported that their fathers and husbands "stayed at the qaygiq [men's house] some part of the time and other times he stayed at their house" (see also Griffin 2004). Elders born in the early 1900s remembered that some men were already living in the households separate from the men's house before the missionaries came. An Elder woman born in the late 1800s recalled her father spending the day at the men's house but returning to the family dwelling for the night. According to one Elder, "there was a time when men live exclusively at the qaygiq" but this was "before her time." Further, when she lived at Kashunak, "some men still lived at the qaygiq but some lived at home with their families." Another's father slept with the family, but her brother stayed in the men's house. These testimonies underscore internal centrifugal stresses in the men's house prior to significant missionary influence.

The men's house also served as a central place to resolve community issues (see e.g., Larson 1991, 1995), but the priests began to undermine this as well, especially through arbitrating disputes among women. Father Llorente (1988, 103) recalled that, upon his arrival in a village, "there were always little problems to settle. They all had great confidence in the priest to settle everything."

However, even if somewhat fractured or undermined by market privatization, when the Jesuits settled at the village of Kashunak in 1927, there was resistance by men. According to the accounts by the priests in the mission daily log, Kashunak men were fairly taciturn (compared to the women) toward the Church, and the priest was more cautious with men. For instance, each morning, Fox would walk to the village mound and ring a small bell in the tunnel entrances of the houses, but he did not enter the sanctuary of the men's house to chime his demands. This may have been because of the powerful men who lived in the men's house, including shamans. The most striking example of residential resistance is the placement of the church compound on the margin of the village. Unlike the men's house that was prominently placed at the center of the village, their option was to reside in relative banishment on the marshy tundra, where high tides and seasonal flooding were constant problems. It was an effective measure to thwart the Church, as the miserable location of the mission was a prominent reason the priests cite for their abandonment of the village.

The first Jesuits on Nelson Island had a fairly benign stance toward the men's house. However, once the magnitude of the unifying and authoritative nature of the men's house as a village institution became apparent to the priests, they worked to undermine the economic and ritual authority of the institution. The recalcitrant reception of Kashunak men as a group may have been because the men's house as a village institution experienced the mission men more as economic and spiritual competitors than as suppliers. Men already had access to trade with Sheppard and would not have been (as yet) dependent on the Church for resources.

Shamans and the Early Mission

During the Advent Phase, opposition may have been spearheaded by shamans. Yup'ik shamans assisted the community in their quest for balance between the natural and the supernatural by serving as mediums and interpreters among worlds. These individuals could be quite influential and both revered and feared (Oswalt 1990; VanStone 1984). On Nelson Island, Lantis (1972, 45) noted that the shaman "could strongly influence and occasionally even order the behavior of others." When Menager (1962, 54) arrived at Kashunak, there were four shamans who "ruled the village with an iron hand." According to the priest (1962, 54), the "medicine men were very angry when I settled in the village because they realized that I was a threat to the continuance of their 'racket.'"

The shaman (along with other successful men) could have more than one wife, which may have given them economic and social advantages (Oswalt 1990). Shamans led daily and annual rituals, formally welcomed village guests, and entered family houses to heal sick patients (Menager 1962; Pierce 1984).Wendell Oswalt (1978, 38) suggests that the "most powerful member of any [Yup'ik] community was the shaman, most of whose performances were designed to diagnose and cure illness." They also acted as leaders during community ceremonies, influenced weather and food harvests, could both cure and cause sickness and catastrophes, visited the dead, and led deadly raids (Michael 1967; Nelson [1889] 1983; Snow 1981; Vitt 1987).

Men and women could be shamans among the Yup'ik. Nelson ([1889] 1983, 427) commented that "possessing power over the invisible world are usually men, but this power is sometimes held by women." Apparently their "principal activity was curing" (Lantis 1946, 200), and during a curing rite, they could use a drum, otherwise associated only with men (Nelson [1889] 1983, 383). An Elder spoke of a woman shaman, Iqlusta, who came from Hooper Bay to Kashunak to "do some doctoring," and she "licked a sick person and he became well" (Aloralrea 1981), and Metrapaagaq, who practiced her art "before the whites or kass'aqs came" (Aloralrea 1981). According to Dick Bunyan (1984), female shamans had the "same powers as the male shamans," and "way before" he was born, they "performed the same things as the male shamans."

Shamans were held accountable for their competence and could be ostracized or even murdered if they "let too many patients die" or were deemed harmfully ineffectual (Nelson [1889] 1983, 429–30). Nelson ([1889] 1983, 429) was told of a shaman that was put to death for "failing to fulfill their predictions and for suspected witchcraft." An Elder woman accused of causing the death of several children was "clubbed to death, her joints severed, and she was burned in oil" by her village (Schwalbe 1951, 30).

Throughout the early colonial period, shamans were in high demand to solve social and medical problems, including outbreaks of infectious disease (Ray 1975). But when missionaries settled, people "flocked to the mission clamoring for salves and medicines" (Oswalt 1990, 87). At Kashunak village Father Menager "became the doctor" and throughout his tenure administered physical and spiritual medicine (Menager 1962, 16). As is common among religious colonialists, God's emissaries strongly linked access to health care and indigenous acquiescence to conversion. People were not blind to this collusion, such that one Elder man commented that people were coerced to "take the Word in one hand and the medicine in the other!" (Schwalbe 1951, 67).

Shamans continued to practice into the 1900s[5] because there was a prevalent distrust of whites as healers, and shamans remained in positions of power (Oswalt 1990). The shamans, seeking to attribute misfortune to human action (and in competition with the shamans of God), would direct blame at missionaries for outbreaks of illness. An outbreak of pneumonia at Akulurak was connected to the Sisters of St. Anne, and a shaman had "told parents that if they let their children attend, they would die" (Fienup-Riordan 1983, 16). But colonists attributed the sickness to wet, cold weather (Ray 1975, 216).

The tensions between the missionaries and the shamans continued to flare up during early twentieth-century epidemics of influenza, measles, and whooping cough, such as during the 1900 "great sickness," when people were said to be too weak to bury their own dead (see Fortuine 1992). Shamans worked to heal and even deflect death from their villages. For example, Ulric Nayamin (1981b) told of a Kashunak shaman who "conjured enough medicine to distract the disease." He essentially quarantined the village, and "he took all the community into the men's house and tied them up with leather thong in order for him to perform successfully."

Nevertheless, Kashunak was eventually hit by illness, and the priests competed with the shamans to save bodies and souls. Father Menager, who had a medical background, arrived at the village "with a lot of medicines" that the people had a "love" for, and he reported "some success in relieving these poor people of some of their ailments" (Menager n.d.). According to the priest, even the "medicine men" came to him for attention and to his mind "acknowledged that their own medicine was a fake" (Menager n.d.). The priests did not dissuade villagers from thinking of them as supernatural healers and rivals of influential shamans. For example, while Menager was at Kashunak: "The custom there was for the men every morning to walk about one hundred feet from the village and empty their bowels all at the same time in a long line, with the loose dogs cleaning up behind them. However, the priest never joined them. It meant to them that the priest was not a regular man and did not need any emptying of any bowels. Maybe he was a different type of human" (Llorente 1988, 57).

As shamans were noted for supernatural acts, such as leaving their bodies to find the stolen soul of an ill patient (Hughes 1984), so, too, were priests known for their mystical feats. Father Llorente (1988, 83–84), who served in the district with Menager and Fox, reveled in this otherworld status, recounting his near drowning, but because he "had made medicine," he lived. Jesus, too, was viewed as a "super-shaman," with the priests his agents on earth in the supernatural realm (Ray 1975, 251). In addition, shamans would attack one another on a spiritual battleground (see e.g., Vidal and Whitehead 2004). For instance, John Kilbuck, a very influential Moravian missionary in the Kuskokwim region (see Fienup-Riordan 1991), was blood poisoned by a shaman when he was ill with an infection. However, Kilbuck gained "enormous prestige" when he survived his shamanic assailant (Rearden 1979, 30).

Elders also remember shamans, such as Agnes George (1981), who, while atop her father's lap, "used to see four shamans" and would "see them dancing." However, over time, shamanistic activities waned (and went underground) in the villages. Ulric Nayamin (1981a) stated that "before the missionaries came, the people have a strong belief in the shaman way of life. These shamans used to help people ... their sickness, heal them and give them a little life longer," and then the "missionaries came and they sort of, uh, kind of scared the people about what the shaman did." When Elder Juliana Aloralrea's (1981) first child was baptized, there "weren't any medicine men in Kashunak anymore."

At first, the priests were acquiescent about feasting and ritual observances in the men's house. In fact, in January 1929, Fox agreed to change the time of evening mass so as not to conflict with the "harmless" native dancing (Fox n.d.-f). However, soon Fox (and the Church generally) grasped the political and religious power seated in the men's house and embodied by shamans. As Nayamin recounts (1981b), "When shamans performed things they have songs and drums and when the missionaries came they even banished the form of an Eskimo dancing thinking that all the Eskimo dancing was connected to that exercise, that practice, of the shamans killing other shamans." The priests were very public in their crusade against shamans, and Menager and Fox "really went after" them (Nanok 1981). "The missionaries scared the people into turning away from the shaman," and they "frightened the old people" (Nayamin 1981b). The missionaries recognized the difficult choices native people made during this colonial crisis of shifting power and belief. Fox wrote in the Kashunak mission log (Fox n.d.-f):

> The native who happens to fall under any of these tabus [sic] has to choose one of two things: either disregard superstitious practices and incur the displeasure of the medicine man and all the hunters, who will blame that native for their bad luck, or carry out the prescribed superstitions and violate the commandments of God. But I get after them pretty hard. As I am a more tangible thing to them than the devil, they cannot afford to incur my displeasure. I know the guilty individuals will be very careful not to repeat their superstitions, at least publicly or before anyone that might tell me about them.

Women and the Early Church

But unlike men in Kashunak, at least some women experienced the early Church differently during the Advent Phase. This may have been because they experienced increased access to trade goods, labor opportunities, ritual, and the warmth and collective space of the chapel. The first priests were highly reliant upon women for local products at this extremely remote mission outpost. Father Menager was not as adept as Father Fox, who eventually became well-known for his ability to get resources and his economic maneuvering. He was so adroit at trade with people that his Church brethren derogatorily labeled him the "Native Santa Claus" (Fox n.d.-f). Fox failed to account for his annual costs at either Kashunak or Hooper Bay missions, as he rarely used cash but most often bartered. While provisioning himself, Fox became quite the trader as well. One of his primary needs was dried fish for himself and his dog team, his lifeblood of conversion in the outlying villages. Acquisition of enough fish was a constant concern and struggle for Fox in the early years, as was getting fuelwood. Fox bartered for seal-poke fish and oil, driftwood, and fish in addition to some manufactured goods such as sealskin boots, fish bags, and small parkas. He both consumed and traded the fish, oil, and wood, and sold the crafts as curios.

Fox did not inject himself into the system of fur trading among the men and the Sheppard trade store, but he did trade in fish. He traded "lots of fish" for tea, sugar, cornmeal and oatmeal, cloth, tobacco and gunpowder, shot, and primers in the surrounding villages (Fox n.d.-a).The mission was supplied hundreds of pounds of fish from the child-labor camp at Akulurak (Fox n.d.-d). Upon arrival of a fish shipment from the northern mission, Fox recorded, "lots of natives come immediately at Father's return to trade curios for flour and fish. After this, no more trading as tea is all gone, and fish and flour are needed for personal use" (Fox n.d.-a; see also Convert n.d.). According to Llorente (1988, 163), people learned that the missionaries gave things away, like tea, medicines, and clothing. It was common for early converts to have ulterior economic motives for acquiescing to the priests' demands of conversion for food. These folks were called "tea converts" and "tended to revert to old ways" after getting goods from the priests (Oswalt 1990, 134). Fish was especially imperative through the difficult period of "spring hunger" (Fienup-Riordan 1986, 26–27) or during a natural crisis (see also Michael 1967; Schwalbe 1951). During the year, people would bring their fish to the store but in the spring could find themselves without. Father Henry Hargreaves, who served at Old Chevak, recalled that the Sheppard trade store would sell back the same fish that people had traded earlier in the year.

But, besides fish, stores were generally disinterested in women's goods or their subsistence products such as seal oil (see also JOPA Chevak Diary; Van-Stone 1984). Fox commented that "no trader at the time cared to bother with, except that they bough[t] a few laftak [tanned hide], and an occasional mukluk skin [bearded seal]. They wanted no seal, nor seal oil at the time"

(Fox n.d.-a). However, Fox regularly traded with women for seal products, and each year he would acquire twelve seal-bag pokes full of oil and dried fish. He would take some pokes north to Akulurak and return with a year's worth of fish for himself and his dogs (Hooper Bay Collection 1945).

Along with subsistence foods, native labor was critical to Jesuit expansionist efforts. As discussed, child labor was the fundamental economic engine of the mission boarding schools and their unpaid subsistence provisioning of satellite missions. At the outlying missions such as Kashunak, women's labor was critical for maintaining the mission. But this was a conundrum at Kashunak since women were more integrated into the church but in general men seemed to remain aloof. For example, according to Church records, unlike women, local men were reluctant to donate labor to the Church. Fox lamented in the early days at Kashunak that it was much harder to get boys interested in volunteering for the Church. "So the problem of finding help was narrowed down to girls" (JOPA 1927–1955; JOPA, Fox Box 8; JOPA 1920–1950). In addition, there may have been parental resistance to allowing boys to participate in the Church, such as the case of a boy who was himself "anxious to be a Catholic," but "his folks are fighting the idea" (Hooper Bay Collection 1928, 1931, 1932). Women, unlike men, generally did not get paid for their Church work; instead, they and children worked for gifts and food (Fox n.d.-c). For instance, on one occasion, Fox's supply boat was loaded down upon return from the north and was caught in the ice and muck of the narrow and shallow Kashunak slough. When he asked for Kashunak men to assist him, he was told that they were all out fishing and hunting and could not pull the boat nearer the village. Reluctantly, he acquiesced to let the women (and a few men) pull his boat up the waterway (see figure 22). After they successfully pulled the boat, he wrote that they "naturally expected a few pinches of tea or flour" for their work. But instead he invited the women for tea and some food at the church and stated that their labor was a donation to the Church (Fox n.d.-c).

Through their closer association with the Church, women also gained access to resources in the chapel complex. The priests introduced a daily schedule that incorporated morning mass, prayers, and formal education for children during the day, and religious instruction for adults in the evening. Each morning, Father Fox would ring his bell in the entrance mouths of the houses, and he remarked that "it takes them just a half a minute to jump up and be on their way to mass at half past six o'clock in the morning" (Fox n.d.-b). Women and their children eagerly sought the morning warmth of the chapel's coal stove (JOPA, Fox Box 1929a), a real luxury for them and a welcome respite from the damp and cold sod houses. Fox wrote that "firewood is extremely

FIGURE 22. Kashunak women and men pulling *The Little Flower* boat with Father Fox. (Courtesy of Jesuit Oregon Province Archives, Special Collections, Foley Center Library, Gonzaga University.)

rare" in this region, and women "do not waste fuel for heating their igloos" but used it for cooking (Fox n.d.-a). Fox often bemoans the scarcity of wood in the village. Native and non-native eyewitness accounts suggest that, if a house had a framed roof, the paucity of available firewood in the late winter required some residents to burn the wood framing their houses for cooking (Fox n.d.-f). According to Fox, this resource strategy forced household members to "move out into tents as soon as the sod roof thawed," as "it might cave in any minute and turn the former igloo into just a square mud hole." Fox indicates that "in the late summer, the hole was cleaned out again, a new frame of split logs put back, and the sod restored to the roof, with a heavy layer of dry grass under it, and a layer of mud from the beach smeared over it to make it more watertight once it froze" (Fox n.d.-f). The household's cautious use of firewood was contrary to the use of wood to stoke the intensely hot firebath enjoyed by the village men each evening in the men's house.

Those who participated in the Church were rewarded for their allegiance, and the priest distributed food, materials, and medicines. Fox often provided incentives for attending Mass, such as soap, combs, and towels, as well as gasoline cans, which were used as small stoves in the houses. The women and girls of Kashunak were present in the chapel "almost all the time." Fox assumed that this was because the "native women have very little housework to do" (Fox n.d.-f). In an attempt to lure men into the church, Fox began a "little evening school" for the village men in 1928 (Convert n.d.). Nevertheless, during the early period, it was primarily women who attended services and who were present in the church compound on a daily basis. The chapel essentially became akin to a woman's communal house. Fox was not entirely comfortable with the overwhelming presence of the women. At one evening mass he complained that there was "nothing except women," although he admitted that "they know that there is always a good warm fire at the mission, their first idea in the morning is to run thither and warm up" and at the same time "talking, looking at pictures, and playing games" (Fox Box 1929a).

Age Groups and the Early Church

Both women and children were important participants of early-stage indigenous involvement with the Church, but Elders were known to be reticent. During the Advent Period, the priests recognized the reluctance of older folks to acquiesce to the priests' attempts to change cultural practices. Father Fox wrote that "old folks are hard to change, and if the children are well protected [by the missionaries], superstition will die with their elders" (Fox n.d.-b). Father Fox (Fox n.d.-b) noted that, at Kashunak, older folks "struggle to part with some of their superstitious practices." In addition, the priests perceived the shaman as a competitor for the training of young people, leading Father Llorente (1988, 38) to suggest that "the only way to penetrate those mentalities would be through the children. Get them before they are taught by the medicine men."

The missionaries would try to integrate sons of prominent shamans into mission work as "helpers" (Schwalbe 1951, 89). For example, Helper Neck, or Uyakok, born circa 1870, was the son of a shaman. In 1885 the Moravians recruited him since he "was of an inquiring nature," and he became an active convert (Schwalbe 1951, 69–71). He soon traveled and "preached" the word in men's houses, especially to other young men. He even wrote a pictographic language book, and when he spoke, the "old medicine men leaned forward. This little book must contain some potent medicine indeed." The young men listened with intent "eagerness" as Uyakok attacked the "darkness of the shaman" (Schwalbe 1951, 70). So, too, in Kashunak did Father Fox seek out young men of prominent families. One of Fox's "best mass servers" was the son of a "patriarch of Kashunak" (Fox n.d.-d). Nonetheless, according to Fox (Fox n.d.-d), the willingness of some boys to serve the Church was met with opposition from their parents.

The missionaries also focused on young people and marriage practices. During the early period of the Church in Kashunak, both Menager and Fox sought to quell arranged marriages (Fox July 1929–May 1952, 1939). First unions were arranged by each young person's family.[6] Fox commented that adults were "accustomed to absolute control over their children, even after they have married them off to another, many times without the approval of the parties to the marriage" (Fox n.d.-c). According to Elder Agnes George (1981), the young women "never had their choice but always the parents made choices." Both the young men and young women never had their own choice. A girl could be promised or even married "before she was born," and the girls would "take a husband even before they get their first menstrual period. When they are told to have this for a husband, they'd be afraid of this man, they didn't have anything to say against him. They had to obey their parents. No matter how scared they were, no matter how scared they were of that man." (Several middle-aged women I've spoken with express relief that arranged marriage customs are no longer practiced.) Marriages were commonly announced in the spring, and a seal caught by the groom was distributed at the men's house and among the households by the bride. The union was formalized in the men's house when the young woman would dance in a garment her mother made for her with hides hunted by the groom (Fox n.d.-b, n.d.-f; see also Lantis 1946). The priests were acutely aware of the authority of adults to arrange these first marriages and counseled young women to refuse or leave an arranged marriage, and they would harbor the young women if there was marital discord (Llorente 1988; Schwalbe 1951).

The End of the Advent Phase

As discussed, women tended to engage with the early Church more than men, and they benefited by this association. The priests, however, were not pleased with just having women as part of their mission work, and eventually the Kashunak mission was abandoned. The official story of the withdrawal of the Church from Kashunak centers on the marginal placement of the church complex and the storm floods of 1931 (Barker 1979). During one storm surge, Father Fox had a harrowing experience wherein an enormous ice wedge was the only thing that prevented him from being swept away to certain death, along with the chapel building. During this same storm, the villagers held a communal feast in the men's house.

Flooding explains the retreat of the Sacred Heart Mission from the village, but before the storm, Fox had been in negotiations with his superiors to relocate the mission. In an annual letter (1929–1930), he stated that the Church mission should move from Kashunak "perhaps next year" (Convert n.d.). He cited that part of the reason for the failure of the Church was the opposition he faced from Kashunak men and his futile efforts to curtail seasonal moves away from the village (Convert n.d.). Clearly the involvement of women with the Church was not enough to keep the mission in the village, and the Church pulled out of Kashunak and instead concentrated their resources in Hooper Bay village. This tactic indeed got the attention of Kashunak men and led to an ensuing return of the Church to Kashunak, but under very different social and economic circumstances.

Retrenchment Phase (1932–1947)

The decision to withdraw and divest from Kashunak was a strategic retrenchment decision which indeed did lead to an eventual return to the village with the mission in a more powerful position. After the withdrawal from Kashunak, the Church invested resources in the village of Hooper Bay, and it grew as a commercial, educational, and religious center of development. This proved an effective turnaround strategy for the Church, as the buildup of Hooper Bay, an allied but competitive village, spurred Kashunak male leaders to ask the mission to return, but it did so on very different terms. The mission complex was no longer marginalized but built in a centralized location on the mound, and villagers (as we will see, especially women and children) began to settle down (see figure 18). This heralded a significant cultural shift, for soon after the mission reopened, the entire village of Kashunak relocated to Old Chevak, the ultimate aim of the Jesuits for many years.

As you will recall, the people of Kashunak and Askinuk (today Hooper Bay) were allied partners during the Bow and Arrow War Days. Nonetheless, even villages that are allied and connected through generations of kin are cooperative and yet extremely competitive (witness an Alaskan native basketball game). When Fox left Kashunak, he carried with him economic access and growth since both the Church and traders facilitated and frustrated distribution and access to resources. They also stimulated economic competition through their own conspicuous consumerism. The priest was the neighbor that always had the latest stuff—especially Fox, who, as discussed, was well-known as a consummate trader and as adventurous and experimental with new technologies. The differential development of Hooper Bay did not go unnoticed, and Kashunak villagers argued that Fox had taken the church and "lost interest" in them (Fox, July 1929–May 1952). My informal discussions of the removal of the mission from Kashunak usually elicited disgruntlement among some Chevak Elder men.

Father Fox, miffed by both the location of the church and the rebuff by the men of Kashunak, took his colonial economic advantage and moved to Hooper Bay. Part of the compulsion for the villagers of Kashunak to acquiesce to the demands of the Jesuits was set in the subsequent economic development of Hooper Bay, which became a boom village and hub of commerce in the region. During the Retrenchment Phase, Hooper Bay was a focal point for increasing colonial market-inspired development. For instance, by 1941, the priests incorporated electrical power initially generated by "wind towers" or "windchargers," which were tall wooden windmill-like structures used in conjunction with six-volt batteries (Fox n.d.-e). Coupled with the use of the fifty-gallon steel drum and the kerosene lamp used in homes for light and heat, electricity was the final blow to the eventual demise of the traditional oil lamp (Harry and Frink 2009).

Hooper Bay also became the center for medical and government services for the coastal villages. Airplanes delivered mail and supplies, and various medical specialists flew in to conduct health checks. (Because of the marshy surroundings of Kashunak, there was no chance to build an airstrip.) One of the most challenging aspects of village life is the lack of affordable access to preventative and emergency health care. Medical visits from health-care professionals (general practitioners, optometrists, veterinarians) are greatly anticipated even today. By the early 1940s, coastal men earned wages (and traveled) if they joined the Alaska Territorial Guard stationed at Hooper Bay. Father Fox applied for and controlled local government assistance and, in 1932, distributed two hundred dollars in government relief money in Kashunak, which he noted was used for tea, flour, and ammunition (Fox 1939).

The Jesuits built up their church complex at Hooper Bay, and five years after Fox moved to Hooper Bay, he founded the Little Sisters of the Snow, an order of indigenous sisters located at Hooper Bay (Frink 2010). The priest was impressed with the willingness of young women to convert and ally with the Church. Under consistent reluctance from and criticism by his superiors, Fox established the order in August 1935 and drew in young women from the surrounding villages. These women were critical to the early functioning of the Church in the region, and, as far as I could tell in the records,

FIGURE 23. Four of the Little Sisters of the Snow pictured with their subsistence gear prior to going out hunting and gathering. (Courtesy of Jesuit Oregon Province Archives, Special Collections, Foley Center Library, Gonzaga University.)

they received no wage compensation, although Anny Sipary (a bilingual mixed-descent Yukon woman), who came with Father Fox, was paid five hundred dollars' worth of cash and food (Fox n.d.-c) in 1927 and eight hundred dollars in 1928. Fox comments that he could "travel around free all I wanted" because of the "cheap" labor (Fox n.d.-a). The young women benefited as well, for three reasons: (1) the Church offered a means to gain access to resources and independence otherwise limited to (young) women, (2) the order was a means to forestall an arranged marriage, and (3) the order made cultural sense, as it functioned much like a polygynous household.

According to Fox, the indigenous sisters were the "domestic helpers of our Alaskan missionaries" (Fox n.d.-a; Hooper Bay Collection 1929–1955). They served several critical roles for the Church on the coast, traveling to outlying villages to perform baptisms and even leading morning prayers in the outlying villages when Fox was absent. The women kept the village schools functioning, as well as Hooper Bay's St. Theresa Catholic School. They also provisioned the priest and themselves fairly autonomously. Fox knew that the sisters "knew how to live off the country, would be easy to support, loved their surroundings, were pious and very practical." On their weekly day off, the women collected firewood and hunted with firearms (see figure 23). One sister could "hunt as well as any Eskimo in the village." They built and tended gardens; grew enormous carrots, radishes, and lettuce; and annually canned more than a ton of turnips, which Fox both bartered with and sold (Fox n.d.-a; Hooper Bay Collection 1929–1955).

The priest would occasionally purchase tea, flour, and sugar for the women, but they built an independent enclave. They provisioned themselves and, to a considerable extent, maintained the mission's ritual and educational activities in the outlying villages. The Little Sisters of the Snow essentially created a women's house. They had economic independence, networking space, and access to ritual authority in the villages. This proved very attractive to young women, and they flocked to the sisterhood. In 1934, Fox had to turn away candidates because the "number of applicants exceeds the means on hand for their support, many vocations have had to be reluctantly put off" (Fox n.d.-a, n.d.-b). In the first year, there were thirteen applicants, and six were accepted, one of whom served at Kashunak village.

Tangential evidence suggests these young women enjoyed an atypical measure of autonomy. For instance, the independent order met with considerable resistance from both the Church and at least some locals. The women acted as priests (shamans), educators (Elders), and traders (men)—a constellation of clout and opportunity quite remarkable for young, unmarried women. There was much ado concerning the autonomous ritual activities that the young women were performing. Jesuit leadership warned Fox that he should not let "these girls do the preaching; let them teach catechism but the preaching belongs to you" and the "preaching of women is not allowed" (Fox n.d.-c). Part of the persistent opposition was also borne by questions of the propriety of the situation. Antagonistic correspondence dogged Fox, especially regarding his predilection for the company of women. A 1935 letter asks him, "Why can't you get along like the rest of our Fathers, alone? Why do you have to keep surrounding yourself with women?" (Hooper Bay Collection 1929–1955).

Renitence toward the order also stemmed from locals. For example, Fox notes in May 1943 that support for the group was "conspicuously absent" among the villagers (Fox n.d.-c). He surmised that the disapproval stemmed from the traditional control over young women the sisterhood tended to thwart. According to Fox, indigenous customs "militate against any such idea as convent life," as Elders were "accustomed to absolute control over their children, even after they have married them off to another, many times without the approval of the parties to marriage" (Fox n.d.-c). The weight of local and Church resistance was ultimately too much and led to the disbanding of the order thirteen years after it was established. Young women still took their vows, but all training and career oversight were centralized at Holy Cross Mission to the north.

Retrenchment Phase Development at Old Chevak

Simultaneous to their economic divestment from Kashunak and investment in Hooper Bay, the Jesuits began to develop Old Chevak, a place the Church ultimately wanted Kashunak villagers to relocate to. For the priests, Old Chevak was better situated along the confluence of two rivers, making transport much easier, and the Sheppard trade store was located at Old Chevak. To the utter dismay of some Kashunak residents, in October 1935, Fox ordered the dismantling of the church buildings at Kashunak and hired the Tununak trader George Aluska (who was of mixed descent—native and Russian) to sink pilings for the new mission at Old Chevak. While dismantling the Kashunak mission compound (in the spring of 1936), people "begged" so much the priest allowed a shed to remain at Kashunak (Fox July 1929–May 1952). Aluska used the Kashunak building materials to construct part of the mission complex at Old Chevak that stands today. The remaining building materials from the razed Kashunak mission were used to assemble mission chapels in Hooper Bay and Tununak.

After building the church complex at Old Chevak, the number of residents increased since it was now the location of both a mission (with a school) and the Sheppard trade store. Catechists did some teaching at Old Chevak, and Bernadette (likely a Sister of the Snow) and Aluska worked there (Fox July 1929–May 1952). In September 1937, according to the Chevak House Diary of the Mission of St. John the Baptist, "quite a crowd gathers at Chevak due to the presence of catechist and school" (Fox July 1929–May 1952).

Reentering Kashunak

But Kashunak villagers had not given up on the Church, and they tried to convince the mission to return, especially to build a school. At one of the Kashunak meetings in 1939, a "good crowd had gathered" (eighty-seven people), and Fox writes that the "chief" with "the counselors" met with the priest to urge him to build a school (Fox July 1929–May 1952). This same year, a small Jesuit school was opened in Kashunak and administered by Ida Hunter, a creole and former Holy Cross student, and her husband, a Russian named Alexis Hunter. Nevertheless, Fox admonished the villagers for their inability to settle down and told them the reason they had lost the mission was their resistance to remain in Kashunak year-round. Fox told people that he wanted to rebuild the mission in Kashunak, but only if the chapel complex was built on the main mound, not in the swampy margins of the village (Fox July 1929–May 1952).

By 1942, approximately ninety people were living at Kashunak, and men had built a new men's house. When Fox visited, he now had significant access to the men's house and "said mass in kazga out of the 3 days he spent at Kashunak" (Fox July 1929–May 1952). Later that year, Father Jules Convert relieved Fox of his coastal parish duties, and in the spring of 1944, the villagers agreed to build an "igloo chapel" instead of a standard, aboveground chapel complex. The reason given was the shortage of materials because of World War II (Barker 1979). The men were paid three hundred dollars for building the chapel complex, and Convert comments that one man, Michael Nayagak, whom he calls "the chief," was the "only one who worked all the time" and "usually kept things going" (Fox July 1929–May 1952). Interestingly, there is a picture of Convert and a Chevak man indicated as "chief" of Kashunak in the JOPA archives and on the back is a handwritten note saying this man was not the chief. When I showed a picture of this later to several Chevak Elders, they, too, in no uncertain terms, said he "was not the chief."

The chapel, priests' residence, and shed were built on the northeast center of the Kashunak village mound (see figure 18; F4, appendix C). The colonial complex took up a space of approximately 12 x 7 m, including a small (3 x 6 m) pit house for Convert's residence (Barker 1979). A dance in the men's house followed the raising of the chapel complex, and the Kashunak men gifted a roll of sealskin to cover the church windows. This was the last regalia held in the men's house until March 1946, when Walt Disney filmed here. Convert had inserted himself in much of the planning for the Disney-inspired regalia in the men's house. He was involved in the "dress rehearsal" and even had a hand in turning away native onlookers: the "crowd brought in by our dancing" were told to "go home and let us have our own fun" (Fox July 1929–May 1952).

After the mission was rebuilt on the Kashunak mound, the demography of the village transformed. Convert writes the Church "attracted more people to come build their house in the village instead of staying year round in their small camps scattered in the vicinity" (Convert March 1948). Seasonal subsistence patterns changed as well. For instance, the priest reports that some people returned to the winter village after spring seal camp, instead of going directly to their fish camp for the summer harvest. Also, more families would come in from fish camp for Mass. To do this, some families may have been setting their fish camps closer to the village, a contemporary trend of increasing centralization of subsistence activities.

People were remaining longer in the village, but there was a significant difference in transience among men, women, and children. Even though households remained seasonally mobile, women were relatively more sedentary than men. For example, traditionally, in the seasonal cycle, though the entire family would move to a harvest location such as fish camp, men were consistently on the go: hunting, fishing, trapping, and trading, pursuits that took them away from both the base and winter camps (as they are even today). However, given the gender-based division of labor, women and children were more tethered to the camp (see also Brumbach and Jarvenpa 1997a, 1997b). The demand of the priests for children to attend school during the day differentially limited women's and children's options to leave the village.

The differential mobility was exacerbated by several other factors, including wage labor and fur trapping. As Father Convert noted in November 1945, the "men begin to leave for [Old] Chevak [for the store] and [fall] camp," and the women and children were left in the village (Fox 1939). Commercial fur trapping could take an extraordinary amount of a man's time; according to one Elder man I spoke with, men could be gone for months. Coastal men also began to work for wages in the canneries during this period. They were hired on at the Bristol Bay cannery to the south, where Convert served as the summer chaplain. Convert notes that about twenty-eight local men worked in the canneries during the summer of 1946, each making around three hundred fifty dollars (Hooper Bay Collection 1929–1955). These wage opportunities were fairly gender-exclusive, and Convert actively undermined women's labor in the commercial subsistence camps. His correspondence with cannery administrators openly opposes women working in the fish factories (Hooper Bay Collection 1929–1955). This is especially poignant since women have long been the sole proprietors of subsistence fish processing.

Transfiguration Phase (1947–1950)

The Transfiguration Phase is marked by the short occupation of Old Chevak by the Kashunak community (and families living on the surrounding tundra). Though they were there only briefly, the site is correlated with intensified colonial engagement. As one Elder woman told me, "When people got to Old Chevak things were changing."

Father Jules Convert, like John Fox before him, was unyielding in his determination to resettle the population of Kashunak to Old Chevak. Convert continued to tell the community the only way to get a church as well as a state-funded school would be to move to Old Chevak. A delegation of state education officials toured the region in 1946 and told villagers they would need to move to Old Chevak, as it was drier and logistically a less complicated location. They also were told that they needed to have enough permanently settled children to warrant the funding of a government school (JOPA Con Box 2). In December 1946, there was a "general meeting for the men" held after the regularly held men's prayer meeting. The council of men agreed to move the village to Old Chevak and to invite other households located on the tundra to join them in their aggregation to the new village location (Fox 1939; JOPA Con Box 2).

Nonetheless, there was a disinclined contingent at Kashunak, specifically the Elder constituency. Convert writes that older people had difficulty with leaving Kashunak because, they told him, "we have always been here" (JOPA Con Box 2). An Elder woman who was born at Kashunak told me that people moved to Old Chevak "little by little" and that there was contention between young and old villagers. As she remembered, "Younger people wanted to move" but the "older people wanted to stay in Kashunak." Foregoing the conflict, "two or three young families who had a good boat" instigated the move to Old Chevak (Barker 1979, 31). By the end of the summer of 1947 there remained only six or seven families at Kashunak; everyone else had permanently resettled at Old Chevak (see figure 24). It was at this historical juncture that people I spoke with knew their lives and their village had irreversibly changed with the move to Old Chevak.

Now located at Old Chevak, the community for the first time was ensconced in the triad of institutional colonial weaponry: the market, the religious mission, and colonial education. However, even with this powerful colonial tactical advantage, people were not just mindlessly acquiescing to changes but were engaged at different levels. The earlier trends of change continued at Old Chevak: struggle over the men's house and public voice, conflict of mobility and subsistence, and trends of economic differential development.

The name "Chevak" in Cup'ik is *Chum'wuk*, or "shortcut made by man." Today, a wide canal connects the Keoklivik and Kashunak Rivers. However, at the turn of the century, the rivers were separated by a thin strip of marshy tundra. Commercial opportunity motivated local men to join the two rivers "just about the time when the trading post was starting" (Friday 1984b). The men used shovels and rope to birth a passage between the major waterways

FIGURE 24. Mission at Old Chevak. Note the house mounds in the background and a possible aboveground storage feature in the left-front corner. The sod church was on the other side of the mission building. (Courtesy of Jesuit Oregon Province Archives, Special Collections, Foley Center Library, Gonzaga University.)

(Friday 1984b; Nayamin 1981b). A cut like this permits the tidal action, ice scouring, and boat travel to widen and deepen a connecting passage. Local men still use this clever method to join major water routes that have grown close.

Two deep pit houses (HP 36 and 49) and an off-site date may demonstrate that Old Chevak was occupied before the indigenous-colonial period (see figure 25; appendix D). People know of Old Chevak as a favored location for certain subsistence activities, occupied before trader or missionary settlement (Ziff, Pratt, and Drozda 1982). It was an ideal site for a camp for fall mink and wolf hunting, and the headwaters of the Keoklivik River were a prime location for beluga whale hunting. Old Chevak was (and still is) used for summer fishing and berry-picking camps by several families (Nayamin 1981a). Across the river from the site is a large fish camp that has been occupied for several generations (Knudson et al. 2004).

Nevertheless, the Church and Father Convert had different designs on the purpose of Old Chevak, and they worked strenuously to settle the population. But as mentioned, there was resistance, and even as late as 1949 there were approximately 120 people still living at Kashunak village. The constant refrain from the priest was that without resettlement there would be no govern-

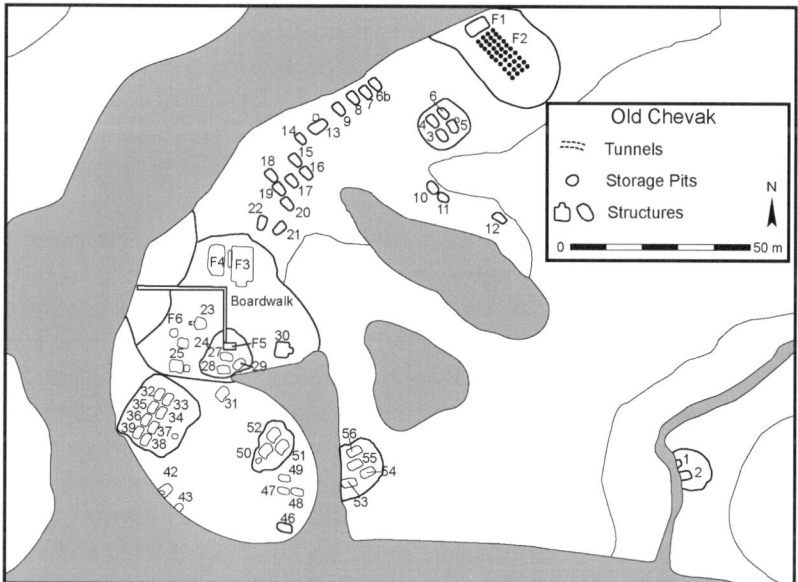

FIGURE 25. Map of Old Chevak.

ment school built for the community. In his correspondence with the director of education of the Alaska Native Schools, Convert pleaded his case and wrote the only way to keep the population settled at Old Chevak was for a school to be built (JOPA Con Box 2). Convert feared the inability to get a school may have led people to "drift again to the tundra" (Convert March 1948). However, there was reticence from the school district to build at Old Chevak, and in protest, Convert accompanied "the village chiefs" to Hooper Bay to argue their case with an Alaska Native Schools representative (Convert March 1949). The Old Chevak contingent was told that they would not get a new school until 1953. Convert routinely visited tundra camps to pressure residents to move to Old Chevak and build up the population. An Elder woman I spoke with, whose family had for many years avoided living at the larger winter villages like Kashunak, remembered Convert's pitch to the family. He told her and her brother and niece that they "had to go to school." Her father thought about it, and "he decided to go" and moved the family to Old Chevak in 1949.

Along with a relative disengagement with the market, women were differentially tethered to the village because of the scheduling demands of colonial education. For example, in March 1949, Father Henry Hargreaves (who replaced Convert) noted in the mission diary that the "families without school children moved to Kashunak or the coast [for seal camp]; the others stay here, with the men going back and forth to the coast" (Fox July 1929–May 1952; Fox 1939). The entire relocation of a family for subsistence harvests was increasingly abridged, and men traveled "back and forth" more than women and children. Today, the last vestige of family relocation for harvesting are fish and berry camps, and even these have changed, with people going out for less time and not as far from Chevak (and some do not go out to camp at all).

Economic investment was also a settlement tactic by the Church, as individual priests controlled the flow of government funding. For example, money from the Eskimo housing program (Alaska Housing Authority) was first offered to Hooper Bay men in 1949. (Father Paul O'Connor, the priest at Hooper Bay, was a member of the Alaska Housing Authority.) Upon the assessment of worth by O'Connor, men could be granted a "character loan" of up to five hundred dollars, with a five-year repayment schedule. This money was to be used for construction materials exclusively for aboveground houses (Hooper Bay Collection 1929–1955). Housing authority employees came to Hooper Bay to demonstrate "how to construct a warm and tight dwelling." Forty-two Hooper Bay men received the loans during the initial year, and "each family head built his own house," often in conjunction with their cannery wages (Hooper Bay Collection 1929–1955).

A year later in Old Chevak, men from the housing commission brought forms for the "men to sign who wished to build new houses next summer [$500], or to buy wooden floors or new roofs [$300]." Father Hargreaves helped the Old Chevak men fill out the paperwork to get funding to build their aboveground houses. However, before the financing arrived, the agency pulled the money. To get funding, the agency demanded that the Old Chevak community find a "drier location," preferably "on a hill" (Hooper Bay Collection 1929–1955).

On the surface, the historical features of Old Chevak look dimly like a traditional coastal archaeological village (see appendix D). By 1947, there were 167 people living at Old Chevak, and thirty houses had been built. Some constructed their houses differently when they moved to Old Chevak, particularly in the eastern flat, marshy area, between the church complex and the store. Though apparently some residents built pit houses, others built directly on the ground, and still others raised their homes on stilts above the wet, marshy tundra (the contemporary style of government housing). During my discussion with Father Hargreaves, he recalled some "fifteen or twenty aboveground log framed houses and sod igloos." According to the priest, there was "always danger of floods" at Old Chevak, and people in pit houses "had to get out" when the waters rose. Because the floodwaters could rise up to a foot in depth, some people "usually built with poles" like the Sheppard trade store, which then rested on thirty-nine poles (the remaining stumps are deteriorating but still visible) before being moved to contemporary Chevak (see F2, appendix D). Most of the Sheppard trade store was relocated to the current village of Chevak in 1950 except for a tin-roofed shed today used by USFWS crews.

The transition of architectural design begun at Kashunak continued at Old Chevak. Elements of both the traditional sod houses and the aboveground houses were implemented. The Elder man that accompanied me to Old Chevak said that "when people built the houses they didn't dig the foundation," but "they built right on the ground." The only surface remains of these houses at the site are slight berms of sod that outline former houses. He explained to me how he built a hybrid-style house for his new bride that was partially set in the ground, but not as deep as a traditional house would have been. He did not use framing wood from dismantled houses at Kashunak (which others did), but instead gathered new driftwood for his house. He described the crafting of his house as "the best" in Old Chevak because he "got the logs and split them and hewed them until they were pretty smooth for the inside part," and then he "put the sod over" the structure, and "when you were inside, you couldn't see sod anywhere because of all the wood." Whenever gussocks [whites] went into his house, he explained, "they just looked all over like they couldn't believe, like, where's the sod?"

Men also placed the roof support beams in a different manner at Old Chevak than they did in the Kashunak pit houses. The Elder stated that the frames "were much closer together for when you put the sod over." The men would use "smaller blocks of sod and they lined them up and one over the other or maybe in between instead of using one or two big pieces" as before at Kashunak. Father Hargreaves described one of the houses that he had been in: "There may be a window, it may be of glass or seal intestine . . . and you see logs split in half along the sides and overhead there's some split logs and sod on the sides and on the roof. . . . I would say the sod igloos were rather confined and tended to be dark . . . people said they were warm. There was only one entrance and usually it was a low entrance." But no longer did the priest have to crawl through an entrance tunnel as Father Menager did at Kashunak.

There are no surface signs of sub-floor storage at Old Chevak. One Elder woman remembered small pits that were used to store containers of water and berries and that people continued to render, store, and preserve oil and other foods in the seal pokes (there are no signs of seal-poke storage pits). This same Elder's father would make "big wooden containers" for the berries to be stored in. According to Hargreaves, the houses had platforms along three sides that were used for sleeping and storing items, and the floor was for sitting and eating. He could not recall large areas for storage inside the houses.

One of the most incredible social changes to occur at Old Chevak was the shift to fully integrated households. Rita Shepard (1997; 2002) suggests that when the men's house as a living quarter ends (like at Old Chevak), then there is noteworthy ideological transformation that leads Alaskan natives to adopt the mission church as a new ceremonial center. Though this profound cultural conversion had been in motion for several decades, the end of the separation of women and men in their living spaces was solidified at Old Chevak. One middle-aged woman I spoke with remembered quite distinctly the day her father came home and told her mother that the priest said they must live together in the village. They were living on the tundra and they had decided to move to Old Chevak. She did not recall exactly what her parents discussed, but she felt tension between her parents, and she had the sense that this was a significant moment of change for her family and community.

In addition, the strategy of usurping the power and position of the men's house institution which had begun at Kashunak continued at Old Chevak. Next to the framed chapel (see F3, appendix D), which was used as a priest's residence, the church built a semisubterranean school with building materials appropriated from the dismantled Kashunak men's house (F4, appendix C). The sod church erected next to the mission chapel was essentially a replica of the men's house at Kashunak (Barker 1979). Ida Hunter taught in the building, and church classes, mass services, and other public activities were held there as well (see figure 26).

The men's relationship with the church was notably different after people moved to Old Chevak. During the Advent Phase, the mission diary was replete with the comings and goings of the Kashunak women, but nearly silent on the activities of the men. However, beginning in the Retrenchment Phase and crystallized during the Transfiguration Phase at Old Chevak is the men's intimate involvement with the church, particularly through the venue of public decision-making and governance of the village. The emphasis on male governance was reinforced by the patriarchal colonial system and in negotiations with the government, law, and education systems. Certain men represent the village, usually alongside either the priest and/or trader. For example, when the Alaska school system rejected Old Chevak's request for a school, "Charlie Peterson [Old Chevak trader] and 2 chiefs (Tom and Joe)" went to Hooper Bay and presented "the village's point of view" (Fox July 1929–May 1952; Fox 1939). (Note here that the administrators flew to Hooper Bay because there was no airstrip at Old Chevak—it is much too marshy of an area

FIGURE 26. Old Chevak mission building (USFWS steam house on the right), July 1998. The sod chapel/men's house is next to the mission building (feature F4 in figure 25). (Photo by author.)

to build a landing area.) When the superintendent of the Alaska Native Schools was planning a visit to Old Chevak, the villagers were instructed to "have a council of 7 men who would meet once a month, draw up laws and propose them to village for acceptance, and once laws are voted on, all should cooperate with council in enforcing them" (Fox 1939). The Old Chevak men then met and chose a council of seven men to represent and govern the village. This is mirrored today in that local Traditional Councils are often composed largely (but not always exclusively) of Elder men.

The men's house was technically gone, but clearly not the institution of authority. At Old Chevak the church's semisubterranean building effectively replaced the men's house, and according to the records, men and boys were more involved in the Church during the Transfiguration Phase. From around 1949, the mission diary shows that boys were involved in services as altar boys and in other Church activities. Men also became more active and, at one point, wanted their own mass separate from Old Chevak women. Father Hargreaves acquiesced to this request and offered women's and men's masses as well as "night prayers and confessions of the men" in the sod church (Fox 1939). Men regularly used the space for meetings to discuss community policy as well as to practice and perform dances. During this period, the men coordinated their dances with Christmas and Easter services. Near the end of the occupation of Old Chevak, men were petitioning for a new church building (Fox 1939), possibly to fully appropriate the sod building.

The loss of the men's house as a public and private institution was an impactful (and contested) development. An Elder woman discussed with me how it was a "really big change for the men" and that they "miss the qaygiq." I have yet to meet an older Yup'ik man who does not mourn its demise. Elder men miss the daily firebath and generally equate the decline of cultural identity and practices to the dissolution of the men's house. It is a common sentiment that this also has been a significant loss to youth and their proper training to be men. With the loss of the men's house, they do not have a common venue and control to teach young men utilitarian and esoteric lessons. As one Elder man told me, "When they used to live at the qaygiq they had strict teaching and rules and values and you know they were taught all kinds of things at the qaygiq."

Firebathing, one of the treasured practices in the men's house, was continued at Old Chevak but on a much smaller scale. Instead of members of the qaygiq bathing together, at Old Chevak they used a little firebath or *maqii* (see F6, appendix D). The structure was small and "almost round," according to an Elder, and the men would enter from a side door and "cover up" the entrance. On the "side close to the ground, they had two little holes where they would breathe through." Because it was quite small, only a few men could bathe at the same time, and the men "took turns."

As discussed, the men's house was also the public theater for shamanic performances, but no longer were the shamans performing their rites in the sod building at Old Chevak (that we know of). These men (and possibly women) instead practiced their arts covertly. For example, Father Hargreaves knew men at Old Chevak but "never knew that they were shamans at the time," but he told me that he had found out in later years they were practicing shamans. He suggested that by the time he had gotten to Old Chevak, "Fox had talked so strongly against the shamans people wouldn't want to admit they were shamans." His Jesuit predecessors had vehemently castigated against the "superstitions" of shamans, and he realized it was to the "benefit of the shamans to be quiet, to keep it hidden if they were still practicing. They probably were [still practicing in the village] but it wasn't as open as it had been in earlier days."

The men lost their exclusive rights to a men's house at Old Chevak, but soon after the villagers moved to contemporary Chevak, they built a men's house. However, they did not sleep in it, but as I was told by an Elder man, used it for "firebaths and to work on whatever their projects, like a workshop." Interestingly, the women I talked with clearly knew that they were not welcome in the building at Chevak (I've also heard this from women in Tununak in reference to their villages' men's houses). Two middle-aged women told me of sneaking into the men's house in Chevak to see what the men did in there. It was empty at the time, but they were very nervous about being caught inside. The men's communal building was used for several decades in Chevak but burnt down sometime in the late 1970s or early 1980s.

Women whom I have spoken with tend not to lament the disbanding of the men's house as do the men. This may have to do with the fact that the men's house was a sanctuary away from household labor, including daily chores and child care. Women talk about the time it took to feed the men in the men's house and that integrated households made their lives much more "easy." The women also thought that, because of integrated households, men's labor was more accessible to them, particularly for child care. For instance, one Elder woman shared that "when they didn't live at the qaygiq," men became more involved in the "family matters, and some of the tasks were shared between men and women."

Along with these social changes, economic development also intensified when people moved to Old Chevak and near the Sheppard trade store. By the time Father Hargreaves arrived at Old Chevak, "most houses had windchargers," whose windmill-like arms were built up on a wood platform and attached to a 6- or 12-volt battery and provided enough energy for a house lightbulb. The towers were built "right next to the igloo." He explained that, in the winter, people would have to climb up the tower and clean off the ice from the wood propellers. Size did matter, as the "industrious shopper" might have a large, 12-volt battery, which required larger propellers and would produce more energy. According to Hargreaves, the priests' residence had an impressive 32-volt battery, which would "hold the electricity for longer and power a lot more lights."

Also at Old Chevak, furs were increasingly exchanged for money, not just barter, or for non-currency coins used by the Sheppard trade store. Father Hargreaves remembered that at Old Chevak men would get seventy-five cents at the store for their muskrat and mink pelts. Sheppard would also purchase bundles of "20 or 25 fish." However, as Hargreaves recalled, it was the men who would "bring their bundles of dried fish to the store, and the store keeper would buy them." Hargreaves reflected that "they would bring them to the store and the storekeeper would put them [bundles of fish] away; and then, in the middle of the winter, when they [villagers] would need fish they buy the fish from the store!"

Hargreaves recalled the reluctance of the store manager, Charlie Peterson, to pay cash for indigenous goods. For instance, the store used stamped "aluminum money," a common colonial practice of economic conscription (Fox 1939). According to Hargreaves, the coins, similar to gambling chips, were worth one dollar but could only be redeemed at the Sheppard trade store. One Chevak man I spoke with recalled that Peterson would cut the chips in half or in quarters to represent different values. Nevertheless, people at Old Chevak struggled for a broader range of goods and financial options beyond the company store. Hargreaves noted that "every house had a Sears Roebuck catalogue . . . so they bought stuff. The store keepers wouldn't like to give money back in change because they knew they [villagers] would spend it on the Sears and Roebuck."

Coastal men accessed currency by working in the canneries or in the National Guard, and this effectively undermined the Church and store practices of in-kind barter or volunteerism. In 1949, Convert suggested that the native men were very unhappy that their labor to move the "igloo-school" (formerly the men's house) to Old Chevak was not compensated with cash. Convert argued that the Old Chevak men were well aware of the "high wages paid in Nunivak [Island] for longshoring or reindeer corralling and butchering. Then they come to us and ask how it is that in their own villages they have to work free all the time" (Convert March 1949). He writes, "All families have big bills in the stores [and] these will absorb most of their coming cannery earnings, so . . . we don't feel it is fair to ask them to donate free work this year again" (Convert March 1949).

The stay at Old Chevak village was quite brief. In 1950, the entire village moved to the present location of Chevak. The village has the standard amenities of Alaskan villages, several stores, a K–12 school, a medical clinic, a post office, several different church sects, and an airstrip. There was no documented evidence there was much if any resistance to moving to Chevak from people in Old Chevak. This may have been because the swampy land of Old Chevak was not appropriate for a village since there is very little elevated ground to be found.

Chapter Summary

When the Jesuits built their first mission on the marshy, unwelcoming margins of the village of Kashunak in 1927, they must have known there was going to be resistance to their advances. And indeed there was, from the local men, but women were more open to interactions with the Church during the Advent Phase. An essential context to this differential response of women and men to the Church, at least in part, is due to the perceived threat or advantage the priests may have represented. Men had come out of the earlier period with commerce squarely in their corner, without a need for the Church. And it rather would have been more a competitor, particularly for powerful shaman and Elder men. During the Advent Phase, the priests needed the villagers to survive—the men's house did not need their assistance or resources yet. In addition, the men's house was still at the time a fairly intact village institution, although there was probably some negotiation going on since Elders remember their fathers sleeping in the family houses. Capitalist marketeering, introductions of new tools, and the loss of warfare were eventually part of the undoing of the tight control over (especially young) men and the physical space of the men's house.

But women as a group did not fare as well with the earlier period of American commerce; their access to commercial goods was largely mediated by their menfolk. The increase in men's oversight or mediums of commerce may be represented in the shift from the prehistoric internal pits found at Qavinaq to the external pits used at Kashunak. Aboveground caches may have also represented the increased privatization of fur hunting and the higher demands for fish, as the number of seal-poke pits could indicate more demand for oil. However, the Church represented a new route to resources for women as well as a communal space, complete with a fire to take off the morning chill. Finally, we can imagine the loss of the tunnel system as a village connective tissue would have curtailed women's interactions, particularly on cold coastal days.

But, the participation of women in the Advent Phase was not enough for the Church. And, the location of the mission exasperated the situation for the priests, and they decided to leave. Not only was the location poor, but the villagers also had not acquiesced to the demands of the Church to stop leaving the village for seasonal harvesting. The Retrenchment Phase is critical because the Church gained strength of position while in Hooper Bay, an allied but competitive village to Kashunak. While there, the Church became a leader in an economic boom, certainly noted by the villagers of Kashunak. And to bring the mission back, the village, now referred to as leading men, agreed with the main requirements of the Church. These included less movement on the landscape, which led to increased tethering to the village for women and children. Also, the mission complex was built directly on the village mound. And along with being in a central location, the mission buildings were made much like traditional buildings. During the Retrenchment Phase, mission schooling was introduced, as were men's groups based in the church. Also during the buildup at Hooper Bay, the Church initiated development at Old Chevak, the village they wanted Kashunak to move to. The Old Chevak mission was constructed with some materials from the original church that stood at Kashunak, and a school was associated with the Old Chevak mission

The Transfiguration Phase is marked by the move of the people of Kashunak to Old Chevak. It seemed young people were more inclined to move first, and though resistant, older people did eventually acquiesce, as did those folks that lived out on the tundra year-round. At Old Chevak, the Church finally had the community and the local trade store in one location. The village of Old Chevak looks nothing like its two predecessors—part of this is undoubtedly cultural change but part of this is the marshy nature of the area. There are very few sod houses, but most were now built on the ground or on stilts, and there is no indication of storage, and no tunnels. A significant shift was that Old Chevak men had access through the priest to funding to purchase building materials for aboveground homes. One of the most significant architectural differences that reflect an enormous cultural shift was that men did not build a men's house at Old Chevak, but rather lived full-time with their families. The Old Chevak men did build a men's house, but at Old Chevak it was instead a church chapel—constructed with materials from the Kashunak men's house. Indeed, this seems a clever symbolic move by the priest as well as a means to retain some semblance of the men's house by the village men. Women and men recall this time as clearly when villagers knew changes were permanent, that their old ways were not to return as they once were.

Conclusion

NORTH AMERICAN SCHOLARSHIP has largely rejected a paradigm of colonialism happening to native people, focusing now on contexts of indigenous-colonial engagement. Since the foundational work of Kent Lightfoot (1995), Patricia Rubertone (2001), and Stephen Silliman (2005, 2010), we are now in a florescence period of scholarship that challenges long-held assumptions of a colonized past and instead seeks to discern indigenous-colonial interactions over time. One of my primary goals in this book is to explore meaningful connections between Yup'ik prehistory and history—and why these links (through food, identity, and use of space) matter when considering their interactions with colonial goods, people, and ideas.

As groups, indigenous women and men, old and young, were affected by and responded to colonial stimuli differently and at times strove to improve their access to material and social resources. Different historical shifts, like the end of warfare, the rise of commerce, or the arrival of missionaries, could prove a boom or a bust for collective groups. Of course, decisions and options were mired in larger interests of family, lineage, and community. Nevertheless, self-interest groups are critical to map during the colonial context (or any context of cultural transformation), specifically because various aspects of colonialism affected interest groups differently. These could be linked to pre-colonial conditions—a significant factor in the responses and outcomes during early indigenous-colonial dealings (Comaroff 1985; Mitchell 2012; Panich and Schneider 2014).

Before colonial material and ideological imports reached the Yukon-Kuskokwim coast, people were not just simply living off the land in perfect harmony. They were dealing with the turbulence of endemic warfare, which was undoubtedly a difficult way of life but also a windfall for some men and women. This prehistoric cultural context is essential to factor in when framing the indigenous-colonial experience that followed. The context of warfare and shift of gender- and age-based opportunities and benefits are vital in assessing the post-warfare integration of commercial market opportunities and later colonial settlers. As discussed in the ethnohistoric documents, warfare was an important avenue for advancement, and rapprochement would have had significant implications for men and women.

Coastal men could raise their social worth through warfare during the Bow and Arrow War Days, but with the early historic cessation of regional fighting, men as a group lost a major route to prestige. There are stories of women cleverly eluding capture and bravely shielding boys and men. There are even tales of women who would accompany raiding parties (Napoleon 1984; Simon 1981; Smith 1984); nevertheless, the preparation and act of warfare was primarily a male avenue to status. The central location of readying for warfare was the men's house, where stories of men who rose to prominence based on their leadership, strategic battle plans, and bravery and abilities in the fight were regaled. Notable warriors were given war names and could wield considerable political influence (Friday 1984a). Therefore, abeyance of conflict culture would have cut off a focal means for men's achievement building. And it is likely that their energies were heavily redirected into the incipient colonial market (see Reedy-Maschner and Maschner 1999).

Some women, too, gained particular distinction for their clever management of subsistence foods and ability to hide or shepherd their men to safety. However, the end of the Bow and Arrow War Days, though certainly embraced, would have diminished the demand for internal surplus so indispensable to stave off siege, delimiting an avenue for women's highly valued authority over food stores. Women also would have benefited from the rigorous preparatory demands of warfare. Raiding was both planned and fortuitous, and people were known to be anxious year-round (Funk 2010). Movement on the landscape was dangerous, and harvesting could be curbed such that people "didn't do as much fishing as they normally did" (Friday 1984a). Therefore, raiding and persistent threat of violence would have proved a benefit to women's complete control over subsistence surplus. In this milieu of unrest and, in particular, the possibility of siege by the enemy, the proper processing, storage, and management of foods would have been at an even higher economic and social premium. Even today, women marvel at their mothers' and grandmothers' extraordinary abilities to produce and closely manage their households' resources, and women's authority was gained from a lifetime of skillful management.

Close on the heels, if not correlated with the end, of regional warfare was indigenous-colonial market intensification. In many ways, the rise of the indigenous-colonial market may have been fueled by the loss of warfare as a route to economic advantage and social elevation. In Alaska, there were several subsistence resource booms that fed the international market, such as fur seals, whale products, and gold. Terrestrial furs were the primary resource extracted for the international market during the mid-nineteenth and early twentieth centuries (see Cassell 2005). On the coast it was indigenous and colonial men who controlled and orchestrated the flow of subsistence furs—from harvest to market. Whether through direct trade, networks of increased supply and demand, or opportunities for employment, men had enhanced economic prospects. Where Russians settled or traveled, economic gain was also open to women. But, as the indigenous-colonial market matured, women were less relied upon for their products and, at least in part because of patriarchal attitudes, were marginalized in the commercial system.

We must also consider the impact of the internal boom of subsistence-based resources, the lifeline for the successful functioning of the early market system. Subsistence-based resources (women's productive purview) were particularly critical in the early stages of colonial development, when traders were deeply dependent on subsistence food products to eat, wear, use, and trade. For example, the Russians traded for furs from their posts but also commonly traveled to outlying villages (Ray 1975). Continued market expansion was deeply dependent upon the fish and sea mammal oil that supplied these traders and their dogs (Wolfe 1984). During this early period, women had significant authority over their products; according to the Russian Zagoskin, "Often a man in his wife's absence decides not to sell anything, particularly provisions of food, as that is her province" (Michael 1967, 108). But the colonial dependence on women's goods waned with the increased availability and variety of foreign foods, technologies, and materials that entered the Alaskan market. Women were edged out of the market, particularly near the end of the nineteenth century, when indigenous and Euro-North American men were the primary business entrepreneurs, and new commercial products replaced women's subsistence production, as in the case of kerosene replacing sea mammal oil for use as lamp fuel (see below).

This diminishment of integration and access into the indigenous-colonial market system is a historical phenomenon played out in other North American regions. In early dealings, native women often had an advantage over men (especially if traders cohabited with or married them), but over time, their access to networks and control over their production were diluted (Sleeper-Smith 2001). This is partially because Euro-North American traders were less beholden to native women's assistance with food and clothing and their trade networks. Also, because native men tended to travel more than women, they had increased access to traders—this attenuated access frustrated (or at the least did not enhance) women's direct distributive control over their products (for excellent examples of this process, see Gonzalez 1981; Murphy and Murphy 1985).

Yet, the phenomenon of differential development cannot be singularly attributed to patriarchal colonial systems since indigenous men would have gained economic and social advantages in their control of commodities networks (see, e.g., Habichte-Mauche 2005; Vehik et al. 2010). The shift in jurisdiction of market-bound resources is a significant indicator of incipient inequalities between women and men as interest groups. For example, Jo-Ann Fiske (1991, 509) found that control of the market subsistence fur trade among the Tsimshian of the Northwest Coast "enhanced" the pecuniary and public position of men, to Tsimshian women's disadvantage. Tsimshian men gained increased control over lineage resources and correlative assumptions of male authority and leadership.

Nearing the twentieth century, the commerce opportunities for Alaskan native men escalated, but for indigenous women, they declined, leading to a changed representation. For instance, instead of the stories of hardy indigenous women who traveled on their own to Russian forts for trade, or even women who gave birth on the tundra while traveling, people now told stories of how women were no longer in charge of trade, such as the Elder man who suggested that "women and children didn't usually travel in the winter months, it was too cold for them to be out and about" (Friday 1983). The priest Father Hargreaves recalled that at Old Chevak it was "probably the men" who traded fish at the store for the women. In addition, several Elders I spoke with remembered that their fathers would go to the store for supplies like sugar and flour. According to one Elder man, it was the duty of the "head of the house" to do the bulk of the trading, and women "hardly ever" went to the store back then.

This shift in women's direct control over their subsistence products in indigenous-colonial commerce was coupled with the fact that over the early commerce trade period the demand for women's surplus products declined as foreign-market foods, technologies, and materials became available. There was both a decline in demand for women's subsistence-based products (particularly fish and oil) and a supplanting of their production. For example, sea mammal oil was a basic dietary element of an Arctic diet and a singularly critical source of fuel (Lucier and VanStone 1992). Yet, while there was likely a boom in oil supply and demand during the early commerce period, by the mid-twentieth century, people were no longer relying on seal oil to light the wicks of their stone lamps but rather used imported kerosene lamps.

A complicating context for the rise in commercial opportunities during the nineteenth century was the abandonment of the village tunnel system. Because the tunnel system's primary function was warfare, the end of regional conflict would have alleviated pressure to build and maintain the system. But the system was multifunctional and especially enhanced village-wide communication among the gender-demarcated village spaces. Not only the Elders' lessons of life but also the quieter conversations from the exclusive province of the men's house would waft through the tunnels. The demise of this subtle village-wide surveillance mechanism likely proved consequential during the period of market intensification and the increase in differential development. Women would have lost a modicum of oversight of economic activities in the men's house, a critical facet of resource decision-making and equity. Without the tunnel communication system, which rendered the men's house more transparent, women were comparatively less privy to business dealings and general information. Without this means of scrutiny, a woman's access to knowledge would be channeled by what she was or was not told rather than by what she herself or a relative overheard. Individually and as a group, men would have been less observed, and relatively less accountable. This, too, would have furthered the mercantilist ideology of privatization that may first have played out in terms of gendered groups before individual households.

Entangled in their loss of surveillance over men's economic activities, women were also differentially affected by male-centered economics, a hallmark of developing colonial commerce. As discussed, although Russians were much more integrated into women's networks of exchange, Euro-North Americans tended not to be. As mercantilism developed over the nineteenth century, neither trade practices nor their benefits were gender-neutral. For instance, recall Nelson's remarks that while men generally were using foreign tools and materials (especially metals), women were not. This may not have been just because of the marginalization of women by patriarchal whites; this also could have been due to native men's preferential economic access and market-based striving—a new venue opened up with the demise of warfare and the influx of colonial goods.

Also accompanying the loss of the tunnel system was a major shift in the ways people stored bulk foods represented in the features at the three sites. At Qavinaq there is a preference for large-scale house-floor storage; this is not the case at Kashunak or Old Chevak. Rather, at Kashunak, deep storage pits are on mounds encircling the village, and no noted sunken storage facilities are anywhere at Old Chevak. Like the tunnel system, oral histories link house-floor storage features to the surplus siege demands of the Bow and Arrow War

Days, when house storage was used for hiding male kin and keeping foods. An Elder stated, "Houses used to have a cellar area where food was stored. They would have to open the wall to go downstairs" (Friday 1984a).

Some did recall pits being used at Kashunak; for instance, a ninety-four-year-old woman I interviewed said her mother used a small floor pit lined with woven grass. Another Elder recalled that small fish were cooked and mashed and then placed "in the holes [on house floors], and they kept a long time." But several Elders who were born at Kashunak (including the Elder man who accompanied me to the site) recalled that their grandmothers and mothers did not use pits for storing foods on the floors of the houses. But recall that Kashunak has abundant evidence of sub-floor pits on the mounds in the marshy areas that are east and west of the main mound. In ANCSA interviews, Elders said that the pits were formerly used as houses but that, in their lifetimes, they had been converted to seal-poke pits (Ziff, Pratt, and Drozda 1982). The Elder I spoke with did not know of the pits being used as houses, only for seal-poke storage.

Though the seal-poke system is found across the circumpolar north coast, little is known about its origins, either for storage or for their use as floats. Starks (2007, 43) suggests that it may be a technology as much as four thousand years old. It was also technology that demanded an impressive set of knowledge and skills. The proper making, filling, and maintenance of these bags was "based on the experience of generations," and the "preparation of a blubber bag of this kind was, in reality, a great art with which only the old people were completely familiar" (Høygaard 1941, 8, as cited in Eidlitz 1969, 114). As Lantis (1984b, 214) recounts, "An effort was made to store large quantities of dried or frozen seal meat and oil, the oil in 'pokes' made of whole sealskins, as well as fish for winter consumption." It was apparently the only means people had to render oil. Margaret Lantis (1984a, 175–76) paraphrases the sentiments toward oil that the Aleuts had (from Veniaminov 1840, 2): "With it, they could eat dried roots, shellfish, or other foods less nutritious or less palatable than meat; and it was regarded as an essential condiment for even favored foods." I have been told that one of the most difficult aspects for older people in travel is that they are hungry all of the time if they do not get sea mammal, fish, and seal oil. Coupled with producer consumption, the oil was absolutely vital in many regions for lamp fuel and as a fundamental trade item of coastal and non-coastal groups (Spencer 1984, 330; VanStone 1967, 128).

The pokes were perfect vessel containers for long-distance trade. The poke oil system likely flourished during the early indigenous-colonial commercial period. Though the system was undoubtedly in use prior to the 1800s and early 1900s, it is easy to imagine there would have been an increase in the demand not only for oil but also for the means to store and transport the oil. Because people were already trading their products inland, it is not unreasonable to suggest that this trade would have increased with the colonial demand for the subsistence commodity. This internal boom and demand for both fish and oil could very well be reflected by the number of seal-poke pits located at Kashunak.

An additional storage feature used at Kashunak and Old Chevak (and apparently not at Qavinaq) was the aboveground storage cache, today ubiquitous in Arctic villages (McGhee 2001; Sheehan 1997). Photographs of early 1900s indigenous villages commonly have the distinctive elevated caches in the background (see Lee and Reinhardt 2003; see figure 24). Despite the prevalence of the caches in the Arctic and Subarctic, few have investigated their use, distribution, or development (but see Darwent, Darwent, et al. 2007; Darwent and Johansen 2010; Lane 1982; Stopp 2002). Susan Fair (1997, 169) speculates that the cache is a storage option that arose during nascent indigenous-colonial interactions and that they are not an "indigenous form" but rather "introduced by early traders, miners, or missionaries" (see also Lane 1982, 406; Lantis 1984b, 215; VanStone 1984, 226). Margaret Lantis (1984b, 215) surmises the aboveground caches replaced belowground storage on Nunivak Island by the turn of the century. According to an Elder consultant I spoke with, house-floor storage was not "used any more when people started building separate storage houses" at Kashunak.

The caches were particularly good for keeping stored products dry and away from dogs and rodents, and they could be locked (VanStone 1984, 226, 228). Three subsistence items in demand during the early indigenous-colonial period and commonly kept in the storage facilities were fish, furs, and sea mammal oil. Since the seal pokes were often removed from their submerged pits for the winter, facilities were used to store them over the winter months (although they could also be left in the pits). And according to an Elder Chevak woman, when the summer fishing season was over, the men hauled the catch from camp and put the dried fish in the aboveground storage units (see also Lantis 1946). To preserve it, the dried fish were bundled like stacks of wood; snow was mixed in with the fish, and the bundles were covered tightly with grass matting (see also Ray 1966). This may have been a clever design to prevent freezer burn and also a great way to package the commoditized subsistence fish for market. For example, when traveling, Nelson ([1889] 1983) traded for bundles of twenty frozen salmon.

The caches were also ideal for storing animal furs. One Elder woman said the features were "used for skins" because the aboveground caches stayed dry and the contents safely away from dogs. During the boom for furs, coastal men hunted and trapped several kinds of furbearers over the years, including mink and white and red fox. Prior to supplying the global fur market, people used these creatures primarily for clothing; animals such as the fox were not a substantial food source. Contrary to every other resource in the Yup'ik harvest, the commoditized fox was the only subsistence resource that women did not process post-harvest. However, in the past, according to Lantis (1946, 179), "Fox skins too would have been handled by the women instead of the men as today." A radical change then was that men managed the entire spectrum of commercial fur: harvest, processing, and distribution. Because of the intensification and privatization of this harvest in the indigenous-colonial market, the men's house may have proved unsuitable as a place to host the burgeoned harvest and as storage for indigenous men's market-bound furs.

The demand for dry storage of surplus fur and fish would have risen during the early commerce period, and the aboveground cache, like the wet-storage seal-poke system, would have been a technological innovation well-suited to the task. The international fur market increased the demand for processed fur pelts, and dried fish was absolutely necessary to feed indigenous and non-native traders and their dog teams (at work, dogs would require about a fish a day). Even if Kashunak men were not always directly trading with Russians or Euro-North American traders, the demands on the entire regional system would have had an impact on supply. Consequently, intra-native trade would likely have intensified to keep step with internal and external demands for both fur and fish. Kashunak men were heavily involved in the fur trade and would trap and hunt for months away from the village. One Elder man I spoke with remembered how many mink and white and red fox his father would bring home and that "after he dried them he'd put them in gunny sacks and take them over to the fur trader." At the trade post men could purchase a firearm with a stack of furs equal to the length of the desired firearm.

A hallmark of the aboveground caches is that the contents are concealed from public inspection. Farther north where the indigenous-colonial market was relatively more intense, padlocked caches were "components of all villages for storage and protection of goods" (Nelson [1889] 1983, 250; Ray 1975, 173). Though the demise of the village tunnel system and access to market goods and information may have been an early boon to the men's house as an institution, privatization of market furs was in part responsible for its decline. The benefits of market privatization, the introduction of technologies that bypassed customary Elder-youth apprentice learning, and the ability of younger men to succeed economically in the indigenous-colonial commerce system whittled away older men's control over younger men and their market activities and rewards. The traditions of authority in the men's house were well under siege before the missionaries arrived.

The separation of women from relatively more direct access to information about indigenous-colonial commerce may have been exacerbated by the dissociation of women from direct jurisdiction over their subsistence stores of fish and oil. The transformation of storage facilities outside of their sphere of domestic control is linked to the usurping of indigenous women's economic authority (Hastorf 1991; Kent 1991). For instance, Cameron Wesson (1999) investigates the connotations of the shift in location of storage facilities over time in southeastern North America. During the emergence of chiefdoms, storage shifted from the household and moved outside of domestic control. The eventual decline of the chiefly political order was coincident with the restoration of domestically controlled storage. In Wesson's (1999) study, the change of storage from inside to outside and back inside houses during the Protohistoric and Historic periods correlates with interactions and conflicts between elites and non-elites. However, I would add that this drama may have also played out among women and men.

Prior to the externalization of bulk storage at Kashunak, women would have had close control over all foods, and their noted domestic/corporate management of these foods could significantly elevate their status. The requirements of warfare would have certainly enhanced the value of surplus foods and the influence of capable Elder women—maybe even more than women are heralded for their production today. But by the early twentieth century, men had monopolized indigenous-colonial commerce. Though women may have started on even ground (or even somewhat-advantaged ground), their access and opportunities faded as the market expanded. Part of the edging out of women may have been exacerbated by the shift from highly controlled subsistence products to externally stored products. As a result of the redirection of their full management of the total harvest, women's relatively diminished authority over subsistence would have been a subtle, but no less influential, cultural and economic shift in process before the missionaries arrived on the delta.

By the time the Jesuit priests settled at Kashunak village, the revaluation and control over subsistence had been a part of coastal life, and the economic position of women had been influenced by differential development. The early Jesuits, however, unlike the traders, bartered with women for their products—surely an economic plus for women in the village. And remember, as with other native North American groups, women and men control their individual earnings. Their resources may go to the "household," but this a decision of the individual (see Hensel 1996). But as is common in other regions, as the availability and access to foreign goods increased, priests were less beholden to women for their goods. And although with the move to Old Chevak women would have had more direct access to the Sheppard trade store, there is some indication that at least some men traded instead of women (which is not the case today).

By comparing the village sites, it is clear that life over this several-hundred-year period changed over time for the people of the southwestern Alaskan coast. The harbinger of dramatic change was not singly the Jesuit preachers but rather transformations that took place beforehand not only between the colonized and indigenous but also among indigenous people themselves. The end of regional warfare and the rise of commercial trading opportunities were a boon for men and their trade of subsistence furs, fish, and oil. Women, nevertheless, may not have benefitted as much as men, given the apparent differential access to metals present in villages before whites settled. But women did benefit upon the arrival of the missionaries. Since these men needed assistance with food and other help, the women had access to their goods. But the men's early reticence toward the priests is a testament to their improved position with the pre-mission system of regional commerce and their relative monopoly on the acquisition of goods (see also Sharp 1952). Nonetheless, this same commercial system undercut the age-based system of authority in the men's house prior to the mission settlement. And it is not unreasonable to suppose that the arrival of the Jesuits (viewed as shamans) stimulated an emphasis of tradition and control in the men's house system.

The earliest phase of mission settlement, the Advent Phase, is a relatively acute time of Church conciliation, not only with the community but also with men and women of the village. As collective groups, Kashunak women and men had different responses to what the priests offered in one hand and demanded in the other. These dissimilar reactions to the Church may very well link to the experiences and trends set in motion prior to the Church's occupation of the village. For the men, the previous indigenous-colonial commerce period ushered in an era of enhanced economic preferential access and abridged communal oversight. It is in this stance of comparative monopolization that men interpreted the Church as competitive interlopers rather than economic or social allies.

The economic advantages of the early indigenous-colonial commerce era were also fraught with risk due to emergent intensified privatization, especially for the institutional authority of the men's house. Enhanced access to wage opportunities and imported technologies threatened to undermine the men's house as a gatekeeping institution, particularly for young men. The faint whispers of the eventual decline of the men's house were heard during the Advent Phase. It was in this milieu that the priests entered the village as an economic and ritual competitor to the collective men.

Contrary to the men's response during the Advent Phase, Kashunak women engaged with the Church and accepted the economic and ritual opportunities that the priests proffered. Kashunak women exchanged their goods directly with the priests, worked for the Church, and blatantly occupied the church. This disparate response is contextualized by their diminished roles in the indigenous-colonial subsistence market and their truncated access to information. Attesting to the patriarchal attitudes of the time, even though village women were substantially involved with the Church, the Kashunak mission was eventually deemed a failure, and the Church relocated to and invested in neighboring Hooper Bay village. It was only when the Church secured a considerable measure of male engagement and spatial centrality in the ensuing Retrenchment Phase that the priests reoccupied Kashunak village. Soon thereafter, the people of Kashunak relocated first to Old Chevak and then eventually to modern Chevak.

Once at Old Chevak, people knew there was no return to the old. There are several key changes represented at Old Chevak. The former men's house at Kashunak was moved to Old Chevak but it now was part of the chapel complex. However, men did not simply forgo the institution of the men's house. They summarily used the building as a men's house and also became the public governing voice of the village and controlled much of the economic resources that were coming into the village.

Connected to the loss of the physical structure of the men's house was that women and men lived together full-time in the family houses for the first time. And these houses were constructed differently than those at Kashunak; this may be partially because the area was so marshy (digging in for a sod house would have proved difficult if not impossible in many areas) and because funding was available to inspire men to build aboveground houses. Old Chevak was the first place that the Church, trader, and education (not state funded yet but through the Church) were together in one space, and the village drew in people from not only Kashunak but also the surrounding tundra. However, Old Chevak, though more convenient for commerce than

Kashunak, was too wet for the Alaskan government to agree to build a school; therefore, the entire village moved to Chevak. The additional analysis of contemporary Chevak and connections to the past are yet another study to unfold, beyond the scope of this research.

In this work I show the tendrils of meaningful connection among the periods of time from the late prehistoric through the historic and show that connecting sequences (and not lumping "history") is essential for getting closer to tracking and interpreting trajectories of change during the indigenous-colonial era. Also, I have demonstrated that interactions among indigenous people through time are absolutely essential to explore, as are the engagements of indigenous people with colonials. And attached to this last paradigm is the critical position of the dynamics of gender and age, especially in any discussion of small-scale indigenous groups and their interactions with colonialism and subsistence. And lastly, this work integrates a rare data set in ethnohistoric studies of indigenous-colonial encounters over time by meaningfully incorporating Alaskan native experiences in order to better frame processes of cultural change and persistence over time.

Appendix A

Site Comparisons

Timeframe and significant events

Site	Timeframe	Significant events
Old Chevak	Historic (AD 1947–1950)	Trade station and mission centralized; loss of men's house
Kashunak	Prehistoric and Historic (circa AD 1640–1947)	End of warfare; rise of market commerce; Anglo settlement
Qavinaq	Late Prehistoric (circa AD 1740–1800)	Bow and Arrow War Days

Site-feature comparisons discussed in text

Feature	Qavinaq	Kashunak	Old Chevak
Number of men's houses	2	2	0
Number of house pits	30	36	57
Storage features on house floor	23	2	1
Storage features, external	12	80	1
Storage features, men's house floor	2	0	0
Evidence for below-ground tunneling	yes	yes	no
Number of pit house features	30	37	28 (> 0.3 m or more below ground surface)
Number of aboveground house features	0	0	30
Attached (no tunnel) entrance	0	1	6

continued

Site-feature comparisons discussed in text (*continued*)

Feature	Qavinaq	Kashunak	Old Chevak
Entry foyer at end of tunnel	0	5	0
Historical non-native structures	0	2 (framed chapel; sod church)	4 (framed chapel; sod church; Sheppard trade store and shed)
Site location	Linear mound site along slough	Roundish mound site along slough	Part of site on mound and in swampy area along major river
Firebath feature	0	0	1
Average pit house size	28 m^2	17 m^2	17 m^2
Average men's house size	177 m^2	96 m^2	
Mean house size	28 m^2	16 m^2	16 m^2
Modal house size	31 m^2	16 m^2	20 m^2

Appendix B

Qavinaq Site

Radiocarbon dates

Sample	Material	Area	Measured age	13C/12C ratio	Calibrated result
Beta 166892 (2001)	wood charcoal	CB1 slough 80 cm below surface	430 ± 60BP	−25.0	AD 1410–1530; AD 1560–1630
Beta 166893 (2001)	wood	CB2 slough 60 cm below surface	420 ± 50BP	−25.0	AD 1420–1530; AD 1560–1630
Beta 166894 (2001)	wood charcoal	HP5 SW corner fox disturbance	320 ± 60BP	−25.0	AD 1140–1670
Beta 166895 (2001)	wood	F20 (men's house) SW corner post	280 ± 60BP	−25.0	AD 1460–1680; AD 1740–1800

Data by Beta Analytic.

Site-feature details

Feature		Dimensions (m)[b]	Description
H1		3 × 3 × 0.4[a]	
H2		6 × 5.5 × 0.6[a]	
H3		4.9 × 4.8 × 0.9	Faint entrance tunnel depression; heavy vegetation
	P1	0.3 × 0.2	Diameter × depth; in SE corner; possible fox disturbance
H4		4.3 × 5 × 0.9	Faint entrance tunnel depression; thick tussock growth; some standing water in center floor

continued

Site-feature details (*continued*)

Feature		Dimensions (m)[b]	Description
H5		5.8 × 5.5 × 0.9	Wood post in NW corner; ground slate ulu piece and pottery sherd found in NE corner from fox digging backfill—dated material (charcoal from same digging); protruding whale bone in NW corner
	Tunnel depression	1.2 × 0.8	Length × width; seems to connect to H6
	P4	1.1 × 0.8 × 0.3	NE corner of interior surface
	P5	0.9 × 0.3	SW corner of interior surface
	P6	0.8 × 1	Center of interior surface
H7		5.8 × 4.8 × 0.9	
	Tunnel depression	1	E of entrance
	Tunnel depression	1	W of entrance
	P7	1.2 × 1 × 0.5	In E corner
H8		4.7 × 6 × 0.9	
	Tunnel depression	2.3 × 0.5	
	P8	1 × 0.6 × 0.5	NE corner of floor
	P9	0.7 × 0.4 × 0.3	NW corner of floor
H9		5.5 × 6.2 × 0.7	
	P10	0.5 × 0.3	W center
H10		6.3 × 6 × 0.6	
	Tunnel entrance	1.8 × 1.6	
	P11	1.5 × 0.6 × 0.3	Floor depression
	P12	0.8 × 0.5 × 0.4	Possible fox disturbance
H11		4 × 4 × 0.4	
	P13	2.7 × 1.4 × 0.3	NE corner of floor
	P14	2.7 × 1.4 × 0.3	SW corner of floor
External pits	P15	0.7 × 0.5 × 0.3	
	P16	0.9 × 0.7 × 0.3	

Site-feature details (*continued*)

Feature		Dimensions (m)[b]	Description
F1		11.5 × 15.5 × 0.6	Men's house; measures given are the wall dimensions; water-filled/saturated depression in center of floor that is not a pit (9.5 × 2.3 × 0.2 m)
	Tunnel entrance	7.5 × 2.3	Distinct
H12		6 × 6 × 0.6	Somewhat internally jumbled feature
	P17	0.8 × 0.5 × 0.4	E center
H13		7.7 × 5.8 × 0.6	
	P18	1 × 0.6 × 0.5	
	Tunnel	8.5 × 0.7 × 0.2	From south wall
H14		5.4 × 5.3 × 0.4	Indistinct berm; floor disturbed by fox digging
H15		5 × 5 × 0.6	
H16		6 × 5.5 × 0.6	
H17		7 × 4.5 × 0.5	
H18		7.4 × 6.8 × 0.5	Connected to F2 by tunnel-like depression
	Tunnel-like depression	1 × 0.7	
	P19	0.9 × 0.5	SE corner; possible fox disturbance
	P20	1.5 × 1.2 × 0.7	NE corner
	P21	1.1 × 0.9 × 0.3	W center
F2		11 × 16 × 0.6	Men's house; with some 2 m wide sod walls; dating material (wood sample from exposed SW corner construction post—from outer part of wood); corner post exposed by fox disturbance
	Entrance tunnel	8.4 × 1.4	
	Tunnel depression	9 × 2.7 × 0.9	Center of floor
	P24	0.8 × 0.3	E center
	P25	0.5 × 0.2	
	Thick wall berm	2.5 × 2	Height × thickness

continued

Site-feature details (*continued*)

Feature		Dimensions (m)[b]	Description
H19		4.6 × 4.6 × 0.5	Indistinct walls
	P23	0.2 × 0.2 × 0.4	N center
H20		4.5 × 5 × 0.4	
H21		6 × 6 × 0.6	Fox disturbance in feature
H22		4.5 × 5 × 0.3	
	P26	0.5 × 0.3	
	P27	0.6 × 0.3	
F3		3.5 × 3.5 × 0.7	Sod strip area
H23		5.2 × 4.9 × 0.8	Tunnel depression visible; thick vegetation growth
	P31	1 × 0.8	NE corner
H24		5.5 × 5.1 × 0.6	Thick vegetation overgrowth
	Tunnel depression	1.4	
	P32	1.6 × 0.3	Floor depression
H25		6 × 5.5 × 0.6	Thick vegetative overgrowth
	Tunnel depression	2.4	
	P33	1.2 × 0.4	NE corner
	P34	0.4 × 0.3	Center
H26		5 × 4 × 0.6	Wood post in NW corner; tunnel depression
H27		5.5 × 3.5 × 0.4	Feature actively being eroded; dating samples taken from slough (D1)[c]
External Pits			
	P35	1.1 × 0.2	
	P36	0.9 × 0.7 × 0.2	
	P37	1.2 × 0.1	
	P38	1 × 0.2	
	P39	1.2 × 0.2	

[a] Ziff, Allan. 1981. Fieldnotes, Old Chevak; Ziff, Allan. 1981. Fieldnotes, Qavinaq.
[b] Depth of feature floors is estimate from house floor to base of surrounding berm; depth of pits are from base of pit to floor.
[c] Corresponds with D1 on map where sample was taken for dating the site.

Appendix C

Kashunak Site

Radiocarbon dates

Sample	Material	Area	Measured age	13C/12C ratio	Calibrated result
Beta 134898 (2001)	wood charcoal	slough bank 1.1 m below surface (CB1)	120 ± 40 BP	−23.0	AD 1655–1950
Beta 166891 (2001)	wood	slough bank 1.3 m below surface (CB2)	180 ± 60 BP	−25.0	AD 1640–1950

Data by Beta Analytic.

Site-feature details

Feature		Dimensions (m)[a]	Description
F1		7 × 11.5 × 3	High walls; men's house
F2		10.5 × 10.5 × 4	High walls; men's house; blue enamelware pot found at center and at entrance; 55-gallon drum on S wall
F3			Maintained sod house; driftwood log, pole, and plank construction; sod floor with plywood boards on floor; 55-gallon converted drum as barrel heater with attached stovepipe; single plastic window; permafrost clearly visible in summer
	Main room	2.4 × 3.3 × 2.1	
	Entryway	2.1 × 1.2 × 1.6	
H1		3.5 × 3.5 × 0.4	Possibly associated with F1
H2		3.5 × 3.4 × 0.4	Visible structural corner post in NW corner

continued

Site-feature details (*continued*)

Feature		Dimensions (m)[a]	Description
H3		4.4 × 6.2 × 2.5	Building sod blocks in SE corner; W wall slumping with wood posts exposed (this could possibly explain why BIA said this house was 6 × 6.5 m); possible tunnel depression between H3 and H2
	P1	2 × 2.6	Depression in center floor
F4		10.5 × 8 × 0.4	Identified as historic sod church "igloo-church" complex (included chapel, shed, and sod house); two entrances (E and W walls) outline identifiable, but fairly irregular (unlike typical sod house)
H5		5 × 5 × 1	Deep and distinct house pit with water saturation on floor
H6		5 × 5 × 1	Deep and distinct with heavy grass overgrowth
H7		7.5 × 6.5 × 0.7	Large for a house pit; walls and rectangular/square shape distinct; non-native residence?
H8		4 × 4.5 × 0.5	Distinct pit but very overgrown
H9		4 × 4	Slumping walls
H10		3 × 4 × 1	Overgrown; construction wooden posts visible
H11		3.5 × 4.5 × 1.3	Slumping walls; grass overgrown
H12		4.5 × 4.5 × 0.6	Distinct walls; wooden posts visible in corners; kerosene lantern on floor
H13		3 × 3 × 0.4	Very overgrown and fairly indistinct
H14			Two possible jumbled walls; too indistinct to categorize
H15		3.5 × 2.5	Very overgrown
H16			Two distinct attached rooms; wall beginning to collapse; fox activity just W of entrance; floor a confused jumble of grassy lumps
	Larger room	3 × 3.7 × 1	
	Smaller room	2 × 2.3 × 0.6	Exposed construction post visible
H17		2.5 × 3.5 × 0.4	Slumping walls
H18		2.5 × 2.5 × 0.3	Very overgrown; slumping walls
H19		4 × 3.6 × 1	Distinct house pit; overgrown; clear entrance depression on W wall

Site-feature details (continued)

Feature		Dimensions (m)[a]	Description
H20			Exposed posts on S wall
	Tunnel	1.4 × 0.6	Connecting the larger pit (P2) and smaller pit (P3)
	P2	3.5 × 3.2 × 1	Contains possible hearth depression in center (P4) and amorphous depression in SE corner
	P3	2.4 × 2.9 × 1	
	P4	1 × 0.5	In center of larger pit (P2); possible hearth depression?
H21		3.8 × 2.3 × 0.6	Thick walls (1.5 m); fox burrow in NW corner; exposed wooden planks visible on S wall; very lumpy floor
	Entrance tunnel	2.5 × 0.5	Exposed wood posts in entrance tunnel
H22			Two very distinct, connected pit features; walls beginning to collapse
	P5	4 × 5.5 × 2	
	P6	3.5 × 3.5 × 1.4	
H23		5.5 × 6 × 0.5	Collapsing walls; clear entrance
H24		4.6 × 5 × 0.4	
H25			Two distinct, connected features; walls collapsing; entry room less distinct
	P7	3.5 × 6 × 2.5	
	P8	2.2 × 2.4 × 0.5	
H26		4 × 4.5 × 0.4	Metal pieces, glass, and wood scattered on floor
H27		3.7 × 4 × 2.5	Distinct house pit; walls beginning to collapse
H28		5 × 5 × 0.4	Wood and sheet metal on floor of pit; walls distinct but beginning to collapse; very overgrown
H29		4 × 4.5 × 0.5	Distinct house pit; walls beginning to collapse; overgrown
H30		5	Length cannot be accurately measured because it is too collapsed and overgrown
H31			Two connected rooms; very distinct; walls beginning to collapse

continued

Site-feature details (*continued*)

Feature	Dimensions (m)[a]	Description
P9	4 × 4 × 0.8	
P10	2.5 × 2.5 × 0.6	
H32	4.5 × 5 × 0.6	Distinct walls; overgrown
H33	4.5 × 5 × 0.6	Overgrown; walls collapsing
H34	3.5 × 4.5 × 0.5	Possible connecting entrance with H34; could be footpath depression
H35	3 × 3 × 0.3	Fairly indistinct; overgrown; collapsed walls
H36	2.3 × 2.5 × 0.3	Fairly distinct; overgrown
H37	4 × 4 × 0.3	Collapsed walls and overgrown; very indistinct
H38	2.5 × 2.5	
H39	2 × 3	
H40	3 × 3	
H41	3 × 3[b]	
	1.7 × 1.1 × 0.7	Amorphous feature
H42	3 × 3.8[b]	
	1.3 × 1.1 × 0.8	Pit is deep but walls have collapsed
H43	2.5 × 4.8[b]	
	1.8 × 0.9 × 0.6	Walls have collapsed
H44	3 × 3.5[b]	
	2 × 1.5 × 0.9	Big lumps of sod on floor; walls collapsed; indistinct E wall
H45	3.2 × 3.7[b]	
	2.8 × 1.4 × 0.8	Possible tunnel entrance depression; rectangular, more definite feature
H46	3 × 3.4	Amorphous feature with jumbled sod; sample taken for dating (0.38 m below surface); pottery (returned to pit), wood, and unidentified bone (left in pit) associated with organic sample; permafrost at 0.35 m
P11	0.9 × 1 × 0.3	Pit near H46
H47	3.5 × 3.5[b]	
	2.1 × 1.3 × 0.5	N wall entrance depression; collapsed and overgrown

Site-feature details (continued)

Feature	Dimensions (m)[a]	Description
H48	3 × 4.3[b]	
H49	3 × 4[b]	
H50	3.2 × 3.5[b]	
H51	3 × 4.8[b]	
H52	2.5 × 4[b]	
H53	3 × 3[b]	
H54	3.5 × 3.5[b]	
H55	[b]	Too jumbled for measurement; very indistinct
H56	2.5 × 3[b]	
H57	2.5 × 2.5[b]	
H58	3 × 3[b]	Snowmobile in pit in 1981 (not there in 2000)
H59	3 × 3[b]	
H60	3 × 4[b]	
H61	2.5 × 3.5[b]	
H62	2.7 × 3.5[b]	
H63	2.7 × 3.5[b]	
H64	2.5 × 3.5[b]	
H65	2.4 × 3.2[b]	W wall entrance depression
H66	2.8 × 3.2[b]	
H67	3 × 3[b]	
H68	3 × 4.7[b]	
H69	3.3 × 4.5[b]	
H70	2.5 × 3[b]	
H71	3 × 4[b]	
H72	2.7 × 2.8[b]	
H73	2 × 3[b]	
H74	3 × 4.5[b]	

[a] Depth of feature floors is estimated from house floor to base of surrounding berm; depth of pits is from base of pit to floor.
[b] Ziff, Allan. 1981. Fieldnotes, Old Chevak; Ziff, Allan. 1981. Fieldnotes, Qavinaq.

Appendix D

Old Chevak Site

Radiocarbon dates

Sample	Material	Area	Measured age	13C/12C ratio	Calibrated result
Beta 166896 (2001)	wood charcoal	eroding house pit associated with site; slough bank 0.5 m below surface	390 ± 60 BP	−25.0	AD 1420–1650

Data by Beta Analytic.

Site-feature details

Feature	Dimensions (m)[a]	Description
H1[c]	2.5 × 2.5[b]	Located on slough SE of site; eroding; associated cache pit identified in 1981 gone (1.5 × 1.5 m)
H2[c]	3 × 3[b]	Located on slough SE of site; eroding; wood sample taken for radiocarbon dating; eroded faces have pottery sherds visible and no identifiable historic artifacts (based on brief examination)
H3	3.5 × 3.5	House floor level with ground surface; piece of porcelain on floor; swampy
H4	3.5 × 2.5	Attached entrance; wall wood and post exposed on S wall; floor on ground level; located in swampy area
H5	3.5 × 4	Floor on ground level; attached entrance; 0.5 m berm; swampy
H6	4 × 3.5	Floor on ground level; post in corner; swampy
H7	3.1 × 2.8	Four distinct corner posts (0.2 m diameter posts); floor level with ground surface; no distinct entrance

continued

Site-feature details (*continued*)

Feature	Dimensions (m)[a]	Description
H8	4 × 4	Floor level with ground surface
H9	5 × 3.5	Very indistinct
H10	5 × 4	Very indistinct
H11	4.5 × 4 × 0.5	E wall abuts elevated (0.6 m) crowberry tundra; S wall entrance; visible wood post 3.8 m off of SE wall (windcharger post?)
H12	4 × 5.5	Abuts crowberry tundra
H13	4 × 4	Abuts crowberry tundra
H14	4 × 3	0.5 m thick berm; attached entrance (1.6 × 0.9 m); floor level with ground surface; two 55-gallon drums on floor; three visible construction posts; located in very swampy area
H15	2.4 × 1.5	Post in corner; floor level with ground surface; swampy
H16	4 × 5 × 0.5	Somewhat indistinct; post in corner; 0.5 m deeper than ground surface; located in very swampy area
H17	4.1 × 4 × 0.1	Floor 0.1 m below ground surface; possible entrance N wall; three interior posts; located in very swampy area
H18	3.9 × 2.5	Floor level with ground surface; visible post 4 m from E wall; swampy
H19	2.8 × 2.8 × 0.2	Floor 0.2 m below ground surface; indistinct berm; visible corner post
H20	3.5 × 3.3	Floor level with ground surface; indistinct feature; sod pit? post in corner; swampy
H21	4.2 × 3.7	Exposed wood (wall?); floor level with ground surface; 0.5 m berms
H22	4.4 × 3.7	Rusted 5-gallon gas can on floor; post 3 m from W corner (dog post?); three corner posts visible
H23	4.6 × 4.1 × 0.2	Located in very swampy area; 0.2 m below ground surface; faint berm
H24	4.5 × 4	Side entrance possible; swampy; floor level with ground surface
H25	3.4 × 3.6 × 0.2	0.2 m below ground surface; swampy
H26	4.5 × 4 × 0.015	Attached entrance; floor 0.15 m below ground surface; depression 2.5 × 2.5 m
H27	5 × 4.5	In 1981, generator directly on house pit, removed in 1985 and replaced in same place by steam house
H28	4 × 4	Somewhat irregularly shaped pit

Site-feature details (*continued*)

Feature	Dimensions (m)[a]	Description
H29	4.5 × 4.5	Floor level with ground surface
H30	4 × 3.5	Modern boardwalk goes through pit; floor surface 0.8 m below ground surface
H31	4 × 4.5 × 0.15	Somewhat indistinct attached feature (2.5 × 2 m); 0.15 m below ground surface
H32	5 × 4.5 × 0.15	No clear entrance; two corner posts visible; 0.15 m below ground surface; identified by Joseph Tuluk as his first aboveground house
H33	4.5 × 4 × 1	1 m below ground surface; distinct berms; two corner posts visible
H34	4 × 3 × 1.3	1.3 m below ground surface; distinct berms
H35	5 × 4 × 0.9	0.9 m below ground surface; distinct berms
H36	4.5 × 5 × 1.1	1.1 m below ground surface; distinct berms
H37	4.5 × 5 × 0.5	0.5 m below ground surface
H38	4 × 3.5 × 0.5	0.5 m below ground surface
H39	5 × 5 × 0.9	0.9 m below ground surface; pit 3.5 m from H38 (0.8 diameter by 0.5 m deep)
H40	3.5 × 4 × 0.8	0.8 m below ground surface
H41	4 × 5.5 × 0.25	0.25 below ground surface
H42	5.5 × 5	2001 did not identify
H43	4.5 × 4.5[b]	Attached room (eroded in 2001); 0.5 m below ground surface; main room had small pit in center (1.2 diameter and 0.5 m deep); historic materials in erosion bank (porcelain pieces; metal); depression (2 × 1.5 m[b])
H44	4.5 × 4.5[b]	Partially eroded canal; historic material in slough bank erosion cut (porcelain, metal)
H45	5.5 × 4.5	Completely eroded; associated cache pit gone (1 × 0.5 m in 1981)
H46	6 × 4.5[b]	
H47	4.5 × 4.5[b]	
H48	3.5 × 4.5 × 0.7	0.7 m below ground surface; relatively indistinct feature
H49	3.5 × 4 × 1.1	1.1 m below ground surface
H50	3.5 × 2 × 1.2	1.2 m below ground surface; relatively indistinct feature

continued

Site-feature details (continued)

Feature	Dimensions (m)[a]	Description
H51	5 × 5 × 0.5	0.5 m below ground surface; distinct house pit; indistinct attached feature (2 × 2 m)
H52	5 × 4 × 0.5	0.5 m below ground surface; possible tunnel entrance
H53	3.2 × 2.2	Indistinct
H54	4 × 3	Floor level with ground surface
H55	3 × 3 × 0.5	0.5 m below ground surface
H56	3.5 × 3[b]	Indistinct feature
H57	4 × 4.5	Indistinct
F1	7 × 5.5 × 3	Dimensions are of walls; Sheppard's shed; wood timber–framed walls; steel siding and roofing; set on wood supports (appears to be on ground); handmade flat-bottomed wood boat near shore (6 m bow to stern; stern 1.5 m wide); 14 m N wall of shed to Keoklivik River edge in 1981 and 10 m in 2001
F2	17.5 × 9	Remains of Sheppard Trade Company store; rectangular area with some 37 posts (average 0.3 to 0.5 m diameter); rectangle approximately 12 × 13 m with entrance rectangle (5.5 × 4 m); berm outlines posts
F3	10.5 × 7.5	Former chapel used as priest's residence; wood framed with steel roofing; side entryway with attached storage area on N wall; building now used for U.S. Fish and Wildlife Service birding crews; boardwalk (1.25 m wide) extends some 50 m to river bank and 27 m to steam house located on H26
F4	10 × 4 × 0.5	"Igloo-school" and chapel; built with materials from sod "igloo-chapel" from Kashunak village; 2.7 m off chapel's N wall; separated by boardwalk; entrance on W side of wall (like chapel); 0.5 m below ground surface
F5	3 × 4	Former generator shed now used as steam for U.S. Fish and Wildlife Service crews; wood framed on raised house mound complex area; sits directly on Joe Friday's former house
F6	3 × 3 × 0.3	Roundish rectangular feature; 4.2 m N/NW of H24; identified in 1988 by Elder as Old Chevak firebath

[a] Depth of feature floors is estimate from house floor to base of surrounding berm; depth of pits are from base of pit to floor.
[b] Ziff, Allan. 1981. Fieldnotes, Old Chevak; Ziff, Allan. 1981. Fieldnotes, Qavinaq.
[c] Where samples for dating were able to be taken from; houses not necessarily part of site.

Notes

Preface

1. The people of Chevak are recognized as Cup'ik; however, the general term for all is Yup'ik. I will use Yup'ik through the text since I often am referring to people in other villages on the coast. Plural for Yup'ik is Yupiit.

Introduction

1. On a regional scale, Arctic and Subarctic ethnographic and ethnohistoric studies have increasingly examined the history and context of colonial encounters and contemporary post-colonial issues. This literature has explored historical trauma and indigenous mental and physical health (Dick 1995; Fortuine 1992; Rosich 2007; Wexler, DiFluvio, and Burke 2009); popular imaginings of Arctic people (Huhndorf 2000); subsistence, development, and identity (Chance 1990; Fienup-Riordan 1983; Hensel 1996; Jolles 1997, 2002a, 2002b, 2006; Ohmagari 2004; Piper and Sandlos 2007; Veltre 2011; Wolfe 1984); native perspectives on culture change (Brody 1976; Krupnik and Chlenov 2013; Oswalt 1990; Petersen 1995; Pratt 2009); resistance and native identities (Feit 2004; Kulchyski and Tester 2007); and missionary interactions and impacts (Fienup-Riordan 1991; Flanders 1984; Kan 1999; Oswalt 1963, 1990). Noteworthy is the groundbreaking archaeological scholarship of James VanStone (1968, 1970, 1972) and his classic study of Crow village, Alaska, with Wendell Oswalt (1967). At the vanguard, VanStone examines Alaskan native and colonial material culture and architecture in pluralistic contexts. His body of work prefaces Kent Lightfoot and colleagues' essential research at Fort Ross, California (Farris 1997; Lightfoot and Martinez 1997; Lightfoot, Martinez, and Schiff 1998; Lightfoot, Wake, and Schiff 1991). Some of our most innovative early indigenous-colonial scholarship stems from work in Labrador (Jordan and Kaplan 1980; Kaplan 1980, 1983). These eastern scholars question several of the critical factors of indigenous-colonial experience that we are closely examining today: measures of indigenous resistance (Kaplan 1985a); the impact of introduced technologies (Kaplan 1985b); the role of foreign imports in prestige-system economies and how these may be reflected in architecture, and the critical context of subsistence in the colonial encounter (Kaplan and Woollett 2000; Woollett 1999); polygynous households and

prestige (Kaplan 1985b; Taylor 1974); and the role of archaeology in testing the ethnohistoric record and the complex nature of relations between native and colonial cultures (Jordan and Kaplan 1980). And of course there is T. Max Friesen's (2012) recent work on nineteenth-century continuities and change over a five-hundred-year span among Inuvialuit of the Canadian Arctic. Additionally, Aron Crowell (1997) explores the complexities of early Russian settlements on Alaska's Pacific coast. And finally, in the delta coastal region, work on the colonial transitional period has been published by Dennis Griffin (2004).

2. In 2001 I examined printed oral history data at the ANCSA repository in the offices of the U.S. Bureau of Indian Affairs in Anchorage, Alaska. These are public records; therefore, the names of the elders that were interviewed are included.

3. For further discussion on the history, management, limitations, and applications of the ANCSA data, see Funk (2010), Griffin (1996), and Pratt (2004, 2009).

4. I conducted interviews with twelve Elders (ranging in age from sixty-six to ninety-one) during my 1997 field season. Eleven of the interviews were with Elder women and were conducted in the village hall. Each discussion was approximately one hour (no longer). Interviews were open-ended and primarily focused on subsistence practices in the past and on how life had changed for the women during their lifetimes. Nine of the women had lived at Kashunak and Old Chevak, and two lived on the tundra prior to their family's move to Old Chevak. In addition, the Traditional Council organized a trip to the three sites, and we boated with an Elder man to the three sites during a day-long excursion. He had been born at Kashunak and moved as a young man to Old Chevak. All of the Elders I spoke with could understand and speak some English, but three were fluent enough to be interviewed solely in English. As is standard in Alaska, all Elders were paid honoraria for the interviews and I received informed consent. I worked with (and paid) a local Yup'ik woman (in her forties and who had previously worked for the BIA ANCSA project) to interpret during the interviews. In the interest of their privacy, I do not include the names of local consultants. In 2001 I interviewed Father Henry Hargreaves in Bethel, Alaska. Because he is a public figure and was stationed at Old Chevak, I include his name. In 2004 I interviewed an Elder man who was one of the first children from the region to go to the Akulurak mission boarding school. Overall I spent seven seasons of field research with the generous people of Chevak. During this time I had many informal discussions with people, stayed in their homes, was taken out on the tundra, and spent several weeks over two summers at a fish camp on the banks of the Kashunak River. A final stage draft copy of this book manuscript was commented upon by the Chevak Traditional Council prior to its publication.

Chapter 1

1. One might suggest that women (unlike men) may have preferred the use of stone knives or that it may have been a form of resistance and clinging to or harboring traditional culture (see also Silliman 2001b). For example, Alaskan seamstresses did not use steel thimbles for clothing decoration, instead preferring the traditional sealskin

tools because they were supple (Nelson [1889] 1983, 109). Or spiritual beliefs could block inclusion of foreign materials; for instance, iron implements were offensive to animal spirits and could bring death to the user. But, even with these caveats, metal knives far exceed the performance of the stone knives and have today completely replaced stone (Frink, Hoffman, and Shaw 2003).

2. The Yukon-Kuskokwim Delta is part of the Clarence Rhode National Wildlife Range, at 2,800 square miles the largest of the 180 national wildlife refuges in North America. Along with fish and fowl, the most heavily relied-upon resource in the north is sea mammals. Along the Central Bering Sea shores and inland river courses are found the northern fur (*Callorhinus ursinus*), ringed (*Pusa hispida*), harbor (*Phoca vitulina*), spotted (*Phoca largha*), and ribbon (*Phoca fasciata*) seal, as well as the Pacific bearded seal (*Erignathus barbatus*), the largest and fiercest. Men also opportunistically hunt migrating Pacific walrus (*Odobenus rosmarus*) and beluga whale (*Delphinapterus leucas*). The coastline is also the summer home to a vast number of migrating waterfowl and shorebirds. It is the nesting habitat for 50 percent of all of the world's brant (*Branta canadensis* and *B. nigricans*), up to 90 percent of all emperor geese (*Philacte canagica*), and nearly all of the white-fronted geese (*Anser albifrons*) that migrate along the Pacific flyway. Each year, ducks breed and produce a fall flock of nearly three million birds. Alas, by mid-October the birds have fled the coming cold weather, and only a few species, such as the rock ptarmigan (*Lagopus muta*), winter over. One of the most important harvests for coastal people is fish, which the Russians termed the "bread of all coastal dwellers" (Michael 1967, 95). Not long after the herring (*Clupea harengus*) run in early summer, the salmon launch their final journey upriver. The delta is a spawning, overwintering, rearing, and migration habitat for five species of salmon: the king or chinook (*Oncorhynchus tshawytscha*), the pink or humpback (*O. gorbuscha*), the silver or coho (*O. kisutch*), the chum (*O. keta*), and the sockeye or red salmon (*O. nerka*). There are many other essential fish such as saffron cod tomcod (*Eleginus gracilis*), Arctic flounder (*Liopsetta glacialis*), and Arctic cod (*Boreogadus saida*). Some species, like whitefish (*Coregonus* spp.), blackfish (*Dallia pectoralis*), ninespine stickleback (*Eleginus gracilis*), and grayling (*Thymallus arcticus*) are harvested throughout the year. Ranging on the tundra are arctic fox (*Vulpes lagopus*), red fox (*V. vulpes*), river otter (*Lontra canadensis*), and tundra hare (*Lepus othus*). In the upland areas are wolverine (*Gulo gulo*), muskrat (*Ondatra zibethicus*), mink (*Mustela vison*), and beaver (*Castor canadensis*).

3. Even when homes have plumbing fixtures, this does not mean they have running water; often they draw from a tank of water filled from central water stations.

4. The kind and number of sea mammal that equate with marriageable manhood varies given the locality (see Lantis 1946).

5. When dogs were used to pull sleds, they were generally fed a fish a day when working, and today they get table and subsistence scraps. Many village homes have at least one dog tethered outside. However, they are no longer used for work—but they still warn occupants of an impending visitor. Recently, people have invited dogs into

their homes, and commercial dog food is sold in village stores (unheard of when I started in 1996).

Chapter 2

1. Robert Ackerman was the first archaeologist to briefly survey the site; later, a crew of BIA/CPSU mapped the site. Based on site features, organization, and diagnostic artifacts eroding from the slough bank, the village was lived in at the precipice of early colonialism (R. Ackerman 1972; Ziff 1981; Ziff, Pratt, and Drozda 1982). My dated samples corroborate this assessment of the age of the site (see appendix C).
2. Based on their morphology and according to the Elder man who came to the site, the floor pits were used for storage and are contemporaneous with site occupation (see also Pratt 1995; Ziff, Pratt, and Drozda 1982). Qavinaq is quite a sacrosanct site for people in the region, and it is highly unlikely that people would dig on the old village site, especially since this could quite literally bring back to the surface buried regional hostilities. Some of the pits may be winter tunnel entrances.
3. Edward Nelson ([1889] 1983, 329) was told of warriors who blackened their faces and could walk among the enemy. This may have been a strategy for neutralizing an ongoing battle through diplomacy.
4. It is well-known that some families are linked to different villages through past warfare captivity (Funk 2010, 534). Sometimes raiders would "give them [the captives] the right to go back to their villages if they want"; however, captivity had a significant negative psychological and social stigma (Buster Smith 1981).
5. A cluster of offsite pits are also at the site of Qavinaq, but Robert Ackerman (1972; see appendix B), as well as my guides, suggest these pits are modern. The small mound pits surrounding Kashunak village may have once been houses (Ziff et al. 1982; appendix C). I was told by my Elder companion who lived at the site that these pits were used as seal-poke storage units. Also, rebuilding episodes to some degree mask the complexity of storage on the house floors over time at Kashunak. Nevertheless, at least by the early twentieth century, deep house-floor pits like those found at Qavinaq were clearly no longer in use at Kashunak.
6. In their report, the ANCSA crew (Ziff, Pratt, and Drozda 1982) mentioned but did not map the presence of posts marking the church foundation; I could not find remains during my follow-up survey.
7. During our site tour, the Elder man suggested this tunnel-like feature may actually be a drainage ditch from the men's house.
8. There are indications (Nelson's discussion of Russian traders in the area and stories of traders in oral histories) that some non-native men made undocumented journeys in the region.
9. Two decades after Nelson's observations, Edmonds, too, commented on the differential distribution of new materials. Edmonds commented that less fur was being utilized by Alaskan native people, and "while new parkies are sold to the miners," local people's coats and other articles of clothing were generally of lower-quality crafting and were "worn till the fur is entirely worn off" (Ray 1966, 36). The "convenience of

cloth trousers and overalls" had "almost wholly driven the fur article out of use," but he found that women were less likely than men to possess manufactured clothing, and this evidently was not from lack of interest, since women relished purchasing "bright calico for gowns, breeches, long stockings and overstockings and underwear" (Ray 1966, 34, 36).

Chapter 3

1. An Elder Chevak man talked to me about his boarding school experience; however, another Elder man would not discuss Akulurak because (I was told by others) of difficult memories.
2. During a 1982 survey, all that remained were the partial remains of eighteen wooden posts protruding from the marshy tundra (Ziff, Pratt, and Drozda 1982).
3. I was told by Chevak residents the Sheppard store manager used poker chips instead of cash in a debt peonage system of economics. This made it more difficult for people to bypass the trade store and purchase goods by mail order, especially out of the Sears catalog (which started in 1894).
4. The names of the two houses were Uniqullermiut and Qaygicuareq ("people of the small qaygiq"). The second and smaller men's house was built to accommodate the influx of immigrants from the battle of Qavinaq (Friday 1984e).
5. I have been told that shamans still actively practice in some villages.
6. One may argue that I am taking liberties with this idea of a polygynous system. However, there is strong indication that there were some intimate relations between Fox and some of the cohort of women. For instance, a young postulate grew an "abdominal tumor" and was taken to Bethel for treatment under the guise of an "ordinary village girl." She was operated on and then sent to Holy Cross Mission (Fox 1939, July 1929–May 1952, n.d.-c). A priest's conversation with the girl led him to believe there were issues of sexual impropriety. When asked why she left the order, the young woman replied that Fox "tell me to take off my dress!" (Fox 1939, July 1929–May 1952, n.d.-c). The Church leadership attributed the comment to language issues, but not long after the accusation, Fox was reassigned and the order disbanded in August 1945 (Hooper Bay Collection 1929–1955).

References

Ackerman, Lillian A. 1995. "Complementary but Equal: Gender Status in the Plateau." In *Women and Power in Native North America*, edited by Laura F. Klein and Lillian A. Ackerman, 75–100. Norman: University of Oklahoma Press.

Ackerman, Robert E. 1972. *Field Report, Survey of Clarence Rhode National Wildlife Refuge*. Anchorage, AK: U.S. Fish and Wildlife Office.

———. 1982. "The Neolithic-Bronze Age Cultures of Asia and the Norton Phase of Alaskan Prehistory." *Arctic Anthropology* 19(2):11–38.

Aloralrea, Julianna. 1981. *Taped interview 81 ROM 034*. Julie Dallara and Marsha Walton, interviewers; Mary Moses, interpreter; Marsha Walton, English transcription.

Barker, James H. 1979. "From Mud Houses to Wood: Kashunak to Chevak." Extracted from the *Tundra Drums*, March 1979. *Alaska Journal* 9(3):3–11.

———. 1993. *Always Getting Ready Upterrlainarluta: Yup'ik Eskimo Subsistence in Southwest Alaska*. Seattle: University of Washington Press.

Bayman, James M. 2010. "The Precarious Middle Ground: Exchange and the Reconfiguration of Social Identity in the Hawaiian Kingdom." In *Trade and Exchange: Archaeological Studies from History and Prehistory*, edited by Carolyn D. Dillian and Carolyn L. White, 129–48. Springer: New York.

Begler, Elsie B. 1978. "Sex, Status, and Authority in Egalitarian Society." *American Anthropologist* 80(3):571–88.

Bell, Kurt. 1984. *Taped interview 84 VAK 007*. James Kurtz, interviewer; Leo Moses, interpreter; Lillian Pingayak, transcription.

Berkes, Fikret, Johan Colding, and Carl Folke. 2000. "Rediscovery of Traditional Ecological Knowledge as Adaptive Management." *Ecological Applications* 10:1251–62.

Binford, Lewis R. 1980. "Willow Smoke and Dogs' Tails: Hunter-Gatherer Settlement Systems and Archaeological Site Formation." *American Antiquity* 45(1):4–20.

Black, Lydia T. 1984. "The Yup'ik of Southwestern Alaska and Russian Impact." *Études/Inuit/Studies* 8:21–44.

Blunt, Alison, and Gillian Rose. 1994. "Introduction: Women's Colonial and Postcolonial Geographies." In *Writing Women and Space: Colonial and Postcolonial Geographies*, edited by Alison Blunt and Gillian Rose, 1–28. New York: Guilford Press.

Bodenhorn, Barbara. 1990. "'I'm Not the Great Hunter, My Wife Is': Inupiat and Anthropological Models of Gender." *Études/Inuit/Studies* 14(1–2):55–74.
Bossen, Laurel. 1975. "Women in Modernizing Societies." *American Ethnologist* 2(4): 587–601.
Bowie, Fiona. 1993. "Introduction: Reclaiming Women's Presence." In *Women and Missions: Past and Present Anthropological and Historical Perceptions*, edited by Fiona Bowie, Deborah Kirkwood, and Shirley Ardener, 1–19. Providence, RI: Berg.
Brightman, Robert A. 1993. *Grateful Prey: Rock Cree Human-Animal Relationships*. Berkeley: University of California Press.
Brody, Hugh. 1976. "Colonialism in the Arctic—Four Reminiscences." *History Workshop Journal* 1(1):245–53.
Brown, Judith K. 1975. "Iroquois Women: An Ethnohistoric Note." In *Toward an Anthropology of Women*, edited by Rayna R. Reiter, 235–51. New York: Monthly Review Press.
Brumbach, Hetty Jo, and Robert Jarvenpa. 1997a. "Ethnoarchaeology of Subsistence Space and Gender: A Subarctic Dene Case." *American Antiquity* 62(3):414–36.
———. 1997b. "Woman the Hunter: Ethnoarchaeological Lessons from Chipewyan Life-Cycle Dynamics." In *Women in Prehistory: North America and Mesoamerica*, edited by Cheryl Claassen and Rosemary A. Joyce, 17–32. Philadelphia: University of Pennsylvania Press.
Bunyan, Dick. 1984. *Taped Interview 84 VAK 074/075*. James Kurtz and Robert Waterworth, interviewers; Lillian Pingayak, interpreter and transcription.
Burch, Ernest S., Jr. 1985. "Eskimo Warfare in Northwest Alaska." *Anthropological Papers of the University of Alaska* 16(2):1–14.
———. 1988. "War and Trade." In *Crossroads of Continents: Cultures of Siberia and Alaska*, edited by William W. Fitzhugh and Aron Crowell, 227–40. Washington, DC: Smithsonian Institution Press.
———. 2005. *Alliance and Conflict: The World System of Inupiaq Eskimos*. Lincoln: University of Nebraska Press.
Cassell, Mark S. 2005. "Gender Visibility and Division of Inupiat Labor in an Arctic Industrial Enterprise." In *Gender and Hide Production*, edited by Lisa Frink and Kathryn Weedman, 105–22. Walnut Creek, CA: AltaMira Press.
Chance, Norman A. 1990. *The Iñupiat and Arctic Alaska: An Ethnography of Development*. Fort Worth, TX: Holt, Rinehart and Winston.
Comaroff, Jean. 1985. *Body of Power, Spirit of Resistance: The Culture and History of a South African People*. Chicago: University of Chicago Press.
Convert, Jules. March 1948. Letter to Dale. Con Box 2, Jesuit Oregon Province Archives. Special Collections, Foley Library, Gonzaga University, Spokane, WA.
———. March 1949. Letter to Foster. Con Box 2, Jesuit Oregon Province Archives. Special Collections, Foley Library, Gonzaga University, Spokane, WA.
———. 1979. *Tundra Drums*, March. Special Collections, Foley Library, Gonzaga University, Spokane, WA.

———. 1997. *Archaeology and the Capitalist World System: A Study from Russian America*. New York: Plenum Press.

———. n.d. Con Box 536-E 13 PTS, Jesuit Oregon Province Archives. Special Collections, Foley Library, Gonzaga University, Spokane, WA.

Crowell, Aron L. 1997. *Archaeology and the Capitalist World System: A Study from Russian America*. Contributions to Global Historical Archaeology. New York: Springer.

Crown, Patricia L., and Susan K. Fish. 1996. "Gender and Status in the Hohokam Pre-Classic to Classic Transition." *American Anthropologist* 98(4):803–17.

Cruikshank, Julie, in collaboration with Angela Sidney, Kitty Smith, and Annie Ned. 1990. *Life Lived Like a Story: Life Stories of Three Yukon Native Elders*. Lincoln: University of Nebraska Press.

Dall, William H. 1870. *Alaska and Its Resources*. Boston: Lee and Shepard Publishers.

d'Anglure, Bernard Saladin. 1984. "Contemporary Inuit of Quebec." In *Handbook of North American Indians*, Vol. 5, *Arctic*, edited by David Damas, 683–88. Washington, DC: Smithsonian Institution Press.

Darwent, John, Christyann M. Darwent, Genevieve LeMoine, and Hans Lang. 2007. "Archaeological Survey of Eastern Inglefield Land, Northwest Greenland." *Arctic Anthropology* 44(2):51–86.

Darwent, John, and Trine Bjorneboe Johansen. 2010. "Archaeological Survey in the Foulke Fjord Region, Inglefield Land, Northwestern Greenland." *Geografisk Tidsskrift–Danish Journal of Geography* 110(2):297–314.

Darwent, John, Owen K. Mason, John F. Hoffecker, and Christyann M. Darwent. 2013. "1,000 Years of House Change at Cape Espenberg, Alaska: A Case Study in Horizontal Stratigraphy." *American Antiquity* 78(3):433–55.

Dawson, Peter C. 2001. "Interpreting Variability in Thule Inuit Architecture: A Case Study from the Canadian High Arctic." *American Antiquity* 66(3):453–70.

Delle, James A. 1998. *An Archaeology of Social Space: Analyzing Coffee Plantations in Jamaica's Blue Mountains*. New York: Plenum Press.

———. 2000. "Gender, Power, and Space: Negotiating Social Relations under Slavery on Coffee Plantations in Jamaica, 1790–1834." In *Lines That Divide: Historical Archaeologies of Race, Class, and Gender*, edited by James A. Delle, Stephen A. Mrozowski, and Robert Paynter, 168–204. Knoxville: University of Tennessee Press.

———. 2007. Comment on Lisa Frink, "Storage and Status in Precolonial and Colonial Coastal Western Alaska." *Current Anthropology* 48(3):349–74.

Devens, Carol. 1992. *Countering Colonization: Native American Women and Great Lakes Missions, 1630–1900*. Berkeley: University of California Press.

Dick, Lyle. 1995. "'Pibloktoq' (Arctic Hysteria): A Construction of European-Inuit Relations?" *Arctic Anthropology* 32(2):1–42.

Dickerson-Putman, Jeanette, and Judith K. Brown. 1994. "Introductory Overview: Women's Age Hierarchies." In *Women Among Women: Anthropological Perspectives on Female Age Hierarchies*, edited by Jeanette Dickerson-Putman and Judith K. Brown, xxi–xvii. Urbana: University of Illinois Press.

Dietler, Michael. 1998. "Consumption, Agency, and Cultural Entanglement: Theoretical Implications of a Mediterranean Colonial Encounter." In *Studies in Culture Contact: Interaction, Culture Change, and Archaeology*, edited by James Cusick, 288–315. Carbondale: Center for Archaeological Investigations Press, University of Southern Illinois.

———. 2001. "Theorizing the Feast: Rituals of Consumption, Commensal Politics, and Power in African Contexts." In *Feasts: Archaeological and Ethnographic Perspectives on Food, Politics, and Power*, edited by Michael Dietler and Brian Hayden, 65–114. Washington, DC: Smithsonian Institution Press.

———. 2010. *Archaeologies of Colonialism: Consumption, Entanglement, and Violence in Ancient Mediterranean France*. Berkeley and Los Angeles: University of California Press.

Dumond, Don E. 2000. "The Norton Tradition." *Arctic Anthropology* 37(2):1–22.

———. 2011. *The Eskimos and the Aleuts*. 2nd ed. New York: Thames and Hudson.

Ehrhardt, Kathleen L. 2005. *European Metals in Native Hands: Rethinking the Dynamics of Technological Change, 1640–1683*. Tuscaloosa: University of Alabama Press.

Eidlitz, Kerstin. 1969. *Food and Emergency Food in the Circumpolar Area*. Studia Ethnographica Upsaliensia 32. Uppsala, Sweden: Almqvist and Wiksells Boktryckert Ab.

Eislet, Sunday B., and J. Andrew Darling. 2012. "Vecino Economics: Gendered Economy and Micaceous Pottery Consumption in Nineteenth Century Northern New Mexico." *American Antiquity* 77(3):424–48.

Ellanna, Linda J., and George K. Sherrod. 1995. "'Big Women': Gender and Economic Management Among King Island and Kobuk River Iñupiat of Northwest Alaska." *Research in Economic Anthropology* 16:15–38.

Evan, Wassilie. 1984. *Taped Interview 84 VAK 033*. James Kurtz and Harley Cochran, interviewers; Lillian Pingayak, interpreter and transcription.

Fair, Susan W. 1997. "Story, Storage, and Symbol: Functional Cache Architecture, Cache Narratives, and Roadside Attractions." In *Exploring Everyday Landscapes: Perspectives in Vernacular Architecture, VII*, edited by Annmarie Adams and Sally McMurry, 167–82. Knoxville: University of Tennessee Press.

Farris, Glenn J. 1997. "Historical Archaeology of the Native Alaskan Village Site." In *The Archaeology and Ethnohistory of Fort Ross, California*, Vol. 2, *The Native Alaskan Neighborhood: A Multiethnic Community at Colony Ross*, edited by Kent G. Lightfoot, Ann M. Schiff, and Thomas A. Wake, 129–35. Contributions of the University of California Archaeological Research Facility 55. Berkeley: University of California.

Feit, Harvey A. 2004. "Contested Identities of 'Indians' and 'Whitemen' at James Bay, or the Power of Reason, Hybridity, and Agency." In *Circumpolar Ethnicity and Identity*, edited by Takashi Irimoto and Takako Yamada, 109–26. Senri Ethnological Studies 66. Osaka, Japan: National Museum of Ethnology.

Ferris, Neal. 2011. *The Archaeology of Native-Lived Colonialism: Challenging History in the Great Lakes*. Tucson: University of Arizona Press.

Fienup-Riordan, Ann. 1983. *The Nelson Island Eskimo: Social Structure and Ritual Distribution*. Anchorage: Alaska Pacific University Press.

———. 1986. *When Our Bad Season Comes: A Cultural Account of Subsistence Harvesting and Harvest Disruption on the Yukon Delta*. Aurora Monograph Series 1. Anchorage: Alaska Anthropological Association.

———. 1988. *The Yup'ik Eskimos: As Described in the Travel Journals and Ethnographic Accounts of John and Edith Kilbuck Who Served with the Alaska Mission of the Moravian Church, 1885–1900*. Kingston, Ontario: Limestone Press.

———. 1991. *The Real People and the Children of Thunder*. Norman: University of Oklahoma Press.

———. 1994. "Eskimo War and Peace." In *Anthropology of the North Pacific Rim*, edited by William W. Fitzhugh and Valérie Chaussonnet, 321–35. Washington, DC: Smithsonian Institution Press.

Fiske, Jo-Anne. 1991. "Colonization and the Decline of Women's Status: The Tsimshian Case." *Feminist Studies* 17(3):509–35.

Fitzhugh, William W. 1985. "Introduction." In *Cultures in Contact: The Impact of European Contacts on Native American Cultural Institutions, A.D. 1000–1800*, edited by William W. Fitzhugh, 1–15. Washington, DC: Smithsonian Institution Press.

Flanders, Nicholas E. 1984. "Religious Conflict and Social Change: A Case from Southwestern Alaska." *Études/Inuit/Studies* 8:141–57.

Fortuine, Robert. 1992. *Chills and Fever: Health and Disease in the Early History of Alaska*. Fairbanks: University of Alaska Press.

Fossett, Renée. 2001. *In Order to Live Untroubled: Inuit of the Central Arctic, 1550–1940*. Winnipeg: University of Manitoba Press.

Foster, George M. 1976. "Disease Etiologies in Non-western Medical Systems." *American Anthropologist* 78(4):773–82.

Fox, Father John P. July 1929–May 1952. Kashunak Mission Diary. Box 585 9PTS, Jesuit Oregon Province Archives. Special Collections, Foley Library, Gonzaga University, Spokane, WA.

———. 1939. "The Founding of Kashunak." Box 585 9PTS, Jesuit Oregon Province Archives. Special Collections, Foley Library, Gonzaga University, Spokane, WA.

———. n.d.-a. Box 10 AM 30: 432–56: 10:3, Jesuit Oregon Province Archives. Special Collections, Foley Library, Gonzaga University, Spokane, WA.

———. n.d.-b. Box Fox 7 AM 30: 410–22, Jesuit Oregon Province Archives. Special Collections, Foley Library, Gonzaga University, Spokane, WA.

———. n.d.-c. Box Fox 8 8:6, Jesuit Oregon Province Archives. Special Collections, Foley Library, Gonzaga University, Spokane, WA.

———. n.d.-d. Box Fox 12 1289–7, Jesuit Oregon Province Archives. Special Collections, Foley Library, Gonzaga University, Spokane, WA.

———. n.d.-e. Box Fox 576–77 8 PTS, Jesuit Oregon Province Archives. Special Collections, Foley Library, Gonzaga University, Spokane, WA.

———. n.d.-f. Miscellaneous Stories. Fox Box 7, Jesuit Oregon Province Archives. Special Collections, Foley Library, Gonzaga University, Spokane, WA.

Friday, Joe. 1983. *Taped Interview 83 VAK 23*. James Kurtz, interviewer; Leo Moses, interpreter; Lillan Pingayak, transcription.

———. 1984a, b. *Taped Interview 84 VAK 015/017/018*. James Kurtz, interviewer; Joe Slats, interpreter; Lillian Pingayak, transcription.

———. 1984c. *Taped Interview 84 VAK 40–45*. James Kurtz, interviewer; John Pingayak, interpreter and transcription.

———. 1984d. *Taped Interview 84 VAK 057*. James Kurtz, interviewer; Lillian Pingayak, interpreter and transcription.

———. 1984e. *Taped Interview 84 VAK 072*. James Kurtz and Theresa Turner, interviewers; Bill Friday, interpreter; Lillian Pingayak, transcription.

Friesen, T. Max. 2012. *When Worlds Collide: Hunter-Gatherer World-System Change in the 19th-Century Arctic*. Tucson: University of Arizona Press.

Friesen, T. Max, and Charles D. Arnold. 2008. "The Timing of the Thule Migration: New Dates from the Western Canadian Arctic." *American Antiquity* 73(3):527–38.

Friesen, T. Max, and Andrew Stewart. 2013. "To Freeze or to Dry: Seasonal Variability in Caribou Processing and Storage in the Barrenlands of Northern Canada." *Anthropozoologica* 48(1):89–109.

Frink, Liam. 2009a. "The Identity Division of Labor in Native Alaska." *American Anthropologist* 11(1):21–29.

———. 2009b. "The Social Role of Technology in Coastal Alaska." *International Journal of Historical Archaeology* 13(3):282–302.

———. 2010. "Identity Collectives and Religious Colonialism in Coastal Southwestern Alaska." In *Across a Great Divide: Continuity and Change in Native North American Societies, 1400–1900*, edited by Laura L. Scheiber and Mark D. Mitchell, 239–57. Tucson: University of Arizona Press.

Frink, Liam, and Celeste Giordano. 2015. "Women and Subsistence Food Technology." *Food and Foodways: Explorations in the History and Culture of Human Nourishment* 23:1–22.

Frink, Liam, and Kelly J. Knudson. 2010. "Using Ethnoarchaeology and Soils Chemistry to Examine Fisheries on the Arctic Alaskan Coast." *North American Archaeologist* 31(2):221–47.

Frink, Lisa. 2002. "Fish Tales: Women and Decision Making in Southwestern Alaska." In *Many Faces of Gender: Roles and Relationships Through Time in Indigenous Northern Communities*, edited by Lisa Frink, Rita S. Shepard, and Gregory A. Reinhardt, 93–110. Boulder: University Press of Colorado.

———. 2006. "Social Identity and the Yup'ik Eskimo Village Tunnel System in Precolonial and Colonial Western Coastal Alaska." In *Integrating the Diversity of Twenty-First-Century Anthropology: The Life and Intellectual Legacies of Susan Kent*, edited by Wendy Ashmore and Susan Kent, 109–25. Arlington, VA: American Anthropological Association.

———. 2007. "Storage and Status in Precolonial and Colonial Coastal Western Alaska." *Current Anthropology* 48(3):349–74.

Frink, Lisa, and Karen G. Harry. 2008. "The Beauty of 'Ugly' Eskimo Cooking Pots." *American Antiquity* 73(1):103–20.

Frink, Lisa, Brian W. Hoffman, and Robert D. Shaw. 2003. "Ulu Knife Use in Western Alaska: A Comparative Ethnoarchaeological Study." *Current Anthropology* 44(1):116–22.

Funk, Caroline. 2010. "The Bow and Arrow War Days on the Yukon-Kuskokwim Delta of Alaska." *Ethnohistory* 57(4):523–69.

Geist, Otto, and Froelich Rainey. 1936. *Archaeological Investigations at Kukulik, St. Lawrence Island*. Miscellaneous Publications of the University of Alaska 2. Washington, DC: U.S. Government Printing Office.

George, Agnes. 1981. *Taped Interview 81 ROM 37*. Marsha Walton and Julie Dallara, interviewers; Mary Moses, interpreter.

Gibson, James R. 1988. "The Maritime Trade of the North Pacific Coast." In *Handbook of North American Indians*, Vol. 4, *History of Indian-White Relations*, edited by Wilcomb E. Washburn, 375–90. Washington, DC: Smithsonian Institution Press.

Giddings, Louis J. 1964. *The Archaeology of Cape Denbigh*. Providence, RI: Brown University Press.

———. 1967. *Ancient Men of the Arctic*. New York: Alfred A. Knopf.

Gifford-Gonzalez, Diane. 1993. "You Can Hide, but You Can't Run: Representation of Women's Work in Illustrations of Paleolithic Life." *Visual Anthropology Review* 9:3–21.

Gonzalez, Ellice B. 1981. *Changing Economic Roles for Micmac Men and Women: An Ethnohistorical Analysis*. National Museum of Man Mercury Series. Ottawa: National Museums of Canada.

Gosden, Chris. 2004. *Archaeology and Colonialism: Cultural Contact from 5000 BC to the Present*. Cambridge: Cambridge University Press.

Griffin, Dennis. 1996. "A Culture in Transition: A History of Acculturation and Settlement near the Mouth of the Yukon River, Alaska." *Arctic Anthropology* 33(1):98–115.

———. 2004. *Ellikarrmiut: Changing Lifeways in an Alaskan Community*. Aurora Monograph Series 7. Anchorage: Alaska Anthropological Association.

Gutierrez, Ramon A. 1991. *When Jesus Came, The Corn Mothers Went Away: Marriage, Sexuality, and Power in New Mexico, 1500–1846*. Stanford: Stanford University Press.

Habicht-Mauche, Judith A. 2005. "The Shifting Role of Women and Women's Labor on the Protohistoric Southern High Plains." In *Gender and Hide Production*, edited by Lisa Frink and Kathryn Weedman, 37–56. Walnut Creek, CA: AltaMira Press.

Hargreaves, Henry. 2001. Liam Frink, interviewer; Bethel, Alaska.

Harry, Karen, and Lisa Frink. 2009. "The Arctic Cooking Pot: Why Was It Adopted?" *American Anthropologist* 111(3):330–43.

Hastorf, Christine A. 1991. "Gender, Space, and Food in Prehistory." In *Engendering Archaeology: Women and Prehistory*, edited by Joan M. Gero and Margaret W. Conkey, 132–62. Oxford: Basil Blackwell Ltd.

Hayden, Brian. 1995. "Pathways to Power: Principles for Creating Socioeconomic Inequalities." In *Foundations of Social Inequality*, edited by T. Douglas Price and Gary M. Feinman, 15–86. New York: Plenum Press.

Helgason, Agnar, Gisli Palsson, Henning Sloth Pedersen, Emily Angulalik, Ellen Drofn Gunnarsdottir, Bryndis Yngvadottir, and Kari Stefansson. 2006. "mtDNA Variation in Inuit Populations of Greenland and Canada: Migration History and Population Structure." *American Journal of Physical Anthropology* 130(1):123–34.

Henry, John. 1984. *Taped Interview 84 VAK 053*. Beth Shide-Cochran, interviewer; Veronica Charlie, interpreter and transcription.

Hensel, Chase. 1996. *Telling Our Selves: Ethnicity and Discourse in Southwestern Alaska*. New York: Oxford University Press.

Herdt, Gilbert H. 1994. *Guardians of the Flutes: Idioms of Masculinity*. Chicago: University of Chicago Press.

Hodder, Ian. 1982. *Symbols in Action: Ethnoarchaeological Studies of Material Culture*. New York: Cambridge University Press.

Hollimon, Sandra E. 2005. "Hideworking and Changes in Women's Status Among the Arikara, 1700–1862." In *Gender and Hide Production*, edited by Lisa Frink and Kathryn Weedman, 77–88. Walnut Creek, CA: AltaMira Press.

Hooper Bay Collection. 1928, 1931, 1932. "Historica Domus." Jesuit Oregon Province Archives. Special Collections, Foley Library, Gonzaga University, Spokane, WA.

———. 1929–1955. "Historica Domus of Hooper Bay District." Jesuit Oregon Province Archives. Special Collections, Foley Library, Gonzaga University, Spokane, WA.

———. 1945. Letter. Jesuit Oregon Province Archives. Special Collections, Foley Library, Gonzago University, Spokane, WA.

Høygaard, Arne. 1941. Studies on the Nutrition and Physio-pathology of Eskimos, Undertaken at Angmagssalik, East-Greenland 1936–1937. *Norske Videnskapsakademi i Oslo, Skrifter 1: Maternatisk-Naturvidenskapelig Klasse* 1940(9).

Hughes, Charles C. 1984. "Siberian Eskimo." In *Handbook of North American Indians*, Vol. 5, *Arctic*, edited by David Damas, 247–61. Washington, DC: Smithsonian Institution Press.

Huhndorf, Shari M. 2000. "Nanook and His Contemporaries: Imagining Eskimos in American Culture, 1897–1922." *Critical Inquiry* 27(1):122–48.

Ingold, Tim. 1983. "The Significance of Storage in Hunting Societies." *Man* 18(3):553–71.

Jarvenpa, Robert, and Hetty Jo Brumbach. 2006. "Revisiting the Sexual Division of Labor: Thoughts on Ethnoarchaeology and Gender." In *Integrating the Diversity of Twenty-First-Century Anthropology: The Life and Intellectual Legacies of Susan Kent*, edited by Wendy Ashmore, Marcia-Anne Dobres, Sarah Milledge Nelson, and Arlene Rosen, 97–108. Archaeological Papers of the American Anthropological Association 16(1). Berkeley: University of California Press.

Jolles, Carol Zane. 1997. "Changing Roles of St. Lawrence Island Women: Clanswomen in the Public Sphere." *Arctic Anthropology* 34(1):86–101.

———. 2002a. "Celebration of a Life: Remembering Linda Womkon Badten, Yupik Educator." In *Many Faces of Gender: Roles and Relationships Through Time in Indigenous Northern Communities*, edited by Lisa Frink, Rita S. Shepard, and Gregory A. Reinhardt, 37–60. Boulder: University Press of Colorado.

———. 2002b. *Faith, Food and Family in an Eskimo Whaling Village*. Seattle: University of Washington Press.

———. 2006. "Iñupiaq Maritime Hunters." In *Circumpolar Lives and Livelihood: A Comparative Ethnoarchaeology of Gender and Subsistence*, edited by Robert Jarvenpa and Hetty Jo Brumbach, 263–86. Lincoln: University of Nebraska Press.

JOPA. Fox Box 8 8:6. Jesuit Oregon Province Archives, Special Collections, Foley Library, Gonzago University, Spokane, WA.

———. 1920–1950. Personal Retreat Reflections. Jesuit Oregon Province Archives, Special Collections, Foley Library, Gonzago University, Spokane, WA.

———. 1927–1955. Con Boxes 583–85. Hooper Bay Collection. Jesuit Oregon Province Archives, Special Collections, Foley Library, Gonzago University, Spokane, WA.

———. 1949–1963. Con Box 2 69.1:536-3 13. Jesuit Oregon Province Archives. Special Collections, Foley Library, Gonzaga University, Spokane, WA.

JOPA Chevak Diary. 1947–1951. Jesuit Oregon Province Archives. Special Collections, Foley Library, Gonzago University, Spokane, WA.

Jordan, R. H., and Susan A. Kaplan. 1980. "An Archaeological View of the Inuit/European Contact Period in Central Labrador." *Études Inuit* 4(1–2):35–45.

Jorgenson, Torre, and Craig Ely. 2001. "Topography and Flooding of Coastal Ecosystems on the Yukon-Kuskokwim Delta, Alaska: Implications for Sea-Level Rise." *Journal of Coastal Research* 17(1):124–36.

Kamp, Katherine A. 2001. "Where Have All the Children Gone?: The Archaeology of Childhood." *Journal of Archaeological Method and Theory* 8(1):1–34.

Kan, Sergei. 1999. *Memory Eternal: Tlingit Culture and Russian Orthodox Christianity Through Two Centuries*. Seattle: University of Washington Press.

Kaplan, Susan A. 1980. "Neo-Eskimo Occupation of the Northern Labrador Coast." *Arctic* 33(3):646–58.

———. 1983. "Economic and Social Change in Labrador Neo-Eskimo Culture." PhD diss., Department of Anthropology, Bryn Mawr College.

———. 1985a. "Eskimo-European Contact Archaeology in Labrador, Canada." *British Archaeological Reports, Int. Ser.* 233:53–76.

———. 1985b. "European Goods and Socio-economic Change in Early Labrador Inuit Society." In *Cultures in Contact: The Impact of European Contacts on Native American Cultural Institutions, A.D. 1000–1800*, edited by William W. Fitzhugh, 45–69. Washington, DC: Smithsonian Institution Press.

Kaplan, Susan A., and Jim M. Woollett. 2000. "Challenges and Choices: Exploring the Interplay of Climate, History, and Culture on Canada's Labrador Coast." *Arctic, Antarctic, and Alpine Research* 32(3):351–59.

Kent, Susan. 1991. "The Relationships Between Mobility Strategies and Site Structure." In *The Interpretation of Archaeological Spatial Patterning*, edited by Ellen M. Kroll and T. Douglas Price, 33–59. New York: Plenum Press.

Knudson, Kelly J., and Liam Frink. 2010. "Soil Chemical Signatures of a Historic Sod House: Activity Area Analysis of an Arctic Semisubterranean Structure on Nelson Island, Alaska." *Archaeological and Anthropological Sciences* 2(4):265–82.

Knudson, Kelly J., Lisa Frink, Brian W. Hoffman, and T. Douglas Price. 2004. "Chemical Characterization of Arctic Soils: Activity Area Analysis in Contemporary Yup'ik Fish Camps Using ICP-AES." *Journal of Archaeological Science* 31(4):443–56.

Koranda, Lorraine D. 1968. "Three Bladder Festival Songs." *Anthropological Papers of the University of Alaska* 14(1):27–32.

Krupnik, Igor, and Michael Chlenov. 2013. *Yupik Transitions: Change and Survival at Bering Strait, 1900–1960*. Fairbanks: University of Alaska Press.

Kuijt, Ian. 2009. "What Do We Really Know About Food Storage, Surplus, and Feasting in Preagricultural Communities?" *Current Anthropology* 50(5):641–44.

Kuijt, Ian, and Bill Finlayson. 2009. "Evidence for Food Storage and Predomestication Granaries 11,000 Years Ago in the Jordan Valley." *Proceedings of the National Academy of Sciences* 102(27):10966–70.

Kulchyski, Peter, and Frank James Tester. 2007. *Kiumajut (Talking Back): Game Management and Inuit Rights, 1900–70*. Vancouver, BC: University of British Columbia Press.

Lane, Robert B. 1982. "Chilcotin." In *Handbook of North American Indians*, Vol. 6, *Subarctic*, edited by June Helm, 402–12. Washington, DC: Smithsonian Institution Press.

Lantis, Margaret. 1946. "The Social Culture of the Nunivak Eskimo." *Transactions of the American Philosophical Society* 35(3):153–323.

———. 1972. "Factionalism and Leadership: A Case Study of Nunivak Island." *Arctic Anthropology* 9(1):43–65.

———. 1984a. "Aleut." In *Handbook of North American Indians*, Vol. 5, *Arctic*, edited by David Dumas, 161–84. Washington, DC: Smithsonian Institution Press.

———. 1984b. "Nunivak Eskimo." In *Handbook of North American Indians*, Vol. 5, *Arctic*, edited by David Dumas, 209–23. Washington, DC: Smithsonian Institution Press.

Larsen, Helge, and Froelich Rainey. 1948. "Ipiutak and the Arctic Whale Hunting Culture." Anthropological Papers of the American Museum of Natural History 42. New York: American Museum of Natural History.

Larson, Mary Ann. 1991. "Determining the Function of a 'Men's House.'" In *The Archaeology of Gender Proceedings of the 22nd Annual Chacmool Conference*, edited by Dale Walde and Noreen D. Willows, 165–76. Calgary, AB: University of Calgary.

———. 1995. "And Then There Were None: The 'Disappearance' of the Qargi in Northern Alaska." In *Hunting the Largest Animals: Native Whaling in the Western Arctic and Subarctic*, edited by Allen P. McCartney, 207–21. Occasional Publications Series. Edmonton: Canadian Circumpolar Institute, University of Alberta.

Lawrence, Susan, and Peter Davies. 2010. *An Archaeology of Australia Since 1788*. New York: Springer.

Leacock, Eleanor. 1978. "Women's Status in Egalitarian Society: Implications for Social Evolution." *Current Anthropology* 19(2):247–75.

———. 1980. "Montagnais Women and the Jesuit Program for Colonization." In *Women and Colonization: Anthropological Perspectives*, edited by Mona Etienne and Eleanor Leacock, 25–42. New York: Praeger Publishers.

———. 1986. "Women, Power, and Authority." In *Visibility and Power: Essays on Women in Society and Development*, edited by Leela Dube, Eleanor Leacock, and Shirley Ardener, 107–35. Delhi: Oxford University Press.

Lee, Molly, and Gregory A. Reinhardt. 2003. *Eskimo Architecture: Dwelling and Structure in the Early Historic Period*. Fairbanks: University of Alaska Press.

Lepowsky, Maria A. 1993. *Fruit of the Motherland: Gender in an Egalitarian Society*. New York: Columbia University Press.

Liebmann, Matthew J. 2012. "The Rest Is History: Devaluing the Recent Past in the Archaeology of the Pueblo Southwest." In *Decolonizing Indigenous Histories: Exploring Prehistoric/Colonial Transitions in Archaeology*, edited by Maxine Oland, Siobhan M. Hart, and Liam Frink, 19–44. Tucson: University of Arizona Press.

———. 2013. *Revolt: An Archaeological History of Pueblo Resistance and Revitalization in 17th Century New Mexico*. Tucson: University of Arizona Press.

Liebmann, Matthew, and Melissa Scott Murphy. 2011. *Enduring Conquests: Rethinking the Archaeology of Resistance to Spanish Colonialism in the Americas*. Santa Fe, NM: School for Advanced Research Press.

Lightfoot, Kent G. 2005. *Indians, Missionaries, and Merchants: The Legacy of Colonial Encounters on the California Frontiers*. Berkeley: University of California Press.

———. 1995. "Culture Contact Studies: Redefining the Relationship Between Prehistoric and Historical Archaeology." *American Antiquity* 60(2):199–217.

Lightfoot, Kent G., and Antoinette Martinez. 1997. "Interethnic Relationships in the Native Alaskan Neighborhood: Consumption Practices, Cultural Innovations, and the Construction of Household Identities." In *The Archaeology and Ethnohistory of Fort Ross, California*, Vol. 2, *The Native Alaskan Neighborhood: A Multiethnic Community at Colony Ross*, edited by Kent G. Lightfoot, Ann M. Schiff, and Thomas A. Wake, 1–22. Contributions of the University of California Archaeological Research Facility 55. Berkeley: University of California.

Lightfoot, Kent G., Antoinette Martinez, and Ann M. Schiff. 1998. "Daily Practice and Material Culture in Pluralistic Social Settings: An Archaeological Study of Culture Change and Persistence from Fort Ross, California." *American Antiquity* 63(2):199–222.

Lightfoot, Kent G., Thomas A. Wake, and Ann M. Schiff. 1991. *The Archaeology and Ethnohistory of Fort Ross, California*, Vol. 1, *Introduction*. Contributions of the University of California Archaeological Research Facility 49. Berkeley: University of California.

Llorente, Sequndo. 1988. *Memoirs of a Yukon Priest*. Washington, DC: Georgetown University Press.

Lucier, Charles V., and James W. VanStone. 1992. *Historic Pottery of the Kotzebue Sound Inupiat*. Fieldiana Anthropology 18. Chicago: Field Museum of Natural History.

Lutkehaus, Nancy C. 1999. "Missionary Materialism: Gendered Images of the Holy Spirit Sisters in Colonial New Guinea." In *Gendered Missions: Women and Men in Missionary Discourse and Practice*, edited by Mary Taylor Huber and Nancy C. Lutkehaus, 207–36. Ann Arbor: University of Michigan Press.

Lutz, Bruce J. 1972. "A Methodology for Determining Regional Intra-cultural Variation Within Norton, an Alaskan Archaeological Culture." PhD diss., Department of Anthropology, University of Pennsylvania.

Lyons, Claire, and John K. Papadopoulas, eds. 2002. *The Archaeology of Colonialism*. Los Angeles: Getty Research Institute.

Lyons, Natasha. 2013. *Where the Wind Blows: Practicing Critical Community Archaeology in the Canadian North*. Tucson: University of Arizona Press.

Maschner, Herbert D. G. 1991. "The Emergence of Cultural Complexity on the Northern Northwest Coast." *Antiquities* 65(249): 924–34.

Maschner, Herbert, and Owen K. Mason. 2013. "The Bow and Arrow in Northern North America." *Evolutionary Anthropology* 22:133–38.

Mason, Owen K. 2012. "Memories of Warfare: Archaeology and Oral History in Assessing the Conflict and Alliance Model of Ernest S. Burch." *Arctic Anthropology* 49(2):72–91.

McGhee, Robert. 2001. *Ancient People of the Arctic*. Vancouver, BC: University of British Columbia Press.

Melbye, Jerry, and Scott I. Fairgrieve. 1994. "A Massacre and Possible Cannibalism in the Canadian Arctic: New Evidence from the Saunaktuk Site (NgTn-1)." *Arctic Anthropology* 31(2):57–77.

Menager, Francis M. 1962. *The Kingdom of the Seal*. Chicago: Loyola University Press.

———. n.d. Men Box 3 3:8, Jesuit Oregon Province Archives. Special Collections, Foley Library, Gonzaga University, Spokane, WA.

Michael, Henry N. 1967. *Lieutenant Zagoskin's Travels in Russian America, 1842–1844*. Arctic Institute of North America, Translations from Russian Sources 7. Toronto: University of Toronto Press.

Mills, Barbara J. 2007. "Performing the Feast: Visual Display and Suprahousehold Commensalism in the Puebloan Southwest." *American Antiquity* 72(2):210–39.

Mitchell, Mark D. 2012. *Crafting History in the Northern Plains: A Political Economy of the Heart River Region, 1400–1750*. Tucson: University of Arizona Press.

Mitchell, Mark D., and Laura L. Scheiber. 2010. "Crossing Divides: Archaeology as Long-Term History." In *Across a Great Divide: Continuity and Change in Native North American Societies, 1400–1900*, edited by Laura L. Scheiber and Mark D. Mitchell, 1–22. Tucson: University of Arizona Press.

Morgan, Christopher. 2012. "Modeling Modes of Hunter-Gatherer Food Storage." *American Antiquity* 77(4):714–36.

Morrow, Phyllis P. 1995. "On Shaky Ground: Folklore, Collaboration, and Problematic Outcomes." In *When Our Words Return: Writing, Hearing and Remembering Oral Traditions of Alaska and the Yukon*, edited by Phyllis P. Morrow and William Schneider, 27–52. Logan: Utah State University Press.

Moss, Madonna L., and Aubrey Cannon. 2011. "The Archaeology of North Pacific Fisheries: An Introduction." In *The Archaeology of North Pacific Fisheries*, edited by Madonna L. Moss and Aubrey Cannon, 1–15. Fairbanks: University of Alaska Press.

Murphy, Yolanda, and Robert F. Murphy. 1985. *Women of the Forest*. New York: Columbia University Press.

Nanok, Peter. 1981. *Taped Interview 81 ROM 35*. Julie Dallara and Kris Andre, interviewers.

Napoleon, George. 1984. *Taped Interview 84 VAK 05*. James Kurtz, Beth Shide-Cochran, and Robert Waterworth, interviewers; Leo Moses, interpreter; Joe Slats, transcription.

Nayamin, Ulric. 1981a. *Taped Interview 81 ROM 21*. Robert Drozda and Kris Andre, interviewers; Peter Tuluk, interpreter; Robert Drozda, transcription.

———. 1981b. *Taped Interview 81 ROM 22*. Robert Drozda and Kris Andre, interviewers; Leo Moses and Peter Tuluk, interpreters.

———. 1981c. *Taped Interview 81 ROM 24*. Robert Drozda and Kris Andre, interviewers; Leo Moses, interpreter; Kris Andre, transcription.

———. 1983. *Taped Interview 83 VAK 013/014*. James Kurtz, interviewer; Leo Moses, interpreter; Lillian Pingayak, transcription.

Nayamin, Ulrich, and Natalia Nyamin. *Taped Interview 84 VAK 067/068*. Theresa Turner, interviewer; Bill Friday, interpreter; Lillian Pingayak, transcription.

Nelson, Edward William. 1877. *Edward William Nelson's Alaska Journals. April 18, 1877 through October 20, 1881*. Smithsonian Institution Archives, Washington, DC.

———. 1882. "A Sledge Journey in the Delta of the Yukon, Northern Alaska." *Proceedings of the Royal Geographical Society and Monthly Record of Geography* 4(11):660–70.

———. [1889] 1983. *The Eskimo About Bering Strait*. Washington, DC: Smithsonian Institution Press.

Norris, Frank, and Becky Saleeby. 2009. "The Cooperative Parks Studies Unit: Dynamic University-Based Research in the Parks." *Alaska Parks Science Journal* 8(1): 21–23.

Nowak, Michael. 1982. "The Norton Period of Nunivak Island: Internal Change and External Influence." *Arctic Anthropology* 19(2):75-91.

Ohmagari, Kayo. 2004. "The Role of Traditional Food in Identity Development Among the Western James Bay Cree." In *Circumpolar Ethnicity and Identity*, edited by Takashi Irimoto and Takako Yamada, 127–38. Senri Ethnological Studies 66. Osaka, Japan: National Museum of Ethnology.

Okada, Hiroaki, Atsuko Okada, Kunio Yajima, Osahito Miyaoka, and Chikuma Oka. 1982. *The Qaluyaarmiut: An Anthropological Survey of Southwestern Alaska Eskimos*. Sapporo, Japan: Faculty of Letters, Hokkaido University.

Oland, Maxine, Siobhan M. Hart, and Liam Frink. 2012. *Decolonizing Indigenous Histories: Exploring Prehistoric/Colonial Transitions in Archaeology*. Tucson: University of Arizona Press.

Oswalt, Wendell H. 1952. "The Archaeology of Hooper Bay Village, Alaska." *Anthropological Papers of the University of Alaska* 1(1):46–91.

———. 1963. *Mission of Change in Alaska: Eskimos and Moravians on the Kuskokwim*. San Marino, CA: The Huntington Library.

———. 1978. *This Land Was Theirs: A Study of North American Indians*. 3rd ed. New York: Wiley.

———. 1990. *Bashful No Longer: An Alaskan Eskimo Ethnohistory, 1778–1988*. Norman: University of Oklahoma Press.

Oswalt, Wendell H., and James W. VanStone. 1967. *The Ethnoarchaeology of Crow Village, Alaska*. Washington, DC: Smithsonian Institution Press.

Panich, Lee M., and Tsim D. Schneider. 2014. *Indigenous Landscapes and Spanish Missions: New Perspectives from Archaeology and Ethnohistory*. Tucson: University of Arizona Press.

Park, Robert W. 2005. "Growing Up North: Childhood in the Thule and Dorset Cultures of Arctic Canada." *Journal of the American Anthropological Association, Special Issue: Children in Action: Perspectives on the Archaeology of Childhood* 15, 53–64.

Petersen, Robert. 1995. "Colonialism as Seen from a Former Colonized Area." *Arctic Anthropology* 32(2):118–26.

Pierce, Richard A. 1984. *The Journals of Iakov Netsvetov: The Yukon Years 1845–1863*. Ontario: Limestone Press.

———. 1988. "Russian and Soviet Eskimo and Indian Policies." In *Handbook of North American Indians*, Vol. 4, *History of Indian-White Relations*, edited by Wilcomb E. Washburn, 394–403. Washington, DC: Smithsonian Institution Press.

Piper, Liza, and John Sandlos. 2007. "A Broken Frontier: Ecological Imperialism in the Canadian North." *Environmental History* 12(4):759–95.

Pratt, Kenneth L. 1981. Fieldnotes, Kashunak, Alaska. On file. Anchorage, AK: Bureau of Indian Affairs, ANCSA Office.

———. 1995. Nunivak Overview: Report of Investigation for BLM AA-9238 et al. Anchorage, AK: Bureau of Indian Affairs, ANCSA Office.

———. 2004. "Observations on Researching and Managing Alaska Native Oral History: A Case Study." *Alaska Journal of Anthropology* 21(1–2):138–53.

———. 2009. *Chasing the Dark: Perspectives on Place, History, and Alaska Native Claims*. Anchorage: United States Department of the Interior, Bureau of Indian Affairs, Alaska Region.

Ray, Dorothy Jean. 1966. "The Eskimo of St. Michael and Vicinity as Related by H.M.W. Edmonds." *Anthropological Papers of the University of Alaska* 13(2).

———. 1975. *The Eskimos of Bering Strait, 1650–1898*. Seattle: University of Washington Press.

Rearden, Jim. 1979. "The Yukon-Kuskokwim Delta." *Alaska Geographic* 6(1).

Redding-Gubitosa, Donna. 1992. "Excavations at Kwigiumpainukamiut: A Multiethnic Historic Site, Southwest, Alaska." PhD dissertation, Department of Anthropology, University of California, Los Angeles.

Reedy-Maschner, Katherine, and Herbert D. G. Maschner. 1999. "Marauding Middlemen: Western Expansion and Violent Conflict, Warfare, and Violence in Ethnohistorical Perspective." *Ethnohistory* 46:703–43.

Rosich, Rosellen M. 2007. "The Human Mosaic." *Annals of the New York Academy of Sciences* 1114(1):310–16.

Rubertone, Patricia E. 2000. "The historical archaeology of Native Americans." *Annual Review of Anthropology* 29:425–446.

———. 2001. *Grave Undertakings: An Archaeology of Roger Williams and the Narragansett Indians*. Washington, DC: Smithsonian Institution Press.

Sahlins, M. 1985. *Islands of History*. Chicago: University of Chicago Press.

Schaaf, Jeanne M. 1995. "Late-Prehistoric Inupiaq Societies, Northern Seward Peninsula, Alaska: An Archaeological Analysis, A.D. 1500–1800." PhD diss., Department of Anthropology, University of Minnesota.

Scheiber, Laura L., and Mark D. Mitchell, eds. 2009. *Across a Great Divide: Continuity and Change in Native North American Societies, 1400–1900*. Tucson: University of Arizona Press.

Schwalbe, Anna Buxbaum. 1951. *Dayspring on the Kuskokwim: The Story of Moravian Missions in Alaska*. Bethlehem, PA: Moravian Press.

Scott, Elizabeth M. 1991. "A Feminist Approach to Historical Archaeology: Eighteenth-Century Fur Trade Society at Michilimackinac." In *Gender and Historical Archaeology*, edited by Donna J. Seifert, 42–53. *Historical Archaeology* 25(4).

Scott, James C. 1990. *Domination and the Arts of Resistance*. New Haven, CT: Yale University Press.

Sharp, Lauriston. 1952. "Steel Axes for Stone-Age Australians." *Human Organization* 11(2):17–22.

Shaw, Robert D. 1983. "The Archaeology of the Manokinak Site: A Study of the Cultural Transition Between Late Norton Tradition and Historic Eskimo." PhD diss., Department of Anthropology, Washington State University.

———. 1998. "An Archaeology of the Central Yupik: A Regional Overview for the Yukon-Kuskokwim Delta, Northern Bristol Bay, and Nunivak Island." *Arctic Anthropology* 35(1):234–46.

Sheehan, Glenn W. 1997. *In the Belly of the Whale: Trade and War in Eskimo Society*. Aurora Monograph Series 7. Anchorage: Alaska Anthropological Association.

Shepard, Rita S. 1997. "Rivers of Change: Eskimo and Athapaskan Domestic Culture in Contact Era Southwestern Alaska." PhD diss., Department of Anthropology, University of California, Los Angeles.

———. 2002. "Changing Residence Patterns and Intradomestic Role Changes: Causes and Effects in Nineteenth-Century Southwestern Alaska." In *Many Faces of Gender: Roles and Relationships Through Time in Indigenous Northern Communities*, edited by Lisa Frink, Rita S. Shepard, and Gregory A. Reinhardt, 61–80. Boulder: University Press of Colorado.

Shnirelman, Victor A. 1994. "*Cherchez le chien*: Perspectives on the Economy of the Traditional Fishing-Oriented People of Kamchatka." In *Key Issues in Hunter-Gatherer Research*, edited by Ernest S. Burch Jr. and Linda J. Ellanna, 169–88. Oxford: Berg.

Silliman, Stephen W. 2001a. "Agency, Practical Politics, and the Archaeology of Culture contact." *Journal of Social Archaeology* 1(2):190–209.

———. 2001b. "Theoretical Perspectives on Labor and Colonialism: Reconsidering the California Missions." *Journal of Anthropological Archaeology* 20(4):379–407.

———. 2004. *Lost Laborers in Colonial California: Native Americans and the Archaeology of Rancho Petaluma*. Tucson: University of Arizona Press.

———. 2005. "Culture Contact or Colonialism? Challenges in the Archaeology of Native North America." *American Antiquity* 70(1):55–74.

———. 2010. "Crossing, Bridging, and Transgressing Divides in the Study of Native North America." In *Across a Great Divide: Continuity and Change in Native North American Societies, 1400–1900*, edited by Laura L. Scheiber and Mark D. Mitchell, 258–76. Tucson: University of Arizona Press.

Simon, David. 1981. *Taped Interview, 81 ROM 14*. Gene Smercheck and Steve Christy, interviewers; Allen Joseph, interpreter; Steve Christy, English transcription.

Skibo, James M., and Michael B. Schiffer. 1995. "The Clay Cooking Pot: An Exploration of Women's Technology." In *Expanding Archaeology*, edited by James M. Skibo, William H. Walker, and Axel E. Nielson, 80–91. Salt Lake City: University of Utah Press.

Sleeper-Smith, Susan. 2001. *Indian Women and French Men: Rethinking Cultural Encounter in the Western Great Lakes*. Amherst: University of Massachusetts Press.

Smith, Bruce D. (ed.) 2011. *Subsistence Economies of Indigenous North American Societies*. Washington, DC: Smithsonian Institution Press.

Smith, Buster. 1981. *Taped Interview 81 ROM 013*. Kris Andre and Ted Maitland, interviewers; Allen Joseph, interpreter; Kris Andre, English transcription.

———. 1984. *Taped Interview 84 VAK 020*. James Kurtz and Robert Waterworth, interviewers; Leo Moses, interpreter; Lillian Pingayak, transcription.

Snow, Jeanne H. 1981. "Ingalik." In *Handbook of North American Indians*, Vol. 6, *Subarctic*, edited by William C. Sturtevant, 602–17. Washington, DC: Smithsonian Institution Press.

Spector, Janet D. 1993. *What This Awl Means: Feminist Archaeology at a Wahpeton Dakota Village*. St. Paul: Minnesota Historical Society Press.

Spencer, Robert F. 1959. *The North Alaskan Eskimo: A Study in Ecology and Society*. Bureau of American Ethnology Bulletin 171. Washington, DC: Smithsonian Institution Press.

———. 1984. "North Alaska Coast Eskimo." In *Handbook of North American Indians*, Vol. 5, *Arctic*, edited by David Damas, 320–37. Washington, DC: Smithsonian Institution Press.

Spielmann, Katherine A., T. Clark, D. Hawkey, K. Rainey, and Susan K. Fish. 2009. "'... Being Weary, They Had Rebelled': Pueblo Subsistence and Labor Under Spanish Colonialism." *Journal of Anthropological Archaeology* 28(1):102–25.

Starks, Zona Spray 2007. "Arctic Foodways and Contemporary Cuisine." *Gastronomica: The Journal of Food and Culture* 7(1):41–49.

Steward, Julian H. [1938] 2002. *Basin-Plateau Aboriginal Sociopolitical Groups*. Smithsonian Institution Bureau of American Ethnology Bulletin 20. Salt Lake City: University of Utah Press.

Stopp, Marianne P. 2002. "Ethnohistoric Analogues for Storage as an Adaptive Strategy in Northeastern Subarctic Prehistory." *Journal of Anthropological Archaeology* 21(3):301–38.

Taylor, Garth J. 1974. *Labrador Eskimo Settlements of the Early Contact Period*. Publications in Ethnology 9. Ottawa: National Museums of Canada.

Testart, Alain. 1982. "The Significance of Food Storage Among Hunter-Gatherers: Residence Patterns, Population Densities, and Social Inequalities." *Current Anthropology* 23(5):523–37.

Tunutmoak, Tom. 1984. *Taped Interview 84 VAK 08, 029*. James Kurtz, Beth Shide-Cochran, and Robert Waterworth, interviewers; Veronica Charlie, interpreter and transcription.

Tushingham, Shannon, and Robert L. Bettinger. 2013. "Why Foragers Choose Acorns over Salmon: Storage, Mobility, and Risk in Aboriginal California." *Journal of Anthropological Archaeology* 32:527–37.

Usher, Peter J. 1976. "Evaluating Country Food in the Northern Native Economy." *Arctic* 29(2):105–20.

Van Kirk, S. 1980. *Many Tender Ties: Women in Fur-Trade Society, 1670–1870*. Norman: University of Oklahoma Press.
Vansina, Jan. 1985. *Oral Traditions as History*. London: James Currey and Heinemann.
VanStone, James W. 1967. *Eskimos of the Nushagak River: An Ethnographic History*. Seattle: University of Washington Press.
———. 1968. *Tikchik Village: A Nineteenth Century Riverine Community in Southwestern Alaska*. Fieldiana Anthropology 56. Chicago: Field Museum of Natural History.
———. 1970. *Akulivikchuk: A Nineteenth Century Eskimo Village on the Nushagak River, Alaska*. Fieldiana Anthropology 60. Chicago: Field Museum of Natural History.
———. 1972. *Nushagak: An Historic Trading Center in Southwestern Alaska*. Fieldiana Anthropology 62. Chicago: Field Museum of Natural History.
———. 1982. "Southern Tutchone Clothing and Tlingit Trade." *Arctic Anthropology* 19(1):51–61.
———. 1984. "Mainland Southwest Alaska Eskimo." In *Handbook of North American Indians*, Vol. 5, *Arctic*, edited by David Dumas, 224–42. Washington, DC: Smithsonian Institution Press.
Vehik, Susan C., Lauren M. Cleeland, Richard R. Drass, Stephen M. Perkins, and Liz Leith. 2010. "The Plains Hide Trade: French Impact on Wichita Technology and Society." In *Across a Great Divide: Continuity and Change in Native North American Societies, 1400–1900*, edited by Laura L. Scheiber and Mark D. Mitchell, 149–73. Tucson: University of Arizona Press.
Veltre, Douglas W. 2011. "Gardening in Colonial Russian America." *Ethnoarchaeology* 3(2):119–38.
Veltre, Douglas W., and Allen P. McCartney. 2002. "Russian Exploitation of Aleuts and Fur Seals: The Archaeology of Eighteenth- and Early Nineteenth-Century Settlements in the Pribilof Islands, Alaska." *Historical Archaeology* 36(3):8–17.
Veniaminov, Ivan Evieevich Popov. 1840. *Zapiski ob ostrovakh Unalashkinskago otdiela {Notes on the Islands of the Unalaska District}*. 3 vols. in 2. Petersburg: Russian-American Co.
Vidal, Silvia, and Neil L. Whitehead. 2004. "Dark Shamans and the Shamanic State: Sorcery and Witchcraft as Political Process in Guyana and the Venezuelan Amazon." In *Darkness and Secrecy: The Anthropology of Assault Sorcery and Witchcraft in Amazonia*, edited by Neil L. Whitehead and Robin Wright, 51–81. Durham, NC: Duke University Press.
Vitt, Kurt H. 1987. *Bernard Bendel: 1870 Kuskokwim Expedition*. Bethel, AK: The Moravian Seminary and Archives.
Voss, Barbara L. 2000. "Colonial Sex: Archaeology, Structured Space, and Sexuality in Alta California's Spanish-Colonial Missions." In *Archaeologies of Sexuality*, edited by Robert A. Schmidt and Barbara L. Voss, 35–61. New York: Routledge.
———. 2005. "From *casta* to *Californio*: Social Identity and the Archaeology of Culture Contact." *American Anthropologist* 7:461–74.
———. 2008. *The Archaeology of Ethnogenesis: Race and Sexuality in Colonial San Francisco*. Berkeley: University of California Press.

Walls, Matthew. 2012. "Kayak Games and Hunting Enskilment: An Archaeological Consideration of Sports and the Situated Learning of Technical Skills." *World Archaeology* 44(2):175–88.
Ward, Margaret C. 2002. *A World Full of Women*. Boston: Allyn and Bacon.
Wernke, Steve. 2007. "Negotiating Community and Landscape in the Peruvian Andes: A Transconquest View." *American Anthropologist* 109(1):130–52.
———. 2011. "Convergences: Producing Early Colonial Hybridity at a *doctrina* in Highland Peru." In *Enduring Conquests: Rethinking the Archaeology of Resistance to Spanish Colonialism in the Americas*, edited by Matthew Liebmann and Melissa Scott Murphy, 77–102. Santa Fe, NM: School for Advanced Research Press.
———. 2013. *Negotiated Settlements: Andean Communities and Landscapes Under Inka and Spanish Colonialism*. Gainesville: University Press of Florida.
Wesson, Cameron B. 1999. "Chiefly Power and Food Storage in Southeastern North America." *World Archaeology* 31(1):145–64.
———. 2010. "When Moral Economies and Capitalism Meet: Creek Factionalism and the Colonial Southeastern Frontier." In *Across a Great Divide: Continuity and Change in Native North American Societies, 1400–1900*, edited by Laura L. Scheiber and Mark D. Mitchell, 61–78. Tucson: University of Arizona Press.
Wexler, L. M., G. DiFluvio, and T. K. Burke. 2009. "Resilience and Marginalized Youth: Making a Case for Personal and Collective Meaning-Making as Part of Resilience Research in Public Health." *Social Science and Medicine* 69(4):565–70.
Whelan, Carly S., Adrian R. Whitaker, Jeffrey S. Rosenthal, and Eric Wohlgemuth. 2013. "Hunter-Gatherer Storage, Settlement, and the Opportunity Costs of Women's Foraging." *American Antiquity* 78(4):662–678.
White, Richard. 1991. *The Middle Ground: Indians, Empires, and the Republics in the Great Lakes Region, 1650–1815*. Cambridge: Cambridge University Press.
Wolfe, Robert J. 1982. "Alaska's Great Sickness, 1900: An Epidemic of Measles and Influenza in a Virgin Soil Population." *Proceedings of the American Philosophical Society* 126(2):91–121.
———. 1984. "Commercial Fishing in the Hunting-Gathering Economy of the Yukon River Yup'ik Society." *Études/Inuit/Studies* 8:159–84.
Woollett, James M. 1999. "Living in the Narrows: Subsistence Economy and Culture Change in Labrador Inuit Society During the Contact Period." *World Archaeology* 30(3):370–87.
Ziff, Allan. 1981. Fieldnotes, Qavinaq. On file. Anchorage, AK: Bureau of Indian Affairs, ANCSA Office.
———. 1981. Fieldnotes, Old Chevak. On file. Anchorage, AK: Bureau of Indian Affairs, ANCSA Office.
Ziff, Allan, Kenneth L. Pratt, and Robert M. Drozda. 1982. Historical Overview of New Chevak. On file. Anchorage, AK: Bureau of Indian Affairs, ANCSA office.

Index

Page numbers in *italics* indicate illustrations.

aboveground housing: at Chevak, 26; first, 71; at Old Chevak, 104–5, 112
aboveground storehouses (caches): advantages of, 120; development of, 119; features of, 51; at Kashunak, 66–68
Ackerman, Robert, 53
Advent Phase (1927–1932): age groups and, 92–93; economic exchanges and, 80–85; end of, 93–94; shamans and, 85–88; women's participation in, 88–92, *91*, 111, 123
age categories: colonialism and, 8–12; early church and, 92–93; in subsistence-based groups, 30
Akulurak, boarding schools at, 77–78, 79
Alaska Native Claims Settlement Act (ANCSA), 18
Alaska Territorial Guard, 95
alcohol, trading of, 22–23
Aleutian archipelago, 21
Aloralrea, Juliana (Elder), 45, 47, 58, 88
Aluska, George, 98
American Commercial Company (ACC), 23
Arctic climate, and storage, 31–33
arranged marriages, 75, 93, 96
artifacts, 51, *52*, 64
Askinuk. *See* Hooper Bay (Askinuk)

bearded seals, 29, 34, 35
Begler, Elsie, 10
Bering Strait, 21–22

Bladder Feast, 23, 45–46
Bow and Arrow War Days: cessation of warfare, 56; oral accounts of, 55–56; preparation/weapons for, 57; Qavinaq massacre, 59–61; strategies, 57–58; women during, 58–59. *See also* warfare
Bunyan, Dick (Elder), 78, 82, 86
Burch, Earnest, 55

ceremonial occasions, women and, 45–46
Chevak: contemporary life in, 26–29, *27*; elevated housing at, 26; moving to, 108–9; overview of, *13*, 16
child labor, missionaries and, 78, 79, 89–90
coastal tundra: earliest habitation of, 20; environmental features of, 19–20, *20*
colonial education. *See* mission schools
colonialism: early interactions, 69–71; indigenous-indigenous interactions and, 9–13; interactive participation in, 4–5. *See also specific periods/phases*
colonial triad, 74
construction jobs, 28–29
Convert, Father Jules, 67, 99–103, 110
Crown, Patricia, 14
cultural change, and use of space, 14–15. *See also* Transfiguration Phase (1947–1950)
currency, 83, 109–10

165

data: ethnohistoric, 16–17; oral traditions/histories, 17–18; site surface, 15–16
Dietler, Michael, 11, 17
differential mobility, 100
divorce, 75–76
Dumond, Don, 20

Early Trade Period (1833–1927): Kashunak village during, 42, 69–71; social/economic changes and, 61–62
economic exchanges: at Hooper Bay, 95–96; of Jesuit missionaries, 82–83; at Old Chevak, 104, 109–10; women removed from, 121
Edmonds, H. M. W., 25
education. *See* mission schools
Elders: interviews with, 18; maintaining tradition, 8, 12–13; missionaries and, 92–93; resistance to relocation, 101; women as, 30–31
electrical power, at Hooper Bay, 95
Ellanna, Linda, 30
endemic warfare. *See* warfare
entrance/exit tunnels, 47–49, 53, 54, 68
epidemic diseases, 23
ethnohistoric information, 16–17
Evin, Wassilie (Elder), 56

Fair, Susan, 119
family house: changes in, 72, 123; men's inclusion into, 44; structure/features of, 46–47, 50
firearms: for hunting, 96, 96–97; trading of, 22–23, 25, 70, 120
firebathing, 59, 91, 108–9
fish: processing of, 24, 38–40, 78, 79; procurement of, 37–38
fish, dried: bartering for, 89; buying/selling, 109; Russian interest in, 22, 24; storage of, 119–20
Fish, Suzanne, 14
fish camps, 24, 28, 39, 40

Fitzhugh, William, 7
food preparation, 27–28. *See also* processing, of food
Fox, Father John: Advent Phase and, 81–83, 88; Little Sisters of the Snow and, 95–98, 96; mission relocation and, 93–95; reentering Kashunak, 98–99; trading skills of, 89–92, 91
Friday, Joseph (Elder), 70–71
front porches, 47, 68
Funk, Caroline, 48
furs: currency for, 109; Russian interest in, 21–22; storage of, 120

gendered economics: acceptance of foreign goods and, 69–70, 72; access to metals and, 25; colonialism and, 10–11, 100; in subsistence-based groups, 7–8, 29–30
George, Agnes (Elder), 87, 93
Giddings, J. Louis, 37
gold prospectors, 23
group identity, subsistence and, 7–9, 29–31

Habicht-Mauche, Judith, 11
Hargreaves, Father Henry, 89, 103–4, 105–6, 108–10
harvesting, 30–31. *See also* processing, of food
healing, shamans and, 86
herring, processing of, 31, 40
Hess, Brother, 80–81
Hohokam culture, 14
Hooper Bay (Askinuk), 23, 48–49, 79, 94–98
houses: in Chevak, 26–27, 27; at Hooper Bay, 48–49; at Old Chevak, 104–6
Hunter, Alexis, 99
Hunter, Ida, 98

identity, subsistence tied to, 7–9, 29–31
illness, shamans/missionaries and, 86–87

indigenous-colonial interactions: early encounters, 21–25; at Kashunak, 69–71; perspectives on, 4–5, 17–18; Russian imports, 22; in southwestern Alaska, 5–7; subsistence and, 3–4
indigenous-indigenous interactions: colonialism and, 9–13; end of warfare, 122
indigenous-mission interactions, 73–74. *See also* missionaries
individual identity, subsistence tied to, 7–9, 29–31
inequities, within indigenous groups, 10
interviews, with Alaskan Elders, 18

Jesuit Oregon Province Archives (JOPA), 17

kashim. *See* men's house (kashim)
Kashunak (Nunaraluq): contemporary use of, 64; early market commerce, 69–71; historic village of, 42; mission building, 65, 66; overview of, *13*, 16; physical layout of, *62–63*, *62–64*, 65; religious colonialism at, 78–80, *80*; return of mission to, 98–100; social/economic changes and, 61–62; storage features of, 65–68, *67*, 117–18; tunnel usage in, 68. *See also* Advent Phase (1927–1932); Transfiguration Phase (1947–1950)
Kilbuck, John, 87
Kinguk (Qavinaq warrior), 58

Lantis, Margaret: on aboveground caches, 119–20; on entrance/exit tunnels, 48; on oil consumption, 36, 118; on shamans, 85; on storage, 31, 33
Late Prehistoric Period (1740–1833), 42
Leacock, Eleanor, 7, 76
Liebmann, Matthew, 4, 16
Lightfoot, Kent, 113

The Little Flower boat, 81, 90, *91*
Little Sisters of the Snow, 95–98, *96*
Llorente, Father, 78, 84, 87, 92

market privatization, 72, 111, 120–21, 123
medical services, 95, 110
men: acceptance of mission, 98–100; in integrated households, 106, 123; procurement and, 32; resistance to mission, 84–85, 122; seal harvesting by, 33–35; social changes for, 106–9; use of foreign goods, 69, 72
Menager, Father Frances, 17, 81–83, 86–87
men's house (kashim): at Chevak, 108–9; decline in primacy of, 72, 123; demise of, 106–8, *107*, 123; missionaries' effect on, 83–84; at Qavinaq, remains of, 54; social position and, 44; structure of, 43; tunnels connecting, 50; women's access to, 44–45
metal tools, 13, 25, 69, 122
missionaries: Advent Phase and, 80–85; choosing Kashunak, 78–80, *80*; on the coast, 76–77; at Kashunak, 65, 66; operating procedures of, 74–76; shamans and, 85–88; trading prior to, 70–71
mission schools: boarding schools, 76–78; jobs associated with, 29, 74; Old Chevak and, 102–3

Natriuluk (Russian entrepreneur), 70–71
Nayagak, Michael, 99
Nayamin, Ulric (Elder), 78–79, 87–88
Nelson, Edward W.: on Bow and Arrow War Days, 55–56, 58; collections/commentary of, 23, 25; on colonial interactions, 69–71; on entrance/exit tunnels, 48; on gender-based tools, 117; on the men's house, 43–44, 46; on shamans, 86

noninvasive investigation, 4
Norton people, 20
Nunaraluq. *See* Kashunak (Nunaraluq)

O'Connor, Father Paul, 104
Old Chevak: advantages of, 102; economic development, 109–10; housing at, 104–6, *107*; map of, *103*; overview of, *13*, 16; Retrenchment Phase at, 98; schooling in, 102–3; social changes at, 106–9, 123; trade store at, 81–82; village relocation to, 100–101, 102
oral historic accounts, 17–18, 55–56, 70
Oswalt, Wendell, 77

Peterson, Charlie, 110
pit storage: features of, 32–33; at Kashunak, 65–66, 67, 118
porches, 47, 68
precolonial cultural influences, 5
precolonial warfare. *See* warfare
processing, of food: fish, 24, 38–40, *39*, 78, 79; production control and, 7–8; seals, 35–37, *36*; in subsistence-based groups, 30–31; women and, 32
procurement system: for fish, 37–38; men and, 32; for seals, 33–35; in subsistence-based groups, 30–31

Qavinaq: aerial view of, *52*; artifacts from, 52; massacre/burning of, 59–61; overview of, *13*, 15–16, 42, 71; physical layout of, 51–54, *53*, *54*; storage at, 117. *See also* Bow and Arrow War Days
Qillerkavialuk (Qavinaq warrior), 58, 60

religious colonialism. *See* missionaries
resource access, within indigenous groups, 10–11
Retrenchment Phase (1932–1947): Little Sisters of the Snow, 95–98, *96*; at Old Chevak, 98; relocation to Hooper Bay, 94–95, 111; return to Kashunak, 98–100
ringed seals, 34
Rubertone, Patricia, 113
Russian-American Company (RAC), 21–22
Russian Orthodox Church, 76
Russians: pacification of, 55–56; trading with, 21–22, 40, 70–71, 115; withdrawal of, 22–23

salmon, 24, 38–40. *See also* fish, dried
schools. *See* mission schools
Scott, James, 9
seal-poke storage system: at Kashunak, 65–66, 67, 72; skill/technology of, 36–37, 118–19
seals: harvesting of, 33–35; processing of, 35–37, *36*
sea mammal oil, 36–37, 118
seasonal relocation, missionaries and, 78–79, 99–100
shamans: functions/influence of, 85–86; as healers/mystics, 86–87; missionaries and, 87–88, 92; at Old Chevak, 108
Sharp, Lauriston, 12
Shaw, Robert, 20
Shepard, Rita, 106, 123
Sheppard, George, 82, 85
Sheppard trade store, 81–82, 105, 109–10
Sherrod, George, 30
Silliman, Stephen, 9, 14, 113
Sipary, Anny, 96
southwestern Alaska: earliest habitation of, 20; environmental features of, 19–20; indigenous-colonial interactions in, 5–7; subsistence and, 3–4, 6
spotted seals, 34
Starks, Zona, 37, 118

stone to steel axes, *12*, 12–13
storage: aboveground, 51, 66–68, 119–20; in Arctic climate, 31–33; facilities for, 51; of fish, 38, 40; at Kashunak, 65–67, 67, 72, 117–18; women's control of, 31–33, 114, 121
subsistence-based resources: for Alaskan coastal people, 3–4; contemporary meals and, 27–28; fisheries and, 37–40; food storage and, 31–33; individual/group identity and, 7–9, 29–31; shift in women's control, 10–13, 115–16

Thule people, 20–21
trade posts, 74, 81–82. *See also* Sheppard trade store
Traditional Council (TC) building, 28
Transfiguration Phase (1947–1950): advantages of Old Chevak, 102; economic development, 109–10; housing and, 104–6, *107*; relocation to Old Chevak, 100–101, *102*; schooling and, 102–3; social changes during, 106–9
Tuntuvak (Russian entrepreneur), 71
Tununak village, 77

Uyakok (Helper Neck), 92

village life: contemporary, 26–29; seasonal relocation in, 25–26. *See also specific villages*
village tunnels: entrance/exit, 48–49, 68; at Kashunak, 68, 72; overview of, 47–48, 50; warfare, 49–50; women's surveillance via, 117
Voss, Barbara, 14

warfare: cessation of, 56, 71–72; during Late Prehistoric Period, 42; oral accounts of, 55–56; preparation/weapons for, 57; Qavinaq massacre, 59–61; social status and, 113–14; strategies for, 57–58; women and, 58–59
warfare tunnels, 49–50
weapons, 57
Wernke, Steven, 14–15
Wesson, Cameron, 9, 121
Western Union Telegraph Expedition, 23
women: acceptance of foreign goods, 69–70, 72; access to men's house, 44–46; control of food storage, 31–33, 114, 121; end of warfare and, 114, 122; family house for, 46–47; in integrated households, 106, 123; interviews with Yup'ik, 18; Little Sisters of the Snow, 95–98, *96*; loss of influence, 10–13, 115–16; processing seals by, 35–37; religious colonialism and, 74–76, 78, 79; response to missionaries, 88–92, *91*, 111, 123; as shamans, 86; subsistence-based resources and, 29–31, 115; trading with, 82; use of tunnel surveillance, 117; during warfare, 58–59

Yir Yoront, *12*, 12–13
youth, 12–13, 57, 75, 84, 92–93
Yukon Kuskokwim Delta region: earliest habitation of, 20; environmental features of, 19–20; subsistence in, 3–4, 6
Yup'ik Eskimos: fisheries and, 37–40; indigenous-colonial interactions of, 5–7; interviews with women, 18; the men's house and, 43–46; seal harvesting/processing, 33–37; shamans, 85–88; subsistence for, 3–4, 29–30

Zagoskin, Lavrentiy, 22, 55–56

About the Author

Professor **Liam Frink** joined the faculty in the Department of Anthropology at the University of Nevada, Las Vegas, in 2005. He received his PhD in anthropology in 2003 from the University of Wisconsin–Madison, and in 2004, he was a Wenner-Gren Foundation for Anthropological Research Richard Carley Hunt Postdoctoral Fellow. Frink has worked in Alaskan native villages since 1996. He has published research on indigenous-colonial studies and ethnoarchaeology/experimental studies in journals such as *American Anthropologist*, *American Antiquity*, *Current Anthropology*, *Food and Foodways*, *International Journal of Historical Archaeology*, *Journal of Archaeological Method and Theory*, and the *Journal of Archaeological Science*. Frink is co-editor of *Many Faces of Gender: Relationships Through Time in Indigenous Northern Communities* (with Rita Shepard and Gregory Reinhardt, University Press of Colorado, 2002), of *Gender and Hide Production* (with Kathryn Weedman, AltaMira, 2005), and of *Decolonizing Indigenous Histories: Exploring Prehistoric/Colonial Transitions in Archaeology* (with Sioban Hart and Maxine Oland, University of Arizona Press, 2012), a *Choice* magazine Outstanding Academic Title.